THE UNIVERSITY OF
WINCHE...

CELEBRATING COLUMBA
Colm Cille á Cheiliúradh

Irish–Scottish Connections 597–1997

Edited by

T.M. DEVINE
and
JAMES F. McMILLAN

John Donald Publishers Limited,
73 Logie Green Road, Edinburgh, EH7 4HF.

ISBN 0 85976 493 1

British Library Cataloguing in Publication Data.

A catalogue record for this book is available
from the British Library.

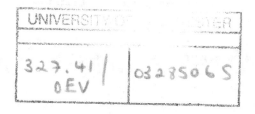
Typesetting and origination by Brinnoven, Livingston.
Printed & bound in Great Britain by Bell & Bain Ltd, Glasgow.

PREFACE

This volume publishes some of the papers given at the first International conference of the Irish–Scottish Academic Initiative held in the University of Strathclyde in September 1997. *Celebrating Columba* was selected as the title of the event because the main purpose was to commemorate the life and achievement of St Columba in the 1400th anniversary year of his death. But rather than devote the entire conference programme to the remarkable influence of Columba himself, it was decided to use the anniversary year as a basis for exploring the full range of Irish–Scottish cultural, religious, political and literary connections over the many centuries from his death to the present day.

This approach produced two days of stimulating lectures, discussions and readings for an audience of nearly 400 academics, students and members of the general public who met in the magnificent surroundings of Strathclyde's Barony Hall. Essentially, there were three parts to the event: lectures on Irish–Scottish history from the time of Columba to the Peace Process in Northern Ireland in the 1990s, discussions between leading public commentators and senior scholars on the future of Scotland and Ireland at a time of profound constitutional change in both countries and literary readings given by distinguished Irish and Scottish poets and novelists. Those taking part included Seamus Heaney, the Nobel Laureate, William McIlvanney, Eiléan Ní Chuilleanáin, Andrew O'Hagan, Fintan O'Toole, the late Iain Crichton Smith and Colm Tóibin.

This book reprints some of the papers which were given as part of the History programme at that event. The intention is not to provide a comprehensive and coherent survey of Irish–Scottish connections over 1400 years but rather to focus on key issues which are the subject of current scholarly research and interest. In the 1970s and 1980s the comparative economic and social history of Scotland and Ireland made enormous advances with the consecutive publication of no fewer than four volumes of conference papers. But much of the focus of these collections was on the history of the two countries since the later seventeenth century. Not only is there much of crucial significance still to be explored in the medieval and early modern periods, but such hugely important issues as religion, popular culture, politics, identity and emigration still await detailed comparative examination for more recent centuries. As Dr Duffy notes in his chapter, the story of Scotland's connection with Ireland in the medieval period remains largely untold. To a large extent this judgement could equally apply to other periods. Until very recently Scottish historians have not surprisingly been fixated on the English connection which has shaped the development of the nation since 1707. Political changes within the Union in the late twentieth century have now encouraged a wider perspective on the history of the British Isles. Non-anglocentric history and the 'New British history' are among the most important growth areas in the historiography of the early modern period and the foundation of ISAI, with the enthusiastic encouragement of the Irish and British governments, is itself a manifestation of a new interest in comparative Irish-Scottish studies. The obsessive preoccupation with England is also waning to some extent as some Scottish historians search for the origins of Scottish identity in the past and in the process discover long-neglected connections with Ireland and Europe. As Duffy notes '…as Scots have gone in pursuit of their Scottishness, their search has brought them to Ireland.'

This is a striking feature of the first three chapters in the book which deal with the era from the sixth to the fifteenth centuries. Professor Herbert demonstrates the enduring impact of Columba's inheritance in Scotland over 600 years. His legacy even survived the Viking attacks on Iona in the ninth and tenth centuries. Columba's missionary and monastic activity had ensured that Iona became the hub of a communications network which spanned the Irish Sea and helped to renew strong contacts between Ireland and Scotland. Because of the effective system of organisation and government which the saint established during his lifetime, the Columban influence from Ireland extended not only throughout Argyll (Dalriada) and the Hebrides but also brought Irish and Christian culture to the Pictish-controlled territories elsewhere on the Scottish mainland. By the end of the seventh century Columban monasteries were already established in Pictland and these areas were also being influenced by the Irish Gaelic vernacular. A bond was forged in this period through a common Christian fellowship between Ireland and northern Scotland which was only weakened fundamentally in the final decades of the eleventh century when Malcolm III took his kingdom of Alba closer to England and the Continent and away from the Gaelic world.

Nevertheless, as Seán Duffy stresses in the next chapter, Irish Gaelic culture was still dominant in Scotland for much of the Middle Ages. The name of the emergent nation was itself derived from its Gaelic roots –

Scotia, the land of the Scotti, 'the original preferred Latin name for the Irish'. The political elites of both nations traced their origins back to a common source through King-lists and the like. Robert Bruce, the hero-king of the Scots, shows in his correspondence that he regarded himself as part of the broad Irish nation, a fact which has only recently been acknowledged by leading scholars of medieval Scotland. Even in the thirteenth century when some authorities see a tendency on the part of the Scottish elites to turn their back on the Gaelic world, accounts of Scottish origins are still proud to proclaim the Irish origins of the nation in order to validate its antiquity and claim to freedom. Indeed, during the reign of Robert Bruce a concerted attempt was made once again to unite Scottish and Irish political interests.

However, it was not to be and under the Stewart successors to the Bruces the process became one of divergence rather than convergence at national level. Instead, Irish–Scottish connections were maintained at a regional level through the flourishing military, economic and family relationships between the Western Isles and Ulster. The complexity of these relationships during the heyday of the Lordship of the Isles is brought out in Simon Kingston's chapter on the MacDomnaills (MacDonalds) who at this time were building up their territorial influence both in the Hebrides and in Antrim. Later, the buannachan or household men, the warrior class of the Highland clans, were in great demand as mercenaries in the north of Ireland. Native Irish chiefs, faced with continuous English attempts throughout the sixteenth century to impose lordship, were able to count on armed support from their kindred among the Scottish clans. This was a profitable business for the clan gentry of the western Highlands because the Irish paid for the services of the buannachan in food and coin. The booming Irish market for men of violence then became a powerful incentive to maximise the fighting strength of the clans. Militarism on this scale posed a serious threat to the centralising Scottish state and in time was bound to invite retribution.

This came in the later sixteenth century and especially after the Union of the Crowns of 1603. From that point a unified and expansionist British state was able to bring its awesome naval and military resources to bear on the two Gaelic societies of the Western Highlands and Ireland. The monarchy of James VI and I annexed the six counties of Ulster, established colonial plantations in the conquered region and initiated the settlement on the confiscated territory of loyal Protestants from mainland Britain who were recruited with the promise of cheap, expropriated land to provide a secure garrison against the native Irish Catholic enemy. Over the course of the seventeenth century, this led to a huge emigration of Scottish farmers, their servants and families, originally to Antrim and Down (associated with the private initiatives of Sir Hugh Montgomery and Sir James Hamilton) and then further west to the six annexed counties. By 1640 at least 20,000 Scots had crossed to Ireland. Thereafter, numbers increased further. Current estimates suggest there may have been as many as between 60,000 and 100,000 migrants after 1650, with most leaving during the series of terrible harvest failures which affected Scotland in the 1690s. This great exodus of presbyterian Scots has left an indelible mark on the history of Ireland down to the present day.

A century later, however, there began the well-chronicled mass movement of the Irish to Scotland. The majority of these migrants were Roman Catholic but a substantial minority were Protestant people from Ulster now returning to the land of their forefathers because of economic distress in textiles and the attraction of new jobs and rising wages in industrialising Scotland. The chapters by Martin Mitchell and Elaine McFarland provide fresh perspectives on key aspects of this great diaspora. Mitchell challenges the stereotype of the Catholic Irish in Scotland as 'a separate and despised community' by demonstrating their widespread involvement in trades unions, reform agitations, Chartism and the temperance movements before 1850. Sectarian riots were rare and mainly confined to 'Orange and Green' disturbances between the migrant Protestant and Catholic Irish. There does not seem to have been the same introspection which characterised the Catholic Irish in the later nineteenth century and afterwards. Commitment to Irish political issues, such as repeal of the Act of Union of 1801, could coexist with support for the democratic causes of their adopted homeland. Elaine McFarland's focus on the career of the remarkable Ulster Protestant, John Ferguson, is also an important corrective to conventional wisdom and simplistic analysis of the experience of Irish immigrants in Scotland. McFarland's account emphasises the subtle complexity of a figure who, while from Ulster Protestant stock, was 'Irish nationalism's most prominent exponent in Scotland' and as equally committed to the cause of Irish liberation as he was to the political emancipation of the working classes in Britain. This connection between the struggle for Irish independence and the Irish in Scotland is also vividly brought to life in John Cooney's chapter on the contribution of the immigrant community to the achievement of self-government in the years 1916 to 1921. Based on the recollections of some of the participants, Cooney shows the extent of the clandestine network in the west of Scotland which managed to channel impressive amounts of cash, explosives and armies across the Irish Sea to sustain the Sinn Fein campaign. De Valera himself declared that the Scottish contribution not only far exceeded that of any other country but in his view was the chief factor in the success of the armed struggle.

The establishment of an Irish Free State, later Republic, under de Valera was hailed by Irish Nationalists as the opportunity to pursue a distinctive style of politics and to embark on a unique cultural and social experiment. The new state was an explicitly confessional state. That did not mean, however, that it was ready to endorse a Christian social order as defined by contemporary Catholic social teaching in papal encyclicals such as *Rerum Novarum* (1891) and *Quadragesimo Anno* (1931) in response to pressure from the Irish Catholic Social Movement. Nevertheless, as Finín O Driscoll demonstrates in his ground-breaking chapter, Irish social Catholicism embodied the Columbian ideal which placed Christianity at the centre of public life and made religion a matter preoccupied with social and political concerns as much as with personal piety. Practical solutions to social problems, such as fiscal reform, were at the heart of its agenda.

During Ireland's most recent and gravest crisis of this century in Ulster, Graham Walker points out in the final chapter in the book, that 'the Scottish voice in debates about the problem has hardly been heard'. Certainly Scottish Catholics and Protestants of Irish descent have given moral support to their coreligionaries in the North and this could even extend sometimes to practical assistance. But the attitude of the vast majority of Scots to the Northern Ireland problem since the 1960s has been conditioned by the vital need to maintain a distance from the Troubles lest they spill over into the west of Scotland where memories of a sectarian past are still fresh. Walker contends that the remarkable progress in the maturing of the Irish peace process, the emphasis in it not simply to strengthen north-south but also east-west links, the innovative idea of a 'Council of the Isles' and the imminence of devolution within the UK all present opportunities for a new Irish-Scottish beginning. Scotland can contribute to the dialogue precisely because the nation has had deep historic affinities with both communities. If such a meeting of minds between the Scots and Irish did come about it would indeed be a continuation and a strengthening of the great tradition established by St Columba and his followers when they landed on Iona so many centuries ago.

ACKNOWLEDGEMENTS

Warm thanks are due to Margaret Hastie of the University of Strathclyde who assisted in the preparation of this book for publication and also bore the primary administrative responsibility for the organisation of the Celebrating Columba conference in September 1997 on which this volume is based. The important contribution of Dr Anne-Marie Kilday, also of Strathclyde, who helped produce the final text is also acknowledged.

It is also a pleasure to acknowledge publicly those who helped to sponsor and support the conference: Mr Martin Naughton, Glen Dimplex, Ireland; the Principal and Vice-Chancellor, University of Strathclyde, Sir John P Arbuthnott; the Royal Society of Edinburgh; the Foreign and Commonwealth Office.

His Excellency, Edward J. Barrington, Ambassador of the Republic of Ireland, opened the conference, and he has been a valued supporter of the Irish–Scottish academic and cultural initiatives. We are grateful to him for his help and wise counsel.

EDITORS

T.M. Devine
University Research Professor in Scottish History and Director of the Research Institute of Irish and Scottish Studies, University of Aberdeen.

J.F. McMillan
Professor of European History at the University of Strathclyde and Vice-Dean of the Faculty of Arts and Social Sciences.

CONTRIBUTORS

John Cooney
Honorary Research Fellow in History, University of Aberdeen.

Seán Duffy
Lecturer in Medieval History, Trinity College, Dublin.

Máire Herbert
Professor of Early and Medieval Irish, University College, Cork.

Simon Kingston
Research student, Oriel College, Oxford.

Elaine W. McFarland
Head of History and Politics, Glasgow Caledonian University.

Martin J. Mitchell
Leverhulme Trust Research Fellow, Research Institute of Irish and Scottish Studies, University of Aberdeen.

Finín O Driscoll
Research student, Wolfson College, Cambridge.

Graham Walker
Reader in Politics, Queen's University of Belfast.

CONTENTS

THE IRISH–SCOTTISH
ACADEMIC INITIATIVE

The Irish–Scottish Academic Initiative (ISAI) is a unique transnational academic partnership formed to support research and scholarship in the field of Irish and Scottish culture. The original founding institutions were Trinity College, Dublin, the University of Aberdeen and the University of Strathclyde. In 1998 a fourth partner, the Queen's University of Belfast, became a member, thus ensuring ISAI membership throughout the island of Ireland.

Ireland and Scotland over the centuries have had a close relationship which, though frequently troubled, has resulted in shared or related experiences which more than ever merit study. At a time when the connection between Ireland and the United Kingdom seems ready to enter a new phase, and when the relationships between the different parts of the United Kingdom are being reassessed, it is especially valuable to foster strong academic links between Scotland and Ireland. History, Language and Literature, the areas of special interest to ISAI, lie at the heart of the two nations' relationship. Research in these disciplines will serve both to highlight common problems – the need to preserve or construct an identity in relation to a powerful neighbouring culture for example – and differences, whether intrinsic or attributable to uneven development of the economics of land usage and industrialisation, language, literary tradition or national sovereignty. The Initiative, in itself a significant manifestation of goodwill in this vital area of concern to both countries, will, when fully functioning, develop that goodwill into an internationally-recognised productive understanding of the past, present and future relations of our two countries, within these islands, Europe, and the world.

Distinctive aims of the Initiative are:

- A collaborative, interdisciplinary approach, which pools the resources and expertise available in the relevant departments of four major universities: Trinity College, Dublin; the University of Aberdeen; the University of Strathclyde; and Queen's University, Belfast.

- Academic exchanges, involving members of staff, postgraduate students and undergraduates in all four universities.

- Joint research projects, rendered possible by the critical mass of key researchers delivered by the Initiative.

- Enhanced supervision of research students, who have the opportunity to access the research resources and research cultures of four universities instead of one.

- Undergraduate exchanges, to encourage 'East-West' contacts in the younger generation.

- Public lectures, seminars, symposia and cultural events to reach out to the wider public in both Ireland and Britain.

Confidence in the Initiative's future success derives in part from the fact that it is being developed from roots laid down in the 70s when the History departments pioneered joint research projects, teaching and Erasmus undergraduate exchanges. The second phase of this development has now been initiated whereby doctoral post-graduates, some under the new Socrates programme, will have the unique advantage of the synergy created by the integration of the archival resources and staff expertise of the four universities. In practical terms this means, for example, that a doctoral candidate working on an Irish/Scottish topic will have the exceptional academic and cultural stimulation of spending one of his/her three research years in another university. It is anticipated that research students of the highest calibre from Britain, Ireland, Europe and North America will be attracted to the Initiative and so establish a critical mass of key researchers (post-graduate, post-doctoral and current staff). Indeed, each discipline has already outlined joint research projects intended to develop (partly through staff exchange) innovative and important publications. ISAI also intends by means of public lectures, seminars, symposia and cultural events to disseminate this research to the widest possible public.

Further information about the Irish-Scottish Academic Initiative can be obtained from Professor T.M. Devine, FBA, Convener ISAI, Research Institute of Irish and Scottish Studies, University of Aberdeen, Humanity Manse, 19 College Bounds, Old Aberdeen, Scotland, AB24 3UG. Email: riis@abdn.ac.uk

For Margaret Hastie
in recognition of her services to the
Research Centre for Scottish History,
University of Strathclyde
until 1998.

1

THE LEGACY OF COLUMBA

Máire Herbert

Saint Columba or Colum Cille left Ireland in the year 563 to live as 'a pilgrim for Christ' in Iona. He founded monasteries both in Ireland and in Northern Britain, and joined them in federation under the mother-church of Iona. He set in place an effective system of organisation and government which ensured the continuity of this monastic enterprise through the centuries after his death in the year 597. While contact across the sea by Columba's successors was reduced in the wake of Viking attacks in the ninth and tenth centuries, the Columban monastic *familia* survived many vicissitudes, including the transfer of headship of the federation from Iona to Ireland. In large measure, the distinctive transinsular identity of Columba's *familia* survived up to the second half of the twelfth century.[1]

For a period of six centuries, then, the Columban monastic federation was influential on both sides of the Irish Sea. Written works, including hagiography, exegesis, and annals, witness to its ecclesiastical and intellectual achievements.[2] Gospel-books and carved monuments attest to its artistic achievements.[3] Yet the contribution of the *familia* of Columba extended beyond these spheres to the social and political world. I propose to focus primarily on this aspect of the Columban legacy, to explore its role in a formative era for Scottish kingship, and for the definition of Irish–Scottish relations.[4]

Columba's career in his adopted land must be set in the context of a pre-existing Irish presence in Dál Riata, the district around present-day Argyll, settled by migrants from the north-east of Ireland some decades previously. We have no contemporary account of the Irish settlement of Dál Riata, but sources from the following century allow us to infer that by Columba's era the colony was organised under its own king, and was not under the rule of a parent-kingdom in Ireland.[5] Loss of power in their Ulster homeland to the neighbouring kingdoms of Dál nAraide and Dál Fiatach may have been a factor in the transfer of Dál Riata peoples and kingship to an underpopulated coastal region across the sea.[6] That this Irish colony in North Britain was the fortuitous landfall of Columba's pilgrim journey seems highly unlikely. Rather, his destination was probably chosen on the basis of prior contact with the Dál Riata leadership.

Columba was a churchman of royal blood, closely related to the rulers of Ireland's most powerful dynasty, the Uí Néill, and though he abandoned his own prospects of secular power for monasticism, nevertheless he was actively involved with kingship on both sides of the Irish Sea.[7] According to his hagiographer and Iona successor, Adomnán, Columba's attitude was that royal governance was divinely bestowed, and should therefore operate in close association with churchmen, the mediators of divine power on earth.[8] While the literary articulation belongs to the seventh century, the recorded actions of Columba and his successors show that this philosophy of church-state relations was a guiding principle. Columba's associations with his Irish Uí Néill kin and with the Dál Riata leadership took active form, as, for instance, in his initiation of a 'conference of kings', which seems to have formalised alliance between his kinsmen at home and his patrons overseas.[9]

Moreover, Columba's outlook transcended the limitations of ethnic and linguistic affiliations. He was a friend of the king of the British kingdom of Strathclyde. He journeyed north to the pagan Pictish king to request protection for sea-faring monks who might land in Pictish-controlled territories.[10] Columba's monastic community included brethren from all four peoples of North Britain, Britons, Picts, Saxons, as well as Gaels.[11] In Ireland, as well as in Britain, his associations were not confined to kin and community. Columba was received with honour by leading Irish churchmen when he visited his homeland. Pilgrims, penitents, aspiring monks, and exiled royalty came to Iona from many parts of Ireland, as indeed they came from various regions of North Britain.[12] Annals recorded on the island, beginning perhaps in the latter part of the sixth century, reveal the extent to which travellers from east and west brought news to Iona about battles, royal successions and ecclesiastical matters in Ireland, in Dál Riata, and in its neighbouring kingdoms.[13] The fact that Iona annalists took a keen interest in worldly as well as in ecclesiastical events further illustrates the engagement of Columban monasticism with secular leadership.

While it is difficult to quantify the extent to which Columba achieved the Christianisation of royal rule, I believe that his life's work had a significant impact on the kingdom of Dál Riata itself. As a fairly inconsiderable Irish settlement, on the margins both of Ireland and of Britain, it might well have become a backwater, destined ultimately to lose its cultural and political identity to neighbouring Picts or Britons. Yet Columba's monastic activity meant that Iona became a magnet drawing visitors and pilgrims, and, as head of the saint's monastic federation, it was at the hub of a communications network spanning the Irish Sea. The periphery became a centre, the focus of revitalised contact with Ireland, and of new contacts with neighbouring territories of North Britain. The whole kingdom of Dál Riata must have gained benefit from the activity generated by Columba, whose monasteries infused Irish and Christian culture and education throughout its territories. Columban association with the kingdom's rulers mutually reinforced church and state, and also linked Dál Riata with powerful Uí Néill dynasts in Ireland. The consolidation of Dál Riata's status and identity, as an Irish kingdom established in the North British political world, was achieved in significant measure, I believe, through association with Columba.

Yet Columba's associations had extended beyond the Gaelic world to Pictland, and the fruits of this contact are in evidence in the decades after his death. His initial journeys probably paved the way for subsequent missionary work in Pictland. Indeed, records of the activities of Pictish rulers by Iona annalists from the 630s may well signal Columban presence in the kingdom.[14] Columba's successor and biographer, Adomnán, provides unambiguous evidence of the presence of Columban monasteries in Pictland by the latter part of the seventh century.[15] Moreover, when Adomnán enacted his *Lex Innocentium,* a ground-breaking church-state legal measure for the protection of non-combatants in time of conflict, this Law was given assent, not only by Irish churchmen and rulers, but also by their Dál Riatan and Pictish counterparts.[16] Thus, humanitarian legislation initiated by Columba's successor in the year 697 joined Ireland, Dál Riata, and Pictland together in a Christian fellowship which transcended political and ethnic boundaries.

There were cultural differences to be accommodated, however, within this unity of the Columban federation in the late seventh century. In Dál Riata the dominant ethos of kingdom and community was Gaelic. But since the Columban community differed in language and in ethnic affiliation from the Picts, what were the cultural consequences of Columban establishment in Pictland? Epigraphic evidence provides some insight. From the seventh century onward we find Pictish vernacular inscriptions written in ogam script. The ogam alphabet clearly comes from the Gaelic world, where it was used for vernacular rather than for Latin inscription. Now, in the wake of Columban introduction into Pictland, we find both alphabet and mode of use being adapted by the Picts to their own cultural context.[17]

Within a still-vigorous Pictish culture, however, Columban monasteries seem to have constituted Gaelic enclaves. Bede's *Historia Ecclesiastica* of the early eighth century relates how the Picts settled in Britain under the direction of the Irish, who provided them with wives and stipulated a role for the female line in royal succession.[18] Bede's account of Columba, moreover, gives precedence to his role as evangeliser of the Picts over his role as priest-abbot of Iona.[19] In effect, these narratives in Bede's work trace the beginnings of both secular and ecclesiastical organisation in Pictland to Irish origins. The content and perspective suggests that the material is likely to have originated in Columban circles in Pictland. This, in turn, implies the maintenance of an Irish-centred mentality in Pictish monasteries of the Columban *familia*.

The Pictish materials of Bede's *Historia* seem to have been transmitted via a delegation sent to Northumbria by Nechtan, king of the Picts, to enquire about Easter observance.[20] This question of universal conformity versus Columban particularity was apparently an issue in Pictish churches as in contemporary Iona. Yet the king's intervention, and his reported expulsion of Columban monks *trans Dorsum Britannie* in the year 717, took place in the context of ongoing leadership struggles in Pictland.[21] There is no indication that these events ended the involvement of Columban monks in Pictland. The Easter question was resolved in Iona by the year 718, and annals of succeeding decades indicate that communication with Columban sources in Pictland continued unabated.[22]

From the 740s surviving annals were recorded in Ireland rather than in Iona.[23] This does not lead to a cessation of information from the Columban *familia* overseas, but the change in perspective coincides with an increase of reports about the activities of Iona abbots in Ireland. The church-state Law of Adomnán in 697 was followed by several such joint enactments throughout Ireland.[24] The proclamation of a 'Law of Colum Cille' by the Southern Uí Néill king in the year 753, however, was followed by a subsequent proclamation of the same Law by the abbot of Iona.[25] The abbot seems to have come to Ireland to ensure that Columba's community received a rightful share in a revenue-generating legal measure named for its patron. Significantly, the next proclamation of the 'Law of Colum Cille' in the year 778 was jointly ascribed to Iona abbot and Uí Néill king.

As the Columban leadership in Iona thus energetically pursued the interests of the saint's *familia* on both sides of the Irish Sea, unforeseen and violent change was imminent. While Viking attacks on Iona from the close of the eighth century brought havoc to the monastic community, these attacks also caused major reverberations within the political milieu in which the Columban community found support. Some change may have been already in progress. Eighth-century conflicts between Dál Riata and the Picts saw the latter dominant in the first half of the century, but Dál Riata on the offensive in the second half. According to an annal of the year 768, the Dál Riata king was waging battle *i Fortrinn*, in the southern Pictish kingdom, and this may signal the beginning of western interest in that area.[26] However, it is after the onset of Viking attacks at the end of the eighth century that annal obits of rulers styled *rex Fortrenn* appear to coincide with cessation of references to *rex Dál Riatai*.[27]

Yet we lack sufficient evidence to determine whether this represented a move by rulers associated with Dál Riata into southern Pictish territory. Moreover, by the year 839 the political situation was again altered by the killing of prominent leaders of southern Pictland in a Viking onslaught. Thereafter, the position of *rex Pictorum* was attained by a Dál Riata dynast, Cináed mac Alpín.[28] Sources from the tenth century onward suggest that Cináed seized power, so it is possible that an existing consensus regarding rulership in southern Pictland was breached by his action.[29] But whatever the affiliations of his immediate predecessors, those of Cináed seem to be linked firmly with the Gaelic west.[30]

Cináed's assumption of power over the Picts may have been an opportunist move, yet his consolidation of his position appears to be shrewdly calculated. He was evidently in touch with contemporary Irish politics, in particular, with the movement toward greater overlordships by powerful Uí Néill rulers. Indeed, Irish records show that a daughter of Cináed was married successively to two Uí Néill kings.[31] Moreover, as he established a Gaelic overlordship over the Picts, Cináed is reported to have transferred relics of Columba to a church which he built, most probably at Dunkeld.[32] Thus, the long association on the western seaboard of Dál Riata kings and Columban monasticism was now being replicated in the new power-centre further east.

Repeated Viking attacks on Iona had been followed by the foundation of Kells in the Irish midlands as a refuge for personnel and valuables from the beleaguered island.[33] Yet Iona had maintained its monastic community. Its abbot, in his role as Columba's successor, went on circuit with the saint's relics to mainland Britain in the year 829, and to Ireland in 831 and 849. Despite the dangers, it was probably imperative to travel with the saint's relics to collect tribute and offerings. Similar circuits in Ireland by the successor of Patrick, for instance, indicate that leading churches were competing for secular support in the face of Viking depredations.[34] By the time that Cináed brought Columban relics and patronage to his new kingdom, the association between monastic community and royal power had been transmuted. Instead of the symbiotic relationship established between church and state in Columba's time, by the mid-ninth century secular power could set the terms of its association with a weakened and embattled ecclesiastical institution.

Cináed channelled Columban prestige in support of his own rule and dynasty. The establishment of the saint's relics at Dunkeld linked royal power with the network of Columban monasteries in Pictish territory, and thereby, with communities culturally disposed to support Gaelic overlordship, and the promotion of Gaelic culture, among the Picts. Cináed's Columban links seems to have pragmatically privileged the monasteries central to his political rule, those which could be agents of Gaelicisation within his new kingdom. The evidence suggests that Iona was sidelined in the pursuit of these policies by Cináed and his family. A downturn in the position of the monastery is indicated by the fact that, on the death of its abbot Flann in the year 891, headship of the Columban *familia* transferred to Ireland.[35]

The achievements of Cináed's reign were reinforced by the fact that his power became a family inheritance. In the *Annals of Ulster* for the year 900 his grandson, Domnall, is accorded the title *rí Alban*. Why does this designation replace *rex Pictorum*, the title used since Cináed's time? In a context in which Cináed's dynasty had close Irish marriage associations, an Irish exemplar may provide a resolution.[36] In Ireland, around the mid-ninth century, the designation *fir Érenn*, 'the men of Ireland', was adopted as an omnibus term for the followers of powerful Irish rulers whose support extended beyond their own kin.[37] An overking like Cináed's contemporary, Máel Sechnaill, whose followers were designated *fir Érenn,* thereby received the title of *rí Erenn*.[38] While annal usage of *rí Alban* precedes that of *fir Alban* 'the men of Alba', the two occur sufficiently close together to posit a sequential relationship parallel to that observable in an Irish context.[39] In my view, the designation *rí Alban* followed from the adoption of the broad collective *fir Alban* (originally 'the men of Britain') for the various kin and ethnic groups under the leadership of Cináed's dynasty. Neither *rí Erenn* or *rí Alban* seems to have had a territorial connotation initially.

Columba is represented as a powerful patron of *fir Alban* in a narrative composed, perhaps, around the latter part of the tenth century.[40] An apparently contemporary account in the *Annals of Ulster* for the year 918 tells how 'the men of Alba' successfully routed Viking attackers, but were lucky to escape from ambush by a hidden battalion. The subsequent narrative, however, presents the encounter as an uncomplicated triumph, gained by *fir Alban* with the assistance of Columba, their apostle. With evident Columban bias, the text declares that the saint's intercession was obtained, not only by prayer, fasting, and almsgiving, but also by the promise that Columba's crosier would be the battle-standard of the men of Alba. The tale of the victory-bringing crosier, called *Cathbhuaidh*, 'battle-triumph', argues for the dependence of the secular power on Columban intercession, mediated on earth by his relic, and by his community. The reality of relations between monastic *familia* and holders of the title of *rí Alban*, however, was rather more complex.

The establishment of a Gaelic-dominant kingdom, centred in former Southern Pictish territory, seems to have been accomplished with the support of an existing Gaelic institution within the territory, that of the Columban monastic federation. Yet the relationship between kingship and Columban community does not appear to have been entirely reciprocal. In effect, succession to Cináed's kingship alternated up to the end of the tenth century between the families of his two sons, Causantín and Áed. The line of Causantín maintained the Columban-Dunkeld association, but the line of Áed seems to have formed its own ecclesiastical alliance with Cenn Ríg Monaid (St Andrews) before the mid-tenth century.[41] In this context, it is hardly surprising to find the Columban community using literary propaganda to assert the position of its patron saint as the dynasty's most powerful conduit to divine favour. Laudatory verse on Columba ascribed to Mugrón, the saint's successor who died in the year 980, introduces its subject as *Colum Cille, cend Alban*.[42] The verse appears to represent Alba as a territorial entity, and this may witness to a political *fait accompli* by the end of the tenth century.[43] The poet's representation of Columba as patron of the kingdom, however, seems to reflect wish rather than actuality. One powerful dynastic line had associated itself with the saint, even in its prominent use of the personal name Máel Coluim.[44] But this partisanship was a barrier to Columba's identification with the kingdom itself, as *cend Alban*, 'Alba's eminence'.

In contemporary Ireland, as in Alba, rulers increasingly sought to requisition the prestige of saints in support of their political objectives. The leaders of Columba's *familia*, prevented by Viking sea-power from travelling regularly from Iona to maintain their influence with Ireland's powerful Uí Néill rulers, were supplanted by the successors of Patrick in Armagh. Armagh support was then co-opted by Brian Bóruma of Munster for his usurpation of Irish overkingship at the beginning of the eleventh century. The demoted Uí Néill sought to renew alliance with the *familia* of their kin-saint Columba, whose successor was now based within their own territories, in the monastery of Kells. A preface composed for the famous vernacular eulogy of Columba, the *Amra*, provides a literary recreation of the saint's era as a template for an eleventh century in which the successor of Columba was again the clerical confrère of leading political powers on both sides of the Irish Sea.[45] But the past could not be revived. Neither Uí Néill nor the Columban *familia* would regain premier position in Ireland. Overseas Gaeldom could no longer be counted as part of Irish polity. The eleventh-century world of the Columban familia was one in which Ireland and Alba were defining themselves as distinct and separate kingdoms.[46]

Yet the Columban *familia* continued as an institution which transcended the political divide. Despite the fact that eleventh-century headship of the *familia* was based in Ireland, annal notices of Iona monastic personnel indicate continuing contact with the island.[47] Other annal notices point to communication between Ireland and Dunkeld, which conveyed information, not only about the monastic community, but also about rulers of Alba.[48] Pastoral visitation from the chief Columban monastery of Kells to Alba is revealed incidentally, when the *Annals of Ulster* in the year 1034 record the drowning, on the return journey, of the Kells lector with his accompanying persons and saints' relics. Particular entries in the Irish annals reveal a Moray bias as they record that dynasty's eleventh-century quest for the kingship of Alba.[49]

[50]

Despite these continuities, however, the latter part of the eleventh century initiated a period of considerable change within Alba, with consequent diminishment of links between its Columban churches and those of Ireland. Internal and external factors worked together, so that the kingdom emerged from royal succession conflicts and dynastic changes to an altered political context in Britain. The reorientation of outlook within the kingdom of Alba from the Gaelic world to that of the Continent and England under the leadership of Máel Coluim III was significant, not only in political terms, but also in ecclesiastical terms, as movement toward ecclesiastical reform shifted the focus toward bishoprics and new monastic orders.[51] As the kingdom and institutions of Alba turned away from Ireland, the Western Isles (including Iona) were ceded to the king of Norway by Edgar, son of Máel Coluim and Margaret, in the year 1098.[52]

Effectively, administrative links between Columban monasteries within Alba and the Irish-based leadership of the saint's *familia* must have all but ceased by the beginning of the twelfth century. Yet the cult of Columba himself survived, even in the royal household. A copy of the *Vita Columbae*, the Life written by Adomnán in Iona at the close of the seventh century, was made under the patronage of King Alexander between the years 1107 and 1114.[53] A Latin poem appended to the copy acknowledges Columba's Irish origins, and asks for his blessing on king and scribe. Moreover, the saint is invoked as 'the sword and defence of the Scots', an echo of his role as guarantor of battle-victory for the men of Alba in vernacular legend two centuries previously.[54]

The extent of the saint's *familia* in the mid-twelfth century is documented in a vernacular Life of Columba written in Derry. The Life's catalogue of the saint's foundations designates the churches over which the current abbot of Derry was claiming headship. All of these foundations are in Ireland, with the exception of Iona.[55] The reasons why Iona links with Ireland persisted are various. Imbued with the presence of the patron saint, the island monastery clearly held a particular place of honour within the Columban *familia*, who maintained monks there despite danger and difficulty. Yet Iona's reputation transcended its ecclesiastical and political affiliations, as it was venerated through the centuries as a centre of religious life and pilgrimage.

Royal devotees of Iona had included Artgal, king of Connacht, who retired to the island in the year 782,[56] an Ulster dynast who died in Iona in the late ninth century,[57] and Amlaib, king of the Dublin Vikings, who retired to the island in the year 978, according to *Chronicon Scottorum*. As Amlaib belonged to a family which had plundered Kells, chief church of the Columban *familia*, the choice of Iona for the Viking king's retirement had evidently less to do with the monastery's Columban connections than with its Christian reputation in the Western Isles.[58] In the early eleventh century a Northern Uí Néill king included Iona in a pilgrim grand tour which began in Clonfert and ended in Rome.[59] A bishop from Tigh Colláin in Meath died 'on his pilgrimage' in the monastery in the year 1047.[60] Moreover, Norse saga recounts a visit by King Magnus of Norway to 'the holy island' in the course of his 1098 expedition to the regions of the Irish Sea.[61]

We know little of Iona's affairs in the half-century after it came under Norwegian overlordship, but it is evident that the political and cultural world to which it belonged had little to do with Norway. Its world was a Hiberno-Norse domain, part of an 'Atlantic community', distanced from an increasingly feudalised kingdom of Alba.[62] Iona's milieu was Irish-connected, while Columban churches in Alba belonged to a milieu increasingly disconnected from Ireland. When the Hebridean leader, Somerled, rebelled in the year 1164 against feudal encroachment on the west by Alba's rulers, he sought to ensure for himself a lordship which would span the Irish Sea.[63] Apparently envisaging Iona once more in the pivotal role of uniting Argyll and the Isles with Ireland, he directed its monastic officials to invite the abbot of Derry, the current head of the Columban *familia*, to move to Iona. [64]

This attempt to transfer Columban leadership back to Iona failed, however, in the face of opposition from leaders of church and state in Ireland.[65] We must assume a degree of self-interest on their part, for both the successor of Patrick and the northern-based King of Ireland had close links with the monastery of Derry.[66] However, Somerled's plan may also have been viewed as transgressing Iona's status as 'the holy isle' by subordinating it to the strategic interests of secular power.

Somerled's machinations came to naught. Yet within a decade, the unity of the Columban *familia* had begun to break up. The immediate causes lay in events in Ireland in the later twelfth century, in particular, the Norman incursion, and the replacement of monastically-oriented church structures by diocesan organisation. The end came less by decision than by a process of attrition.[67] But a long history had left its traces behind.

In seventh-century Iona, Adomnán had written of Columba 'that one who dwelt on this little island on the edge of the ocean should have earned a reputation that is famous not only in our own Ireland and in Britain, the largest of the ocean's islands, but has also reached the three corners of Spain and Gaul and Italy beyond the Alps, and even Rome itself'.[68] Yet Columba achieved more than widely-acknowledged sainthood. His career in Iona was fundamental to the maintenance of a Gaelic kingdom of Dál Riata. His monastic community had a significant supporting role in the establishment of Gaelic culture and overlordship in Pictish lands. The ecclesiastical organisation which he founded linked peoples on both sides of the Irish Sea across political and ethnic barriers. Moreover, Iona, the place of his pilgrimage, remains an enduring reminder of how a tiny and remote island was transformed into a centre which united Scots and Irish, and reached out to the world.

REFERENCES

1. For a detailed history of the *familia*, focusing in particular on its leadership, see M. Herbert, *Iona, Kells, and Derry: The History and Hagiography of the Monastic Familia of Columba* (Oxford, 1988, repr. Dublin, 1996).

2. See, for instance, A.O. Anderson, M.O. Anderson and Revd M.O. Anderson (eds.), *Adomnán's Life of Columba* (Oxford, 1991); D. Meehan (ed.), *Adamnan's De Locis Sanctis* (Dublin, 1958); J. Bannerman, 'Notes on the Scottish Entries in the Early Irish Annals' in *Studies in the History of Dalriada* (Edinburgh, 1974), 9–26.

3. See, for instance, G. Henderson, *From Durrow to Kells: The Insular Gospel-books 650–800* (London, 1987); Royal Commission on the Ancient and Historical Monuments of Scotland, *Argyll: An Inventory of the Monuments, iv, Iona* (Edinburgh, HMSO, 1982).

4. I have relied on primary sources, those which are contemporary, or those as nearly contemporaneous as possible. I have avoided sources such as king-lists insofar as much remains to be done to analyze their evidence. I have tried to

avoid constructing a narrative which synthesizes a variety of materials of varying historical status, and, in general, my references are directed at the primary material. I am indebted to much valuable secondary literature, and wish to acknowledge that this indebtedness greatly exceeds the acknowledgements possible in the notes. Responsibility for all interpretations, however, is entirely mine.

5. This conclusion is based on a reading of the Irish annals. Inferences to the contrary have relied on non-contemporary materials such as an early-eleventh-century account of the Convention of Druim Cet.

6. G. Mac Niocaill (*Ireland before the Vikings* (Dublin, 1972), 75) suggests that the migration could have been encouraged by the British kingdom of Strathclyde so that Dál Riata might constitute a barrier against Pictish attack. However, there is no evidence to support this contention.

7. For evidence of Columba's genealogy, see Herbert, *Iona, Kells, and Derry,* 10.

8. Anderson (ed.), *Adomnán's Life of Columba* (hereafter abbreviated as *Life*, with textual references to book and chapter) I.14, I.36.

9. M. Herbert, 'The Preface to *Amra Coluim Cille*' in D. Ó Corráin *et al.* (eds.), *Sages, Saints and Storytellers: Celtic Studies in Honour of Professor James Carney* (Maynooth, 1989), 67–75 (in particular, 69–71).

10. *Life*, I.15; II.42.

11. *Adomnán of Iona: Life of St Columba*, tr. R. Sharpe (Harmondsworth, 1995), Introduction, 21.

12. *Life*, I.3; I.50; I.18; I.4; I.5; I.22; I.26; I.30; I.32; I.; 44; I.13.

13. Bannerman, 'Scottish Entries'; Herbert, *Iona, Kells and Derry*, 22–23.

14. S. Mac Airt and G. Mac Niocaill (eds.), *The Annals of Ulster (to 1131)*, (hereafter *AU*), beginning in the year 631.

15. *Life*, II.46.

16. Kuno Meyer (ed.), *Cáin Adamnáin: An Old-Irish Treatise on the Law of Adamnán* (Oxford, 1905); M. Ní Dhonnchadha, 'The Guarantor List of *Cáin Adamnáin*, 697', *Peritia* 1 (1982), 178–215.

17. K. Forsyth, 'Literacy in Pictland', in H. Pryce (ed.), *Literacy in Medieval Celtic Societies* (Cambridge, 1998), 39–61; T.M. Charles-Edwards, 'The context and uses of literacy in early Christian Ireland', *Ibid.* 62–82.

18. B. Colgrave and R.A.B. Mynors (eds.), *Bede's Ecclesiastical History of the English People* (Oxford, 1969, repr. 1979) (hereafter *Ecclesiastical History*, citation by book and chapter numbers) I.1.

19. *Ibid.* III.4.

20. *Ibid. V.21.* See also A.A.M. Duncan, 'Bede, Iona, and the Picts', in R.H.C. Davis and J.M. Wallace-Hadrill (eds.), *The Writing of History in the Middle Ages* (Oxford, 1981), 1–42.

21. *AU* 717.4; also *AU* 713.4, 713.7; W. Stokes (ed.), *The Annals of Tigernach* (*Revue Celtique* 16 (1895), 374–419; 17 (1896), 6–33, 119–263, 337–420; 18 (1897), 9–59, 150–97, 267–303; (repr. Felinfach, 1993), hereafter *ATig*, s.a. 723; *AU* 726.1; 728.4, 729.2, 3.

22. *AU* 716.4; *ATig*, s.a. 717.

23. Bannerman, 'Scottish Entries', 12–13; 25–26; G. Mac Niocaill, *The Medieval Irish Annals* (Dublin, 1975), 18–23.

24. *AU* 734.3; 736.10; 742.7; 744.9; 748.8.

25. *AU* 753.4; 754.3; 757.9.

26. Note, for instance, *AU* 736.1; 741.10; 768.7; 789.11.

27. *AU* 792.4; 820.3; 834.1.

28. *AU* 839.9; 858.2.

29. I note, for instance, the pseudo-prophecy in the *Tripartite Life* of Patrick, probably completed in the tenth century, which refers to the taking of Alba *ar éicin*, 'by force', by [a descendant of] Áedán mac Gabráin. See K. Mulchrone (ed.), *Bethu Phátraic: The Tripartite Life of Patrick* (Dublin, 1939), lines 1884–91. Material in the 'Chronicle of the Kings of Alba', dated to 954–62, attributes the destruction of the Picts to Cináed. See text published by M.O. Anderson in *Kings and Kingship in Early Scotland*, 282–83, and commentary by Dauvit Broun, 'Dunkeld and the origin of Scottish identity', *The Innes Review*, 48.2 (1997), 112–24 (especially 113–15). Dr Broun rightly draws attention to the propaganda element in the text, and the possibility that it is retrospectively paralleling the success of Cináed's dynasty with the fall of the Picts. The Irish reference is less *parti pris*, however, hence my tentative conclusion that force was involved in Cináed's succession.

30. The same two tenth-century sources (n. 28 above) seem to provide the earliest supporting evidence. The 'Chronicle' refers to Cináed as *primus Scottorum* in the kingship, and as having previously held the kingship of Dál Riata. The *Tripartite Life* presents Aédán mac Gabráin, the late sixth-century king of Dál Riata, as surrogate for contemporary rulers of his line. An eleventh-century Irish genealogy shows Cináed and his dynasty in direct line of descent from Áedán, and ultimately from Fergus, son of Erc, and his Irish ancestors. See M.A. O'Brien (ed.), *Corpus Genealogiarum Hiberniae* (Dublin, 1962, repr. 1976), 162 c44, and J. Bannerman (ed.), *Senchus Fer nAlban* in *Studies*, 65–67.

31. The Irish source is the twelfth-century *Banshenchus* 'The Lore of Women', detailing females mainly through their association with prominent men, whether by descent, marriage, or motherhood. See M.E. Dobbs, 'The Banshenchus', *Revue Celtique* 47 (1930), 282–339; 48 (1931), 163–234; 49 (1932), 437–89 (in particular, 48: 186–188), and *AU* 879.1; 913.1; 916.1.

32. Our authority is the 'Chronicle'. On the identification of Dunkeld as the site of the transfer of relics, see Broun, 'Dunkeld and the origin of Scottish identity', 118–21.

33. See Herbert, *Iona, Kells, and Derry*, 68–70.

34. *AU* 829.3; 831.1; 849.7. Patrician-related entries at *AU* 818.5; 836.4; 846.9. The view that Columban entries must be interpreted in the context of contemporary annal reports has also been advanced by M. Lapidge, 'The cult of St Indract at Glastonbury' in D. Whitelock *et al.* (eds.), *Ireland in Early Medieval Europe* (Cambridge, 1982), 179–212 (in particular n. 57). For a variant interpretation of information about Columban relics see J. Bannerman, 'The Scottish takeover of Pictland and the relics of Columba', *The Innes Review*, 48.1 (1997), 27–44.

35. On these matters, see Herbert, *Iona, Kells, and Derry*, 72–84.

36. See note 31 above.

37. Usage of the term *fir Érenn* was first noted by D. Ó Corráin, 'Nationality and kingship in pre-Norman Ireland', in T.W. Moody (ed.), *Nationality and the Pursuit of National Independence* (Belfast, 1978), 1–35 (in particular p. 8), but a different inference has been drawn.

38. *AU* 858.4; 862.5.

39. *AU* 900.6; 919.4.

40. The text is found as part of a chronicle of Viking-Age events, probably compiled in the mid-eleventh century, but drawing on existing narratives, including some concerning the activities of Irish-based Vikings in Britain, to which context the present narrative belongs. For edition, see J.N. Radner (ed.), *Fragmentary Annals of Ireland* (Dublin, 1978),168–71 (forming part of section 429), Commentary, *Ibid.* xxii–xxvi; 206–07.

41. The 'Chronicle' states that Cusantín son of Áed entered religion in his old age. Subsequent tradition, such as the *Prophecy of Berchán* indicate that his place of retirement and death was St Andrews. See A.O. Anderson, 'The Prophecy of Berchán', *Zeitschrift fur Celtische Philologie* 18 (1929), 1–56 (at stanza 154). Note also the acknowledgement of St Andrews implicit in the pilgrimage to the monastery by Áed mac Máelmithid, an Irish grandson of Cináed mac Alpín, for the notice of whose death in St qAndrews in the year 963, see W.M. Hennessy (ed.), *Chronicon Scottorum* (hereafter *CS)* (London, HMSO, 1866, repr. Wiesbaden, 1964), 216–17.

42. The text is in Bodleian MS Laud 615, p. 105.

43. I suggest that this may also mark the transition in meaning of *Alba* to signify the area which had previously been the territory of Southern Pictland. See also Dauvit Broun, 'Defining Scotland and the Scots before the Wars of Independence' in D. Broun *et al.* (eds.), *Image and Identity: The Making and Remaking of Scotland through the Ages* (Edinburgh, 1997), 6–20.

44. *AU* 954.2; 1034.1; 1093.5.

45. See M. Herbert, 'The Preface to *Amra Coluim Cille*', 72–73; 'Sea-divided Gaels? constructing relationships between Irish and Scots c. 800–1169' in B. Smith (ed.), *Britain and Ireland 800–1300* (Cambridge, forthcoming).

46. Herbert, 'Sea-divided Gaels' (forthcoming).

47. *AU* 1005.1; 1025.1; 1062.2; 1070.6; 1099.6.

48. *AU* 1027.7; 1033.7; 1034.1; *AU, CS* 1040; *AU, ATig* 1045.

49. *AU* 1020.6; *ATig* 1029; *AU* 1032.2; 1058.2, .6, 1085.1.

50. K. Jackson (ed.), *The Gaelic Notes in the Book of Deer* (Cambridge, 1972), 30–32, 42, 52–53.

51. For discussion of these matters, see, for instance, A.A.M. Duncan, *Scotland : The Making of the Kingdom* (Edinburgh, 1975), 117–32; G.W.S. Barrow, *Kingship and Unity: Scotland 1000–1306* (London, 1981), 24–34.

52. A.O. Anderson, *Early Sources of Scottish History A.D. 500 to 1286* (Edinburgh, 1922, repr. Stamford, 1990), vol. II, 105–06, 112–13.

53. Anderson, *Life*, Introduction, lix–lx.

54. For a transcript of the text, see W. Reeves (ed.), *The Life of St Columba, founder of Hy* (Dublin, 1857), Preface, xxix.

55. Text ed. M. Herbert, *Iona, Kells, and Derry*, 218–69. See also 189–202.

56. *AU* 782.2, 791.1.

57. The evidence is found in the poem *Clann Ollaman Uaisle Emna* (F. J. Byrne (ed.), *Studia Hibernica* 4 (1964), 54–71). This twelfth-century account of Christian kings of Ulster presents problems, as the present Iona information does not occur in all manuscript copies, and there are problems regarding the name of the ruler. Nevertheless, I include it as witness to Ulster tradition that a member of the royal line died in Iona. See Byrne, 69.43A; 78; 86.

58. *AU* 951.1; 970.1.

59. S. Mac Airt (ed.), *The Annals of Inisfallen* (Dublin, 1951), at the year 1026.

60. J. O'Donovan (ed.), *Annála Rioghachta Éireann: Annals of the Kingdom of Ireland by the Four Masters* (Dublin, 1848–51), at the year 1047.

61. *Anderson, Early Sources*, II, 107–09.

62. On the concept of an Atlantic community, see R.A. McDonald and S. A. McLean, 'Somerled of Argyll: A New Look at Old Problems', *The Scottish Historical Review*, LXXI (1992), 3–22.

63. *Ibid.* 13–22.

64. W.M. Hennessy and B. MacCarthy (eds.), *Annála Uladh: The Annals of Ulster* (4 vols, Dublin, 1887–1901), at the year 1164.

65. *Ibid.*

66. Herbert, *Iona, Kells, and Derry*, 111–17.

67. *Ibid.*, 114–23.

68. *Life* III.23; Translation, Sharpe, *Adomnán of Iona*, 233.

2

THE ANGLO NORMAN ERA IN SCOTLAND: CONVERGENCE AND DIVERGENCE

Seán Duffy

The kingdom of Ireland ended with the lecherous king Roderick, descended from a branch of our own stock, who most improperly for a Christian king wished to have six wives at the same time, nor did he wish to give them up even if it meant losing his kingdom, although he was often warned by the whole church both by archbishops and bishops, and reprimanded with terrible threats by all the inhabitants both magnates and private individuals. So he was despised by them all. They refused to obey him in future, and to this day they decline to obey any king at all. Therefore that kingdom for long distinguished in the days of our ancestors is now, as you see, miserably divided into thirty or more kingdoms.

So says John of Fordun, the great chronicler of Scotland's past, writing in the 1380s.[1] He is a little confused, because the king Roderick in question is Ruaidrí Ua Conchobair, the last high-king of Ireland, who died in 1198, whereas, in the chronicle, the story is related by Scotland's famous king Máel Coluim Cennmór (Malcolm Canmore), who died just over a century earlier! But the jist of it is correct. An insertion in the *Annals of Connacht* for 1233 states: 'Here ends the rule of the children of Ruaidrí Ua Conchobair, king of Ireland. For the Pope offered him the title to Ireland for himself and his seed after him for ever, and six wives, if he would renounce the sin of adultery from then on; and since Ruaidrí would not accept that, God took the rule and sovereignty from his seed for ever in punishment for adultery'.[2] And the Irish antiquarian, Geoffrey Keating, writing in the seventeenth century, repeats a similar version of this moralising tale in his religious tract *Trí Bior-Ghaoithe an Bháis* ('The Three Shafts of Death').[3]

What is interesting about the occurrence of this story in Fordun's chronicle, apart from the light it may shed on his access to Irish sources of

15

information, is the view of Ireland which lies behind it, and which we can perhaps take as reflecting some section of Scottish opinion in the late fourteenth century. John is calling his contemporaries' attention to the decline in Ireland's fortunes in recent times. It is a kingdom which was once renowned, whose rulers, indeed, descended from the same stock as Scotland's, but it is now torn apart by the rivalries of petty kings, none of whom receives the obedience of the entire nation. And as Ireland has slumped, so Scotland has prospered. There is not much sympathy apparent in the account. John, of course, was a cleric and hardly likely to condone moral impropriety, but, over and above that, one senses a certain contemptuous attitude to Ireland, to the Irish, and to their purported barbarous ways. Clearly, in his view, while the Scots might retain a lingering memory of the ties which bound them to Ireland, their paths had long since diverged.

But to what extent had those paths ever run parallel or converged? In some respects, medieval Ireland had a great deal more in common with Wales than with Scotland. The similarities become apparent when one seeks to offer a definition of the peoples and countries in question. It is very easy to define what Ireland was, because it is an island. But Wales was only part of an island. So, where did its territory end? And who decided the matter? The answer, of course, is that Wales was the land of the Welsh, and Wales was, therefore, wherever the Welsh were. They were the pre-Roman inhabitants of Britain, continuing to regard themselves as the true Britons even after intruders stole their clothes. Though its borders might fluctuate according to the vicissitudes of war, Wales was a place inhabited by this people, and they *were* a people, a nation, because, whatever else divided them, they were united by language: they were the Cymry and their language was Cymraeg.[4]

Likewise, throughout its early history, at least until the arrival of the Vikings at the end of the eighth century, Ireland was inhabited by a people who spoke a common language and who believed themselves to be one nation: they were the Goídil, and their language was the language of the Goídil, taking its name, Goídelc, from them.[5] It was this exclusive insular domination which made it easy for the Irish to convince themselves that they were a nation; but it also made the inhabitants of that island very sensitive to new arrivals and conscious of their distinctiveness. Thus, throughout the Middle Ages, the indigenous inhabitants were always the Goídil, and newcomers, however long they had been in Ireland, were always the Gaill. Therefore, in Ireland there never emerged, at any stage in the Middle Ages, a willingness to 'accept' foreigners and to offer them, as it were, membership of the Irish nation.

Scotland, however, was not an island; like Wales, it was part of an island, and was surrounded to north and west by many smaller offshore islands. But medieval Scotland was, as Ireland and Wales were not, a heterogeneous society. Before a single Anglo-Norman set foot in it, Scottish society was multi-ethnic. In Caithness, in Argyll, in Galloway, and in the Western Isles, there was a strong Scandinavian input as a result of settlement in the Viking era. From an earlier age still, stretching south from Dumbarton on the Firth of Clyde to the Lake District in north-west England, were the people who had inhabited the ancient kingdom of Cumbria or Strathclyde. Ethnically, these people were predominantly Brittonic or British, related, in other words, to the people of Wales. They were matched on the east coast by the northern part of the Anglian kingdom of Northumbria, which is usually called Lothian, and provides the very important English element in the mix. To the north of these lay people descended from the Picts, but, whatever became of them, they were in time subsumed into the Gaelic social order, which had been imposed on northern Britain as a result of the Dalriadic invasion and colonisation from Ireland.

As a result of this heterogeneity, it was much more difficult for the inhabitants of that part of northern Britain that became Scotland to be exclusive. Foreigners who settled in Scotland could very quickly, within the space of a generation or two, 'become' Scots. This partly explains why it is that, although there was a massive programme of Anglo-Norman settlement and colonisation in both Ireland and Scotland in the twelfth century and later, in Ireland those Anglo-Normans remained a separate nation to the Irish, whereas in Scotland they became part of the Scots nation. They did not become 'the English of the land of Scotland' as their counterparts in Ireland were 'the English of the land of Ireland'. Instead, they became Scots, they came to see themselves as every bit as Scottish as the people they found there on their arrival, and Scotland and Scottishness, the Scots identity, adapted itself to make room for them.

Hence, for instance, the Irish sent a famous Remonstrance to the Pope in 1317 saying of the Anglo-Irish that they were so different from them in customs and language (*in condicionibus et lingua sunt nobis aliisque multum dissimiliores*) that there was, and never in the future could be, sincere concord between them (*quod sicut nec fuit actenus nec unquam de cetero inter nos et illos sincera concordia esse*);[6] on the other hand, three years later, the Scots also wrote off to the Pope – the famous Declaration of Arbroath – in which they boasted of their ancestral triumphs in Scotland over the Britons, and the Picts, the Norwegians, the Danes, and the English, and yet many of those in whose name this letter was sent were the grandsons and great-grandsons of men who had migrated, usually via England, from Normandy and Brittany and Flanders, and had only settled in Scotland in the comparatively recent past.[7] The fact that they now proudly proclaimed that they were Scots, part of a nation that had inhabited the northern part of Britain since the dawn of history, surely indicates that, unlike Irishness, Scottishness was not an exclusive club; membership was wide open, and it was that openness, that receptiveness, that adaptability that contributed to the emergence of Scotland as a highly respected (if second-rank) monarchy on the western European model, from the twelfth century onwards.

However, at the time when Scotland first truly emerged into the pages of history, it was its Gaelic culture which was supreme. It was this, in fact, which gave the land its very name, Scotia, the land of the Sco[t]ti, the original preferred Latin name for the Irish. So, whilst there may be quite stark comparisons between Scotland and Ireland in the Middle Ages, there is no escaping this one overriding link. The Irish and the Scots – that is to say, the dominant political elite within what we call Scotland – traced their descent back to a common origin. They were, taken to the logical extreme, of the same nation.

And yet, with a few notable exceptions, historians of medieval Scotland have frequently in the past paid little more than lip-service to this most fundamental of facts. What is worse, they have sometimes ignored if not actually expunged the evidence. For instance, in the 1950s, the great Scottish medievalist, Professor Archie Duncan, discovered in Edinburgh University Library, Borland MS 207, a formulary containing drafts of letters, one of which in particular bears all the indications of having been originally drawn up for Robert Bruce. This letter, in Latin, as one would expect, was apparently sent, or intended to be sent, by Robert to Ireland. Professor Duncan would have been the first to recognise it as an important document, and he has since provided two editions of it, one along with the rest of the documents in the formulary, and another in his marvellous collection of the acts of Robert I.[8] But the first person to publish the letter was, in fact, Ranald Nicholson, untranslated and without much in the way of commentary, in an appendix to an article which appeared in the *Scottish Historical Review* in 1963.[9] Two years later, another giant of medieval Scottish historiography, Geoffrey Barrow, produced his classic biography of Robert Bruce, in which he provided a translation of this letter, from which the following extract is taken:

> The king sends greetings to all the kings of Ireland, to the prelates and clergy, and to the inhabitants of all Ireland, his friends.
>   Whereas we and you and our people and your people, free since ancient times, share the same national ancestry and are urged to come together more eagerly and joyfully in friendship by a common language and by common

custom, we have sent over to you our beloved kinsmen, the bearers of this letter, to negotiate with you in our name about permanently strengthening and maintaining inviolate the special friendship between us and you, so that with God's will *your nation* may be able to recover her ancient liberty...[10]

Professor Barrow translated the letter thus, in spite of the fact that both the original manuscript and Ranald Nicholson's edition did not contain the phrase 'vestra nacio', but 'nostra nacio' – 'our nation'. If the letter is indeed the product of his chancery, Robert Bruce wrote seeking an alliance with the Irish so that 'our nation', the Scots and Irish nation, might be able to recover her ancient freedom.

It should be stressed that in a subsequent edition Geoffrey Barrow amended his translation so that it now does indeed read 'our nation',[11] but one wonders whether his original decision to translate this phrase as he did – in effect, to assume that the manuscript contained a scribal error – stemmed from an unwillingness, perhaps even an inability, to accept that a man like Robert Bruce, a Scottish nobleman in the fourteenth century, other than perhaps an inhabitant of the Highlands and Islands, might regard himself or seek to pass himself off as of the same nation as the Irish. And yet, it seems that this is the case, and must therefore be confronted as, to his great credit, Professor Barrow has done in his important pamphlet, *Robert the Bruce and the Scottish Identity*.[12] In fact, one cannot but be impressed by the openness of Scottish historians in recent years to the Irish dimension in Scottish history, a development which has done much to break down barriers previously erected, and to remind us that medieval Scots, including the kings of medieval Scotland, were indeed conscious of their Irish links, whether in a strictly ethnic sense in the form of genealogies and king-lists which linked them into the Irish chain of descent,[13] or in the broader cultural, social, and ecclesiastical sense with which we have perhaps in the past been more familiar.

This has undoubtedly been a very positive development, since it has helped to a certain extent to free us from the shackles of hindsight. Because Scotland has had a constitutional link with England for the last four centuries, there is something of a tendency to write its history as if that had always been the case, or had always been fated. At the very least, historical writing has been focussed on examining how that state of affairs arose. This is useful to the extent that it helps us to understand how things came to be the way they are. It is not helpful, however, if it involves airbrushing the picture to remove those images which might have suggested a different story. If the story that is to be told is of the emergence of a distinct kingdom of the Scots, the development of the Scottish monarchy and parliament, and eventual union of both crown and parliament with England, then the exercise will produce an abundant supply of red herrings for which there is no market. And Ireland will be one of them. For so long as eyes are firmly focussed on Scotland's frontier to the south, rather than the damp and misty west, telling the story of Scotland's relationship with Ireland in the Middle Ages is not going to be part of the enterprise of Scottish historiography.

One must admit, of course, to the existence of a similar situation in Ireland, where the historiography of the country from the twelfth century onwards is dominated by discussion of Anglo-Irish relations. The inevitable consequence for both Scotland and Ireland, though, is that the book shelves and the academic journals are heavy with works on medieval Anglo-Scottish relations and on Anglo-Irish relations, but the story of Scotland's connection with Ireland in this period still remains largely untold. This is not because there is very little to say on the subject, and neither is it, surely, because the connection was not viewed as being important in its own day. The shelves remain empty, and the story remains untold, because *we* do not regard it as important.

An obvious example of this springs to mind, again involving Robert Bruce and Geoffrey Barrow, though this is most emphatically not intended as a criticism of the latter. As has recently been succinctly stated (by someone better equipped than most to judge): 'There are two great books about Robert Bruce, one written in the fourteenth century by John Barbour, the other in our time by G.W.S. Barrow'.[14] Bruce died in 1329, but did not find a biographer as such until Barbour, archdeacon of Aberdeen, wrote his epic poem, 'The Bruce', some fifty or so years later. As it has come down to us, this fourteenth-century metrical biography has 13, 645 lines. From an Irish point of view, one of the most remarkable things about Bruce's career is his decision, not long after his great victory at Bannockburn, to launch an invasion of Ireland, led by his brother Edward, whom he set up as king there. Archdeacon Barbour obviously thought this important too, because he devoted a full 1407 lines to it, some 10% of his poem. In fact, if one bears in mind, as is well known, that Barbour's poem is in a sense a double biography, of both Bruce and Sir James Douglas, Barbour making ample use of a now lost work on the latter, and one attempts to isolate and quantify the contents of this lost record, it comes to not far short of another 3,000 lines; if this source were excluded from the calculation, the proportion of 'The Bruce' given over to Edward Bruce's Irish invasion would be in the region of 13%. Professor Barrow's biography is the definitive twentieth-century work on Bruce, and first appeared, as already noted, in 1965. It contains over 450 pages of text, but of this, the Irish invasion as such occupies only one paragraph.

Now, Geoffrey Barrow was not being a 'bad historian' in relegating the Irish aspect of Bruce's career to this position; but he was being a man of his time. In the 1370s, when Archdeacon Barbour was writing, the affairs of Ireland and Scotland (or, to be more accurate, of parts of Ireland and parts of Scotland) were quite closely entwined. Of course, they had been even more closely-knit in the past, but Barbour was not to know that they were now irreversibly drifting apart. He simply told it as he – or his source(s) – saw it, and gave Ireland the coverage he thought it deserved. The plans which the Scots had had for Ireland a generation or two earlier still seemed important, even though Edward Bruce had been killed in battle there, and the Scottish kingship of Ireland had died with him. Barbour was, one presumes, merely expressing a contemporary belief that Scottish involvement in Ireland in the time of Robert Bruce was relevant, was not an aberration from the main story of Scotland. By the mid-1960s, on the other hand, things looked rather different. No one can deny that Ireland and Scotland had indeed drifted very far apart in the intervening centuries.[15] Ireland had come to occupy a very peripheral role in Scottish affairs, and anyone writing about Robert Bruce, and trying to assess his contribution to Scottish history, would not spill too much ink on waxing lyrical about his Hibernophilia.

That was the 1960s, and that was the norm then. But something has happened since. It may be part of a change of mood in Scotland, a growing sense of being or of wanting to be more distinctively Scottish.[16] It certainly seems to be the case that work produced in recent years on the history of medieval Scotland is less preoccupied with England. It is not simply that other neglected aspects of Scottish life in the Middle Ages are getting the attention they deserve, but that Scottish links with other places besides England are being investigated. Neither has the Auld Alliance with France monopolised this expansion of interest: in the last decade or so, we have witnessed an explosion of publications on Scotland and Europe generally;[17] on the Scandinavian world to which northern and western Scotland and the kingdom of the Isles belonged since the Viking Age;[18] North Sea trading contacts;[19] Scotland's contribution to European art, architecture, and intellectual movements;[20] and links with Ireland that, of course, reach back further still.[21] (And it is interesting to note that Geoffrey Barrow's recently re-worked edition of his *Robert Bruce* devotes somewhat more space to Ireland than the earlier editions.)

In Scotland today, therefore, there would appear to be a growing interest in Ireland; but if so, why is it the case? Regrettably, there has not been in Ireland a corresponding growth of interest in medieval Scotland, with the notable, if misdirected, exception of those in whose work one is inclined to detect contemporary political animus.[22] Could it be that, as Scots have gone in pursuit of their Scottishness, their search has brought them to Ireland, and Scottish historians, trying to understand what made medieval Scotland tick, have come to conclude that, perhaps, in the past, they have underestimated the significance of the Gaelic component in that society? One would not, of course, want to make too much of this point by arguing, for instance, that in, let us say, the reign of Robert Bruce, its Gaelic inheritance was still the oxygen in the lifeblood of the Scots nation. Nevertheless, it is demonstrable that throughout this period a vital ingredient in the dynamic of Scottish society continued to be supplied by Ireland. Dauvit Broun has shown that accounts of Scottish origins produced (probably by individuals who did not belong to the Gaelic learned classes) in the thirteenth century, at a time when we tend to view Scotland's elite as turning its back on the Gaelic world, still proclaim the Irish roots of the Scots, and do not dilute earlier definitions of Ireland as their divinely-ordained homeland.[23] These accounts are not moribund antiquarian scrapbooks, but are intended, partly at least, to serve a contemporary political purpose: their redactors and their patrons hope that they will assist in proving (or reminding others, and perhaps themselves, of) the antiquity of Scotland's royal line, and vindicate their country's claim to freedom, long before the first war of independence provided a greater urgency for such a line of defence. At a time when, as we know especially from the work of the likes of John Gillingham, Rees Davies, and Robert Bartlett, the pressure should have been on the Scots to deny their Irish origin,[24] they seem to be trumpeting it from the very rooftops.

Admittedly, the documents presented by Scottish clerical lobbyists to counter Edward I's diplomatic offensive at the papal curia in 1301 give an account of the wanderings of the ancient Scoti which records only a temporary stopover in Ireland,[25] while the account of Scottish origins in the Declaration of Arbroath blithely bypasses Ireland altogether! But there may have been special circumstances at work here: Scotland's case for independence from English lordship might have been undermined if it included an admission of Irish descent at a time when the papacy acknowledged the legitimacy of English rule over Ireland. The fact is that the evidence for a continued Scottish belief in the importance of their bond with the Irish has been there for all to see in Robert Bruce's aforementioned letter to Ireland, when he spoke of the Scots and Irish sharing 'the same national ancestry', or, to give a more direct translation, stemming from 'one seed of birth (*ab vno processimus germine nacionis*)' [26]

Scottish, and, indeed, Irish historians would perhaps be inclined to take that with a pinch of salt, and one can argue that Robert had a brazen nerve talking in such terms since the Bruces were of Anglo-Norman extraction. However, the extent of Bruce's immersion in the Gaelic world is well known, and he did, of course, have direct Gaelic ancestry, admittedly on his mother's side, being the daughter of Niall (Latinized Nigellus), earl of Carrick. What is more, we have solid evidence that an awareness of this connection existed among his family's Irish supporters. When Domnall Ua Néill of Ulster sent his Remonstrance to the pope during the course of Edward Bruce's invasion of Ireland, explaining why he supported the Scots' attempt to overthrow English rule, he said of the English that 'in order to shake off the harsh and insufferable yoke of servitude to them and to recover our native freedom which for the time being we have lost through them...we call to our help and assistance the illustrious Edward de Bruce earl of Carrick, the brother of the Lord Robert by the grace of God the most illustrious king of Scots, and sprung from our noblest ancestors (*de nobilioribus progenitoribus nostris ortum*)'.[27]

Precisely what connection Ua Néill had in mind between the Bruce family and his own 'noblest ancestors' (or those of the Irish in general, on whose behalf he purported to write) is difficult now to say. Assuming that the Gall-Goídil from whom Galloway takes its name were partly of Dalriadic ancestry, Bruce's Carrick forbears could, no doubt, have been fitted into the Irish genealogical pyramid, but one has to travel back a great distance into the purely mythical to find the link: if one began one's journey at Cináed mac Alpín (Kenneth MacAlpin) and travelled back perhaps ten generations to Fergus mac Eircc, supposed founder of Scottish Dál Riata, one would still have the best part of another forty generations to go before reaching the apical figure, Óengus Turbech Temra, from whom both the Uí Néill of the northern half of Ireland and the royal house of Scotland traced their descent![28] There is, though, a shortcut. The eponymous ancestor of the O'Neills of later medieval Ulster, including, of course, Domnall Ua Néill, was the high-king Niall Glúndub, who died in 919. His mother, Máel Muire (d. 913), was Cináed mac Alpín's daughter.[29] If the rulers of greater Galloway could claim descent from Cináed, they were indeed related to Domnall Ua Néill, but at a remove of perhaps as much as fourteen generations. The possibility of a yet closer connection should not be dismissed. The Bruce family sought to perpetuate their links with their Gaelic ancestors in Carrick by retaining the name Niall in the family. Robert Bruce had a brother of this name, called after their maternal grandfather, the last 'native' earl of Carrick (d. 1256). The latter was a son of Duncan of Carrick (d. 1250) who, intermittently since at least 1197, held lands in Ulster granted to him by its Cumbrian conqueror, John de Courcy.[30] For much of the quarter of a century in which de Courcy ruled

Ulster he was allied to the O'Neills. The *floruit* of Domnall Ua Néill's own grandfather was at this precise point – he died in 1223 – and his name was Niall Ruad ('the Red'). Did Duncan of Carrick give his heir the same name because of an alliance with Niall's family? If so, Robert and Edward Bruce did indeed spring from Domnall Ua Néill's 'noblest ancestors'.

Whatever the precise connection, in this period we are not simply dealing with the Bruces exploiting some vague memories of primordial links which may have survived among the naive Irish, and thereby manipulating Irish dissidence or restiveness for their own ends. Ua Néill, perhaps the most powerful king in Ireland, is striving of his own accord and for his own purposes to convince the outside world that Edward Bruce is more entitled to rule the Irish than Edward II because he is 'sprung from our noblest ancestors'. Hence, a major faction within Gaelic Ireland, led by Domnall Ua Néill, voluntarily joined forces with the king of Scots and his brother in a campaign against their common enemy, England, and both sought to harness the potency of the contemporary consciousness of the shared progeny of the Scots and Irish. It was this shared Gaelic inheritance, therefore, which provided something of the inspiration for the Bruce invasion of Ireland. On this point, it is worth recalling an observation made by Professor Archie Duncan, in a recent paper on this subject, in which he stated his conclusion that the invasion is 'an expedition which cannot be explained by a close or continuous inter-relationship of Irish and Scottish families or politics'.[31] One does not choose lightly to disagree with such an authority, but I would suggest rather that the Bruce invasion cannot be explained by any means *other* than a close and continuous inter-relationship between Irish and Scottish families and politics. If Professor Duncan's verdict was correct, there is nothing in the long-term political relationship between Ireland and Scotland in this era which explains why the Scots launched an invasion of Ireland; and there is nothing by way of long-running family connections between the peoples of both countries which might explain why some individuals in Ireland and Scotland supported the enterprise, and others not.

Needless to say, to refute such a conclusion, and to do so succinctly, is not easy, since it involves an examination, on the one hand, of relationships over a lengthy time-scale between families with points of contact on both sides of the North Channel, and, on the other, of the politics of the north Irish Sea area. But, while we await a full study, perhaps a few benchmarks could be laid down here.[32] Above all else, it is vital to examine events in the Irish Sea world, of which the Bruce invasion is simply one of the most dramatic and best-documented, in a sufficiently long-term context. Over the centuries, extraordinary things happened that involved men from

Ireland in Scotland and men from Scotland in Ireland. But if each is looked at in isolation, they naturally have the appearance of happening out of the blue, and it is impossible, therefore, to build up a contextual framework for them. So, the result is that they have tended to be ignored, or relegated to the realm of anecdote, or just explained away as once-off random eccentricities of the Celtic world. On the other hand, a long-term study of the subject, even though it may still not prove possible to explain each incident fully, allows us at least to say that we had seen similar such occurrences on other occasions, and that they fit into a long-standing pattern.

Such a study suggests, for instance, that the relationship between Ireland and Scotland in the thirteenth and early fourteenth centuries was a good deal closer and more complex than sometimes allowed. It has long been an article of faith among historians (and hence has received little real investigation) that a steady undercurrent of contact flowed between Gaelic Ireland and Gaelic Scotland. By contradistinction, the tendency has been to minimise the extent of interfusion between the Scots and the Anglo-Norman colonists in Ireland. Yet this was an everyday fact of life, and it played a part in sowing the seeds that produced the Bruce invasion, and in dictating its outcome. For all of the time that he was in Ireland, attempting to establish his claim to its kingship, Edward Bruce's centre of power was in east Ulster, occupying the lands of its earl, Richard de Burgh; the latter was Robert's father-in-law, though they had undoubtedly parted company by now. By and large, the Anglo-Irish tenants of the earldom of Ulster also resisted the temptation to commit treason by joining the Scots, and instead remained loyal to Edward II.[33] No doubt, many factors were at play here, but one of their reasons was because they were heavily involved on the English side in the war in Scotland. Let us take the example of the fitz Warin family. They had a long pedigree in Ulster, their ancestors having come there during the reign of King John.[34] In the early 1270s, during Richard de Burgh's minority, Sir William fitz Warin was seneschal of the earldom of Ulster.[35] But after the battle of Stirling Bridge in September 1297, he was entrusted with holding Stirling Castle for the English,[36] and shortly afterwards Alexander Comyn wrote a letter of recommendation on his behalf to Edward I.[37] In the period 1297–9, Comyn was involved with, among others, John Comyn of Badenoch, murdered by Robert Bruce in 1306, and Alexander Mac Dubgaill of Argyll, later one of Bruce's most inveterate opponents, in a violent campaign in the west highlands and islands, which was directed in part at least against one of Bruce's most loyal supporters in Ireland, Clann Domnaill of Islay.[38] It seems more than likely that William fitz Warin was also involved in this rivalry between Clann Dubgaill and Clann Domnaill, because he was married at this point to

Alexander Mac Dubgaill's much-married sister Mary; and, apart from fitz Warin's lands in Ulster, we know that he had a stake across the North Channel also since, when he died in 1299, his heir quitclaimed any rights he had to 'all Sir William's goods in Scotland'.[39]

But that is just one example of the complicated family background to the Bruce invasion. Prior to William fitz Warin, the seneschal of Ulster had been Sir Henry de Mandeville. The latter was killed in north Antrim in the 1270s, but in 1319 another Henry de Mandeville was involved in the death of a son of Domnall Ua Néill, Bruce's great ally.[40] Surely they were related to the Sir Henry de Mandeville who was among the magnates of Scotland to do homage to Edward I in March 1296, who was a juror that August at an inquisition into the holdings in Wigtownshire of Elana la Zouche, who was written to by Edward I on 24 May 1297, who received £20 in 1311–12 for a horse killed in action against the Scots in the service of Edward II, and who was in the English garrison in Berwick in 1312.[41] The de Mandevilles had been in Ulster since the early thirteenth century, and became widely ramified there, so that it is not surprising to find one or two of them taking the side of the Scots during the 1315–18 invasion,[42] but most did not, including the head of the family, Sir Thomas de Mandeville. A copy of a suspicious-looking document survives purporting to be a conveyence by Duncan earl of Carrick (d. 1250) to Sir Thomas (d. 1316) of the Carrick lands in Ulster,[43] but it seems a fair bet that when Edward Bruce, newly created earl of Carrick, and would-be heir to this estate, landed on the coast of Antrim in the early summer of 1315, he had as one of his more straightforward objectives the recovery of these family lands .

Another analogous family are the Logans, prominent in Ulster since the days of de Courcy. They may have been related to Walter Logan, lord of Hartside in East Lothian, who had a grant of Luce in Annandale from the Bruce family in 1298, was among those whose lands were confiscated by Edward I for adhering to Robert in 1306, and witnessed at least two charters in the company of Reginald Crawford, sometime sheriff of Ayr (who was executed in 1307 when he landed in Galloway with an Irish army in the company of Thomas and Alexander Bruce).[44] Walter seems afterwards to have deserted the Bruce cause since on the very eve of the Bruce invasion, on 4 May 1315, Edward II assigned him the task of sending from Ireland to England a force of 500 hobelars and armed foot.[45] During the Bruce invasion the head of the Irish-based family was John Logan, who had been among those Anglo-Irish requested by Edward II to take part in a proposed expedition to Scotland in 1310, and who was conspicious by his opposition to the Bruces in 1315–18.[46] But was he simply being loyal to his lord, the king of England? One of Robert Bruce's most enduring contributions to the history of western Scotland was his displacement of the Mac Dubgaill lordship of Argyll and the stimulus he provided to their Mac Domnaill collaterals in creating what became their great 'Lordship of the Isles': in Ireland, the latter stood shoulder to shoulder with Edward Bruce (the head of the family dying with him at Fochart) while Eógan Bacach Mac Dubgaill (John de Ergadia or 'of Argyll') spent his last days in a rather pathetic effort to undermine them.[47] John Logan did indeed join in his efforts, but had this anything to do with the fact that when he was a minor, back in 1299, his wardship had been granted to Eógan Bacach Mac Dubgaill's sister, Mary, the widow of William fitz Warin?[48]

One of Alan Logan's more notable successes against the Scots was the capture, in 1316, of Alan Steward of Jedburgh.[49] He did so in the company of one John Sandal, again a member of a family with a long history in Ulster,[50] but what relationship, if any, had the latter with Sir John Sandal, Edward I's chamberlain for Scotland a decade or so earlier?[51] Joining them in their success was Hugh Bisset, a member of a family who had been prominent in Ulster since the 1240s, and whose important place in contemporary Scottish history needs no rehearsal here.[52] Edward Bruce's arrival in Ireland must have struck terror into the hearts of those occupying the estate of his great-grandfather, Duncan of Carrick: that estate was centred around Glenarm in County Antrim, and Hugh Bisset claimed to be lord of Glenarm. He was therefore the first in Bruce's line of fire, and provides no better illustration of the way in which Edward's Irish invasion *must* be viewed as, in part at least, a manifestation of the close and continuous inter-relationship of Irish and Scottish families and politics.

It is undoubtedly the case that there were many more families caught in this net, but it is not the purpose of this chapter to analyse the subject in the detailed manner it deserves, merely to call attention to the intimacy of the cross-channel relationships at this point, so that the apparently intensified interactions of the Bruce years may be viewed in a better perspective. An insensitivity to this context has been one of the failings in the past in terms of the historical assessment of the Bruce wars in general and Edward Bruce's invasion of Ireland in particular.[53] Awareness of it does not make the Bruce invasion any less remarkable, but it does serve to make aspects of it somewhat easier to explain. Above all else, the familiarity with Ireland of those at the highest level of Scottish society, both in the Gaelic world and beyond, meant that when a crisis erupted in Scotland in 1286, and especially after war with England broke out there a decade later, it was bound to have implications for Ireland, and it was very likely indeed that that war would spill over unto Irish soil.

In that sense, the Bruce invasion is an example of continuity and convergence in Hiberno-Scottish relations. There is, though, one way in which the events of Robert Bruce's reign mark a divergence, and do not fit into an earlier pattern. Professor Rees Davies recently published an important set of essays entitled *Domination and Conquest. The Experience of Ireland, Scotland and Wales, 1100–1300*, in which he analyses the process by which the Anglo-Norman (later, English) kings gained an ever-increasing dominance over the other peoples inhabiting these islands. It is a very persuasive argument and he brings out extremely well the similarities and the differences in the experience of the Scots, Irish and Welsh, at English hands, and the gradual intensification – the tightening of the screw – of English overlordship over each. But for much of the time, as he himself would be the first to admit, in trying to treat of the affairs and experience of Scotland in the same breath as Ireland and Wales, one gets the feeling that one is pushing a square peg into a round hole. The reason, as mentioned earlier, is that Ireland and Wales had very similar experiences of Anglo-Norman aggression, albeit, in the case of the Welsh, a century before the Irish, shortly after the Norman conquest. And that experience included dispossession, colonisation, denial of access to the law, erosion of the power of the native rulers, and ultimately the assertion of English lordship over both countries.

Now, at the same time in Scotland something very different was happening. Unlike Ireland and Wales, Scotland had only one king, and far from being invaded by Normans, he was inviting them in, using them as instruments in the assertion and expansion of his own royal authority. So when, for instance, the Anglo-Normans invaded Ireland, the Scots, at least the Scots nobility many of whom had good Anglo-Norman pedigrees, felt no great sympathy for the native rulers whose lands were removed and power eroded. Their sympathies, in fact, lay full square with the invaders, the contemporary Melrose chronicle, for instance, pointing out proudly that their leader Strongbow was a first-cousin of the Scottish king.[54] And when Edward I conquered Wales in the early 1280s, Alexander III was still comfortably on the Scottish throne, and there is no reason to think that he felt any unease at this development. However, twelve years later when Alexander was dead and his direct royal line extinct, the Scots found themselves in a very different position, facing war with England, and an attempt by Edward I to repeat there his earlier success in Wales.

It is at this point that a major sea-change takes place in the affairs and attitudes of the Scots. They very quickly found that hand in hand with a campaign of opposition to the king of England went the attempt to foment trouble for him elsewhere. The Welsh, in the past, had been able to benefit from sympathetic outbursts of rebellion across the Irish Sea,[55] because they themselves were free of ties with the Anglo-Norman colonists there, and in many cases, as already noted, suffered at their hands in the same way that the native Irish did. The problem for the Scots, when their breakdown in relations with the English occurred, was that they could not make such ready recourse to Irish support, since they themselves were products of the Anglo-Norman world, and their ties and sympathies had lain hitherto with the colonial community in Ireland.

Here, therefore, we find one of the most remarkable consequences of the rupture with England that took place in the 1290s, and that is that the Scots, most spectacularly in the case of the Bruces, in trying to sow the seeds of trouble for the domineering Edward I and for his weak son and successor Edward II, were forced into the camp of the native Irish. In fact, Bruce's actions in the immediate aftermath of his coup, in particular his seizure of several of the more strategic fortresses commanding the firth of Clyde,[56] virtually necessitate the conclusion that securing the route to Ireland was an integral part of his plan of action in grabbing the kingship. The wisdom of so doing soon became clear when, within weeks, he was a hunted fugitive seeking refuge in Rathlin off the coast of Antrim and elsewhere in the Isles. It was surely at this point that he sent his letter to the Irish,[57] which provides us with a dramatic insight into Robert's policy and strategy in the initial stages of his kingship.

One of the more remarkable features of this letter is that, in spite of the fact that he had married the daughter of the Anglo-Irish earl of Ulster only some four years earlier, the document had an appeal limited to the native Irish. When Bruce talks about the Scots and Irish coming from 'one seed of birth', having been free since ancient times, and sharing a common language and customs, and when he speaks of 'permanently strengthening and maintaining inviolate the special friendship between us and you, so that with God's will our nation may be able to recover her ancient liberty', his address could not but ring hollow in the ears of Anglo-Irishmen. This, therefore, was Robert Bruce's attempt, however unqualified for the task he may appear to modern eyes, to appeal to the common Gaelic inheritance of Ireland and Scotland, reminding the Irish that they too have lost their freedom at English hands, and suggesting that the way forward lies in joint action.

In a sense, the Irish letter shows the Scots, amid the crisis they faced in the winter of 1306–7, being forced to re-discover their identity, or, in the case of the new King Robert perhaps, re-inventing their identity, including their links with their ancestral homeland. Had the embassy, and the Bruce family's subsequent efforts in Ireland, achieved their intended purpose, this juncture would have marked a re-convergence of Scottish and Irish interests. In some small respect, therefore, Robert Bruce's *Littera directa ad Yberniam* may be said to have marked Scotland's rediscovery of itself, its Scottishness, and, accordingly, its Irishness. But his plans came to nothing. Edward Bruce 'by God's grace king of Ireland' died there in 1318, and Robert, though addressed on at least one subsequent occasion as 'by God's grace king of Scotland and Ireland,'[58] did not long outlive him. What seemed, under the Bruces, the prospect of a spectacular convergence gave way, under their Stewart successors, to a gradual, inexorable, and unhappy divergence.

REFERENCES

1. The quotation is from the later elaboration of Fordun, *Scotichronicon by Walter Bower*, vol 3, J. MacQueen, W. MacQueen and D.E.R. Watt (eds.) (Edinburgh, 1995); but see also John of Fordun, *Chronica Gentis Scotorum*, in W.F. Skene (ed.), *Historians of Scotland*, vols I and IV (Edinburgh, 1871–2), IV, 186.

2. A.M. Freeman (ed.), *Annála Connacht. The Annals of Connacht* (Dublin, 1944), 47.

3. Osborn Bergin (ed.), *Trí Bior-Ghaoithe an Bháis. The Three Shafts of Death* (Dublin, 1931), 171.

4. See R.R. Davies, *Conquest, Coexistence, and Change: Wales 1063–1415* (Oxford, 1987), chap. 1; and the latter's presidential addresses to the Royal Historical Society, on the theme of 'The peoples of Britain and Ireland 1100–1400', esp. I, 'Identities', *Royal Hist. Soc. Trans.*, 6th ser., iv (1994), 1–20, and IV, 'Language and historical mythology', ibid., vii (1997), 1–24.

5. Donnchadh Ó Corráin, 'Nationality and kingship in pre-Norman Ireland', in T.W. Moody (ed.), *Nationality and the Pursuit of National Independence: Historical Studies XI* (Belfast, 1978), 1–35; see also, F.J. Byrne, 'Senchas: the nature of Gaelic historical tradition', in John Barry (ed.), *Historical Studies IX* (Belfast, 1974), 137–59.

6. Bower, *Scotichronicon*, Watt (ed.), vol. 6, 396–9.

7. For the text and discussion, see A.A.M. Duncan, *The Nation of Scots and the Declaration of Arbroath*, Historical Association Pamphlet, 75 (London, 1970).

8. A.A.M. Duncan (ed.), *Formulary E. Scottish Letters and Brieves 1286–1424* (Glasgow, 1976), 44; *Regesta Regum Scottorum V: The Acts of Robert I* (Edinburgh, 1988), 695.

9. 'A sequel to Edward Bruce's invasion of Ireland', *Scot. Hist. Rev.*, xlii (1963), 30–40.

10. G.W.S. Barrow, *Robert Bruce and the Community of the Realm of Scotland* (London, 1965), 434 (my italics).

11. *Robert Bruce*, 3rd edn (Edinburgh, 1988), 314 and 379, note 9.

12. It is interesting that, whereas in the second edition of *Robert Bruce*, Barrow commented that 'I remain not wholly convinced...that the Irish question was central to Robert I's political strategy, at any rate for more than a few years' (Edinburgh, 1976, 446), in his pamphlet he refers to Bruce's 'constant preoccupation with Ireland' (*Robert the Bruce and the Scottish Identity*, Saltire Pamphlets, new ser., 4 (Edinburgh, 1984), 17).

13. The great pioneer of modern research into Scottish and Irish genealogical links has been W.D.H. Sellar. See, for example, 'The origins and ancestry of Somerled', *Scot. Hist. Rev.*, vl (1966), 123–42; 'Family origins in Cowal and Knapdale', *Scottish Studies*, 15 (1971), 21–37; 'The earliest Campbells – Norman, Briton or Gael?', ibid., 17 (1973), 109–25; 'Highland family origins – pedigree making and pedigree faking', in Loraine Maclean (ed.), *The Middle Ages in the Highlands* (Inverness, 1981), 103–16. For Scottish royal consciousness of Ireland, one may note, for instance, E.J. Cowan, 'Myth and identity in early medieval Scotland', *Scot. Hist. Rev.*, lxiii (1984), 111–35; John Bannerman, 'The king's poet and the inauguration of Alexander III', *Scot. Hist. Rev.*, lxviii (1989), 120–49; Seán Duffy, 'The Bruce brothers and the Irish Sea world, 1306–29', *Cambridge Medieval Celtic Studies*, xxi (1991), 55–86; Dauvit Broun, 'The origin of Scottish identity', in C. Bjørn, A. Grant, K.J. Stringer (eds.), *The Formation of Social Identities in the European Past* (Copenhagen, 1994), 35–55. The latter has really made this subject his own, and I am very grateful to him for making available to me a draft of his important forthcoming paper, 'Anglo-French acculturation and the Irish element in Scottish identity'.

14. A.A.M. Duncan, in the preface to his recent edition of John Barbour, *The Bruce* (Edinburgh, 1997), vii.

15. I exclude, of course, the strong Ulster-Scots links established as a consequence of the seventeenth-century Plantations as these were, in most respects, quite distinct from earlier medieval patterns of contact.

16. In his introduction to Barbour's *Bruce*, Professor Duncan remarks that one of the reasons it recommends itself to its readers is because of its 'invocation of freedom for our land which resonates so powerfully in the late twentieth century' (1).

17. For instance, Alan Macquarrie, *Scotland and the Crusades, 1096–1560* (Edinburgh, 1985); T.C. Smout (ed.), *Scotland and Europe 1200–1850* (Edinburgh, 1986); G.G. Simpson (ed.), *The Scottish Soldier Abroad, 1247–1967* (Edinburgh, 1992); T.C. Smout (ed.), *Scotland and the Sea* (Edinburgh, 1992); Barbara Crawford (ed.), *Scotland in Dark Age Europe* (St Andrews, 1994); G.G. Simpson, *Scotland and the Low Countries, 1124–1994* (East Linton, 1996).

18. A. Fenton and H. Pálsson (eds.), *The Northern and Western Isles in the Viking World* (Edinburgh, 1984); Barbara Crawford, *Scandinavian Scotland* (Leicester, 1987); Knut Helle, 'Norwegian foreign policy and the Maid of Norway', *Scot. Hist. Rev.*, lxix (1990), 142–56; G.G. Simpson, *Scotland and Scandinavia, 800–*

1800 (Edinburgh, 1990); C.E. Batey, J. Jesch, C.D. Morris (eds.), *The Viking Age in Caithness, Orkney, and the North Atlantic* (Edinburgh, 1993); R. Andrew McDonald, *The Kingdom of the Isles. Scotland's Western Seaboard in the Central Middle Ages, c. 1100–c. 1336* (East Linton, 1997).

19. David Ditchburn's work has been especially important here: see, for instance, 'Trade with Northern Europe, 1297–1540', in M. Lynch, M. Spearman, G. Stell (eds.), *The Scottish Medieval Town* (Edinburgh, 1988), 161–79; ibid., 'Cargoes and commodities: Aberdeen's trade with Scandinavian and the Baltic, c.1302–c.1542', *Northern Studies*, xxvii (1990), 12–22; and contributions to volumes cited in note 17 above.

20. J.D. McClure and M.R.G. Spiller (eds.), *Bryght Lanternis: Essays on the Language and Literature of Medieval and Renaissance Scotland* (Aberdeen, 1989); G. Williams and R.O. Jones (eds.), *The Celts and the Renaissance: Tradition and Innovations* (Cardiff, 1990); R.M. Spearman and J. Higgitt (eds.), *The Age of Migrating Ideas: Early Medieval Art in Northern Britain and Ireland* (Edinburgh, 1993); A.A. MacDonald, M. Lynch, I.B. Cowan (eds), *The Renaissance in Scotland* (Leiden, 1994); P. Dukes (ed.), *The Universities of Scotland and Europe: The First Three Centuries* (Aberdeen, 1995).

21. See, for example, S.T. Driscoll and M.R. Nieke (eds.), *Power and Politics in Early Medieval Britain and Ireland* (Edinburgh, 1988); Máire Herbert, *Iona, Kells and Derry. The History and Hagiography of the Monastic Familia of Columba* (Oxford, 1988); R.R. Davies, *Domination and Conquest. The Experience of Ireland, Scotland and Wales 1100–1300* (Cambridge, 1990); B.T. Hudson, *Kings of Celtic Scotland* (Westport, Conn., 1994); Colm McNamee, *The Wars of the Bruces. Scotland, England and Ireland, 1306–1328* (East Linton, 1997).

22. The leading light here is Ian Adamson: *Cruithin: the Ancient Kindred* (Conlig, Co. Down, 1974); *The Identity of Ulster: the Land, the Language* [sic]*, and the People* (s.l., 1982); *The Ulster People: Ancient, Medieval, and Modern* (Bangor, Co. Down, 1991).

23. Broun, 'Anglo-French acculturation and the Irish element in Scottish identity' (forthcoming).

24. John Gillingham, 'The beginnings of English imperialism', *Journal of Historical Sociology*, 5 (1992), 392–409; idem, 'Conquering the barbarians: war and chivalry in twelfth-century Britain', *Haskins Society Journal*, iv (1993), 67–84; idem, 'The English invasion of Ireland', in B. Bradshaw, A. Hadfield, W. Maley (eds.), *Representing Ireland: Literature and the Origins of Conflict, 1534–1660* (Cambridge, 1993), 24–42; Davies, *Domination and Conquest, passim*; and 'The peoples of Britain and Ireland 1100–1400' [Parts 1–4], *Royal Hist. Soc. Trans.*, 6th ser., iv–vii (1994–7); Robert Bartlett, *The Making of Europe. Conquest, Colonization and Cultural change 950–1350* (London, 1993), esp. chap. 8.

25. Bower, *Scotichronicon*, Watt (ed.), vol. 6, 143.

26. Duncan (ed.), *Regesta Regum Scottorum V*, 695.

27. Bower, *Scotichronicon*, Watt (ed.), vol. 6, 401.

28. M.A. O'Brien (ed.), *Corpus Genealogiarum Hiberniae* (Dublin, 1962), 137 b 36–8, 143 bc 29, 162 d 42; see also, R.A.S. Macalister, *Lebor Gabála Érenn*, 5 vols (London, 1938–56), v, 285; Bower, *Scotichronicon*, Watt (ed.), vol. 1, 163–4.

29. M.E. Dobbs, 'The Ban-shenchus', *Revue Celtique*, xlviii (1931), 186, 225.

30. Seán Duffy, 'The first Ulster plantation: John de Courcy and the men of Cumbria', in T.B. Barry, Robin Frame and Katharine Simms (eds.), *Colony and Frontier in Medieval Ireland* (London, 1995), 24.

31. A.A.M. Duncan, 'The Scots' invasion of Ireland, 1315', in R.R. Davies (ed.), *The British Isles 1100–1500 Comparisons, Contrasts and Connections* (Edinburgh, 1988), 102.

32. I have a more detailed discussion of it in my doctoral dissertation, 'Ireland and the Irish Sea Region, 1014–1318' (University of Dublin, Trinity College, 1993), which is currently being prepared for publication.

33. See Robin Frame, 'The Bruces in Ireland, 1315–18', *Irish Historical Studies*, 19 (1974–5), at pp. 25–37.

34. M.C. Griffith (ed.), *Calendar of the Justiciary Rolls of Ireland, 1308–1314*, (Dublin, 1956), 56.

35. H.S. Sweetman (ed.), *Calendar of Documents relating to Ireland, 1171–1307*, 5 vols (London, 1875–6), ii, no. 929.

36. Barrow, *Robert Bruce*, 3rd edn, 88, 344, n. 10.

37. *Calendar of Documents relating to Scotland*, 5 vols (Edinburgh, 1881–1986), vols i–iv, ed. Joseph Bain , vol. v, ed. G.G. Simpson and J.D. Galbraith; v, no. 211.

38. G.W.S. Barrow, *The Kingdom of the Scots* (London, 1973), 381–2.

39. *Cal. Docs. Scot.*, ii, no. 1117.

40. John O'Donovan (ed.), *The Annals of the Kingdom of Ireland by the Four Masters*, 7 vols (Dublin, 1851), s.a. 1319 (under the guise of 'Annraoi Mac Dauill').

41. Francis Palgrave (ed.), *Documents and Records illustrating the History of Scotland* (London, 1837), no. cviii; *Cal. Docs. Scot.*, ii, nos. 730, 824, 884; iii, pp. 393, 394. See also, J.R.H. Greeves, 'Robert I and the de Mandevilles of Ulster', *Trans. Dumfriesshire & Galloway Nat. Hist. Soc.*, 3rd ser., 34 (1955–6), 59–73.

42. Frame, 'The Bruces in Ireland', 29.

43. K.W. Nicholls, 'Abstracts of Mandeville deeds', *Analecta Hibernica*, 32 (1985), 5–6.

44. Barrow, *Robert Bruce*, 3rd edn, 146, 358, n. 88, 354, n. 1; Charles Johnson, 'Robert Bruce's rebellion in 1306', *English History Review*, 33 (1918), 366–7; Cosmo Innes (ed.), *Registrum S. Marie de Neubotle* (Edinburgh, 1849), no. 139, cf. 146.

45. *Rotuli Scotiae*, 2 vols, Record Commission (London, 1814–19), ii, 143.

46. E. Tresham (ed.), *Rotulorum Patentium et Clausorum Cancellariae Hiberniae Calendarium* (London, 1828), 13; J.T. Gilbert (ed.), *Chartularies of St Mary's Abey, Dublin*, 2 vols (London, 1885–8), ii, 298, 349.

47. Duffy, 'The Bruce brothers', 75.

48. *Cal. Docs. Ire.*, iv, 698.

49. *Chartularies of St Mary's, Dublin*, ii, 298, 349.

50. Duffy, 'John de Courcy and the men of Cumbria', 21.

51. For whom, see *DNB*, s.n.

52. See, for instance, the account of the Bisset lords of Aboyne in E.C. Batten (ed.), *The Charters of the Priory of Beauly* (London, 1877).

53. Though an excellent corrective is now available in Magee, *The Wars of the Bruces*.

54. Quoted in A.O. Anderson (ed.), *Early Sources of Scottish History AD 500 to 1286*, 2 vols (Edinburgh, 1922), ii, 269.

55. See Seán Duffy, '1169 as a turning-point in Irish–Welsh relations', in Brendan Smith (ed.), *Britain and Ireland, 900–1300* (forthcoming).

56. Barrow, *Robert Bruce*, 3rd edn, 148–9; McNamee, *Wars of the Bruces*, 29.

57. I present some of the evidence for date in Duffy, 'The Bruce brothers', 64–5.

58. BL Addit. Charter 3320; see Barrow, *Robert Bruce*, 2nd edn, 446.

3

TRANS-INSULAR LORDSHIP IN THE FIFTEENTH CENTURY

Simon Kingston

In the summer of 1425 the party of the Albany Stewart rebel James the Fat fled from western Scotland to Antrim. His fortunes and whereabouts in the next four years remain an enigma but it was to Carrickfergus that a fleet came from the Isles to meet him in 1429. The hysterical reaction of contemporary national governments to his movement across the Irish Sea illustrates how suspicious they were of the region and its people. The Scottish parliament responded to news of the flight of these 'notourious rebellours' with legislation banning all unauthorised contact between Scotland and adjacent parts of Ireland. No ship was to pass between the Isles and Ulster without license and on entering a Scottish harbour each ship was to remain at anchor without disembarking its passengers until they had been inspected by the King's baillies. In addition to the threat from the Albany faction, a fear was expressed that 'men that ar under Erschry subiect to the King of Ingland mycht espy the pryuates of this realm'.[1] None of this however was to prejudice the Scots King's relations with his 'gude alde frends of Erschry'.

The Scottish government was not alone; the Anglo-Irish administration was constantly regaled with stories of the threat represented by alliance between Scots and Ulster Irish. When the fleet came to James the Fat in 1429 as usual the English of Ulster panicked; in response a letter close was dispatched by the English government directing 'all lieges of Ireland now in England...[to]...speed...thence to their native land for the defence thereof'. The stated reason for this raising of the alarm was information which had come to the king which suggested 'that the rebels in Ireland and other his enemies of the northern parts banding themselves together are purposing...to invade Ireland in order to destroy his true lieges there and to lay waste his country.'[2] The Irish annalist maintains that the intention of whoever sent the fleet was to bear James the Fat back to Scotland and install him as king in place of his cousin James I. Whilst this may have been precisely the threat about which the Scots king had been so anxious, it was of little comfort to the English king's subjects in Ulster. James White, the castellan of Carrickfergus, was paid compensation in March 1429 for the sufferings endured at the hands of 'Odomnyll and a great multitude of Scots'.[3] The Scots at whose hands White suffered may very well have been from the fleet sent for James; since the Albany lord rather inconsiderately died the moment his Scottish supporters arrived in Ulster they may have been endeavouring to make the best of a bad job.

Both Scots and English administrations believed that invasion of their territories from the North Irish Sea region was feasible; even if it was not orchestrated by the government of the other kingdom then it would surely be connived at. Central to this opinion was the belief that since the region was beyond the ken of one government it must necessarily be alive with partisans of the other. There certainly were population movements in the early fifteenth century caused principally by successive Scots royal offensives in the Isles: these led at intervals to the emigration to Ulster of significant numbers of the Clann Domnaill affinity. MacDonald of Sleat in his account of affairs in the Isles describes the two time-honoured options for Scottish rebels: '...either to betake themselves to the hills, or to go to Ireland...'[4] In the fifteenth century many of the émigré Hebrideans moved into what was already a well established Clann Domnaill lordship in Antrim; they were not the roving *gallóglaigh* of earlier centuries, nor yet the seasonal 'redshanks' of later years. The events surrounding James the Fat's arrival in Ulster indicate how confusing the interwoven identities and loyalties of this region might appear from the outside.

Sweeney in his mad peregrinations delimits the region concerned rather well:

I went raving with grief
on the top of Slieve Patrick,
from Glen Bolcain to Islay,
from Kintyre to Mourne.[5]

Lordship was exercised in both Ulster and western Scotland by men who were familiar with both the cultural and the geographical lineaments of Sweeney's world. For English commentators however describing the peoples who lived in the territories of the North Irish Sea Rim was always difficult: 'Scottyshe Irysshe' or 'Irish Scotish', both were tried.[6] Bagenal was to describe the Mac Domnaill of Antrim as a 'bastard kind of Scottes'; however, they were more than simply raiding *routiers*, full-time possession of a lordship in Ulster had changed Clann Eoin Mhóir.[7] Irish authors too displayed varying degrees of misapprehension in dealing with the strange category of Unidentified Flying Scotsman that appeared at intervals in the affairs of Ulster. Clann Eoin Mhóir was the mixed metaphor at the centre of an area which historians have frequently seen as without form and unworthy of treatment as a unit. Possessed of territories on either side of the Irish Sea the kindred presents a great problem of classification to external commentators. In the middle years of the fifteenth century its leader was Domnall Ballach and he was the paragon of the Trans-Insular lord; it is hoped he will serve to illustrate the nature of the connection between Ulster and the Isles.

Domnall Ballach began his career at the head of as diverse a range of the Clann Domnaill affinity as any Lord of the Isles in the early fifteenth century could have mustered. In 1431 Alexander head of the greater Clann Domnaill and Lord of the Isles was in crown custody, and an expeditionary force under the earl of Mar marched on Inverlochy with the intention of bringing the Isles to heel. Domnall, still only 18, gathered a host which incorporated the MacIans of Ardnamurchan, MacLeans of Coll, Ragnall Bán from Antrim, MacQuarry from Ulva and MacGee from the Rhinns of Islay. The home territories of these kindreds were spread the length of the Isles and formed an impressive general hosting. They were also sufficient to rout the royal expeditionary force in a defeat that led to the release of Alexander Lord of the Isles and a period of expansion for Clann Domnaill which included the recognition of the Mac Domnaill title to the earldom of Ross. This facility to command the support of the client families, in the Isles, was to characterise the whole of Domnall's career.

In spite of his extensive lordship in Antrim Domnall remained intimately involved in the politics of the Isles and their relations with the larger Scots polity. Just how involved is suggested by a closer reading of what, traditionally, has been one of the least convincingly addressed aspects of Clann Domnaill behaviour: that is its role in the Douglas / Crawford / Ross bond of 1445. This arrangement was 'ane offensive and defensive League & Combinatione against all none excepted' and was used by James II to impute treasonous intentions to William Douglas. It has been assumed that the Ross element of this Bond was the above mentioned Alexander lord of the Isles and earl of Ross: this it seems to me is problematic given Alexander's delicate position in relation to the crown and, more obviously, his complete failure to act as if he had been party to the bond. Alexander of Ross, then, was an unlikely candidate for 'third man' in the bond with Crawford and Douglas; his heir John II of the Isles may also be ruled out of any such league by his youth and character: the question of who the Islesman involved was remains unanswered. Contemporary records and the accounts of events as they came to be chronicled suggest that the individual in question was Domnall Ballach. Certainly his actions in 1452, when the king moved against William Douglas, stand in stark contrast to the inactivity of his kinsmen who were supposedly obliged by the bond. Domnall led the response of the Isles to the King's actions by raiding Inverkip and other points on the west coast; this happened after a visit to the Isles by the new earl of Douglas and was done in the company of at least one Douglas family member.[8] Domnall is a plausible ally for Douglas for other reasons too; of the major Hebridean leaders only he had emerged from the early 1430s without having suffered the humiliation of defeat or imprisonment at the hands of the king. It is also apparent that Domnall did not simply remain in the Glens of Antrim after Inverlochy, instead he remained active in the Isles. In October 1433, for example, he was recorded as 'Johannis de Insulis Ballac, grandson of the lord of the Isles' in a supplication to Rome witnessed in the Isles.[9] Mobility clearly remained a feature of his life. In practice Domnall could very easily have played the role of lord of the Isles during the minority of his kinsman. He was indeed confused for the Lord of the Isles at times.

The entry in the Asloan manuscript which describes the embassy of James Douglas to the Isles is informative; the new earl of Douglas it states came to Knapdale, to see the partners in his father's bond,

> And spak thar with the erll of Ross and Lord of Ilis And maid thaim all richt rewarde of wyne...[10]

The reference to the earl of Ross and lord of the Isles as if they were two different individuals is significant given that Domnall Ballach is described as 'Donald of the ylis' two entries later. The only record of the Douglas/Crawford/Ross bond, which may not have been written in the first place, also suggests Domnall Ballach's participation. It states that the co-signatory with Douglas and Crawford was one 'Donald lord of the Isles'.[11] This is generally regarded as an error but it is not the only such reference. Pitscottie writes, admittedly well after the events took place, that it was 'Donald Lord of the Iles' who was in association with Douglas after 1455.[12] In addition the writer of the 'Brieve Cronicle of the Earlis of Ross', records that when Douglas fled to the Isles, he turned to 'Donald, earle of Ross and Lord of the Iylis, [and] he procurit to him...to mak war in his favour against the King.'[13] There was some confusion in the minds of chroniclers but Domnall clearly featured as a powerful figure. However unlikely the title earl seems, given his powerful position might Domnall Ballach not have been styled Lord of the Isles, especially after 1449 when he may well have been in effective control of the lordship?[14] A number of other literary references lend credibility to the assertion that Domnall Ballach was involved in the 1445 bond. Space does not permit a complete rehearsal of them here.[15]

In the context of his career as a whole, Domnall Ballach's possible involvement in the bond of 1445 with Douglas and Crawford, seems neither surprising nor out of character. The bond represents one part of a life the compass of which was as trans-insular as that of his father Eoin Mór who first established a Mac Domnaill lordship in Antrim. A continuing role in the Isles for Domnall made sense: after Alexander's death in 1449 he was the most senior kindred leader in the Hebrides. It has been suggested that Domnall was guardian to the new Lord of the Isles after Alexander's death; this practice was not without a precedent.[16] Certainly Domnall Ballach was enormously influential as chief advisor to John for much of his career and in the years after 1445 he dominated the affairs of the Isles to an extent which is frequently ignored by historians of the period. With lands in Islay, Antrim, Kintyre and Ardnamurchan, in addition to responsibility for Greenan in Carrick, Domnall Ballach possessed what amounted to a controlling stake in the Lordship of the Isles.[17] The influence wielded by Domnall Ballach was not simply a function of his individual capability, it was predicated upon the coherence of Clann Eoin Mhóir. Working in concert with Domnall were other members of the kindred about whom the records of the period say very little but who constituted a second tier of leadership. One such figure was Ragnall Bán, a brother of Domnall and his 'fixer' in Ulster. Domnall's influence was also exercised through attendance at meetings of the council of the Isles. A number of charters survive in which Domnall was a witness: in each he was the chief councillor present and was always listed first. From 1456 to 1476 he was evidently the senior member of the council of the Isles.[18] There is also evidence that, in his own right, he granted lands in Jura to MacIan of Ardnamurchan.[19] Despite his demonstrably superior qualities as a leader Domnall Ballach remained loyal to John II Lord of the Isles throughout his life, an ability to exert influence as a councillor granting him all the power he required.

Simultaneous with this activity in the Isles, Domnall was building up his patrimony in the Glynns in Antrim, the strategic value of which was to be important to Domnall's descendants for generations. The importance of 'na seacht tuaithe' [the seven countries of Antrim] lay not simply in the territory itself but in its situation: 'Groined by deep glens and walled along the west by the bare hilltops and the tufted moors, this rim of arable that ends in foam' was a safe refuge, physically secure from land ward and seaward sides; it was to the Glynns that Domnall repaired in the immediate aftermath of the battle of Inverlochy.[20] During the 1430's howver, Domnall Ballach succeeded in turning his lordship of the Glens into something more than just a bolthole. Turning his focus away from the Isles, for Domnall the Glynns were a propitiously positioned base for engagement in the affairs of Ulster. Domnall made new alliances; the most striking example of the province-wide nature of these was the campaign of 1433 in which Clann Domnaill and Uí Neill forces combined to inflict a series of defeats on Uí Neill enemies. The Annals of Ulster record that Eoghan Ua Neill was assisted in his protracted struggle with Niall Garbh Ua Domnaill by a large fleet [*coblach mór*] led by Mac Domnaill of the Isles. It is very hard to believe that the Mac Domnaill in question was not Domnall; his capacity to organise such an expeditionary force had been proven in 1431. Later raids carried out by him in Scotland were noted for the size of the fleets involved. The raids of 1451 and 1453 on Inverness and Inverkip, for example, were similar sea-borne raiding operations of fairly short duration. Furthermore the base which Domnall possessed in Ulster would have been invaluable in such an operation and leaving him out of the scheme would have been well nigh impossible, even if the impetus had originated with Alexander, lord of the Isles.[21] The conspicuous success of the operation of 1433 illustrated that the Mac Domnaill presence in Ulster could alter the pattern of events across the whole province. The magic ingredient in this campaign was sea power; Clann Domnaill amphibious troops acted as a hammer to the anvil of Uí Neill land-based forces, twice catching Ua Domnaill and his allies in between. The style of this campaign was that of an operation in the Isles and employed marine resources, used there commonly, which were almost never seen amongst the Irish of Ulster. Ordinarily Domnall's Ulster alliances were on a smaller scale and, until the 1460s, with the Clann Aodha Buidhe segment of the Uí Neill rather than the main Tír Eoghain family.

The critical role of the Scots fleet is not commented on in detail by the annals; Cosgrove characterises it as the last large scale intervention by Scots from the Isles in the affairs of Ulster during the period.[22] As such, it would be virtually inexplicable if it was assumed to have been the work of Alexander Mac Domnaill himself. If, however, Domnall Ballach is seen as the prime mover, it fits quite neatly into the pattern of his behaviour as described above. Clann Eoin Mhóir as both Scots of the Isles and Ulster were taking their place as part of a newly constituted *cóiced* rolled into province-wide hostings by the Uí Niall during their hegemonic flourishes across Ulster. Clann Eoin Mhóir succeeded however in creating an Ulster identity independent of Uí Neill proper of which it never became a client kindred. Nevertheless, and perhaps uniquely among the families of eastern Ulster, Clann Eoin Mhóir is not recorded as ever being actively hostile to the Tír Eoghain Uí Neill in the period. That Domnall Ballach should choose positively to ally himself with Uí Neill proper was by no means inevitable. His first marriage to Siobhan Ua Domnaill suggests a certain hedging of bets; the second marriage to Johanna Ua Neill of Clann Aodha Buidhe also kept alliance options open.[23] This bond was further strengthened by the marriage of Domnall's daughter Mary to Conn who was to be head of the Clann Aodha Buidhe.[24] Aside from his heir Eoin, Domnall had at least one other son Aengus, who was killed in 1465 by the son of a bishop Mac Domnaill.[25] There are no references to either of Domnall's wives in the annals, but it is evident that Clann Eoin Mhóir could court the advances of kindreds which were at least periodically hostile to the Uí Neill. Domnall virtually disappears from record on either side of the north channel in the twenty years following 1431, but it must have been in this period that his marriages occurred. In 1445 he was mentioned in a petition to Rome by 'Donald Machoagaill' who had given land at Glenarm for the establishment of a friary. The grant of land had been made to him initially by one 'Semiquinus Machcon' captain of his nation, according to the petition, along with 'Donald Ballach Machdomnaill' and 'Alexander Machdomnaill'. Costello in editing the entry in 1909 identified the first named grantor as the Mac Eoin Bisset; it has been argued elsewhere that the man in question may have been leader of the MacUibhilin.[26] In either case there is no doubt that Clann Eoin Mhóir leaders were a significant power in the land. An element of uncertainty existed in the mind of the grantee: Machoagaill lodged the petition because he doubted 'for certain reasons that his aforesaid gift and grant have inherent force'. Clearly whether it was the Bissets or the Mac Uibhilin who were granting land in north Antrim it could not be done without the support of the Mac Domnaill and even then might be uncertain. The building up of the 'strong country' by Clann Eoin Mhóir in the Glynns was an ongoing process, but no details remain of relations between, for example, Domnall Ballach and the Uí Catháin to the west or indeed of the nature of practical contacts with Clann Aodha Buidhe if any existed. That links with the Uí Catháin were developed is certain; Domnall's best known grandson was Eoin Cathanach, a name which suggests that he was fostered by that kindred.[27] In the context of the feud between the Uí Catháin and the Mac Uibhilin this contact was highly significant and remained so in the 1480s and 1490s.[28] To the south-east of the Glynns the link established by Eoin Mór with the English crown when he entered into indentures with Henry IV, was elaborated by Domnall who was later to be involved in negotiations with Edward IV. Such links and the propinquity of the Glynns to Carrickfergus and Larne must have involved engagement with the Anglo-Irish of eastern

Ulster. Larne itself was a point of contact with Scotland, albeit one which the Anglo-Irish must have viewed with some ambivalence, given that both Bruce brothers had used it in the course of the invasion of 1315–18.[29]

Perhaps Domnall Ballach's most dramatic engagement in trans-insular lordship was his role in the negotiation of the Treaty of Westminster/ Ardtornish. The agreement is generally regarded as a rather ineffectual and almost reflexive attempt by the English to stir up trouble within the kingdom of Scotland. There is, however, an explicit concentration on Clann Eoin Mhóir in the wording of the document which suggests English intentions were rather more positive. The kindred was employed in a conflation of English policy interests: it represented the most vibrant element in the greater Clann Domnaill and was therefore a potential ally versus the Scot crown; simultaneously Clann Eoin Mhóir leaders were identifiable and responsive elements within the 'Scots of Ulster' – a group which often appeared amorphous and potentially threatening to the English interest in Ulster. Conversely for the Scots crown Clann Domnaill was increasingly seen to be irredeemable as a part of the community of the realm; other leaders on the western seaboard were to prove more malleable as its agents. James III and IV both needed to be persuaded that Clann Domnaill was worth the effort; such evidence was not forthcoming rather the reverse. The treaty, and the consequences of its discovery, is thus a paradigm for Clann Domnaill relations with the crown in the latter half of the century. The discovery of its existence by James III gives it the significance for Clann Domnaill that the 1445 bond had had for Douglas.[30]

As a dominant voice on the council of the Isles, Domnall seems to have used it to legitimise his efforts to reach an agreement with the English king. After a council meeting on 10 October at which the negotiations were surely discussed, John, Lord of the Isles, issued letters patent from Ardtornish on 19th October 1461. The terms in which the treaty is usually discussed, that is solely Scottish ones, relegate it to the status of a standard manoeuvre of no lasting significance in the course of Anglo-Scottish conflict.[31] When viewed in the context of trans-insular activity its stature grows. Domnall's influence, and Irish considerations, are evident in the arrangements from the outset with the appointment of Ragnall Bán as one of the ambassadors to Edward; the pre-occupation of the treaty with Ulster follows from this. The treaty, signed in February 1462, names Domnall as the principal figure with John II on the Mac Domnaill side.[32] Domnall and Eoin, his son, continue to be mentioned by name along with John II throughout the document.[33] That the English felt they were coming to grips with an Ulster problem is clear; nevertheless the fear of invasion led by the Scottish crown seems to have been a lingering one and the Mac Domnaill are enjoined to fight against the 'Scottes in Irlande' if necessary. The purely Scottish element of the treaty is in contrast to this; it refers to the rights of James Douglas in the event of an English conquest of Scotland, and is a combination of vague aspiration and non-specific *politesse*. The prospect of bringing Scotland, or even 'the more part thereof', to obeisance to the English crown with the particular aid of the Douglas faction was a remote one.[34] The cursory references to James Douglas are unconvincing as declarations of serious intent. The realistic ends the English had in view are further signified by the appointment in March 1463 of Richard, bishop of Down and Connor, who was empowered by Edward IV to receive the oaths of the three Mac Domnaill.[35]

The substance of the treaty and its associated negotiations suggest that it was concerned as much with Ulster as with Scotland; other factors seem to support such an interpretation. In Clann Eoin Mhóir Edward was presented with a family which had an established record of self-interested co-operation with the English crown. In the 1480s and '90s Eoin Mór was listed as an ally of the English in a series of treaties; this continued a policy adopted by John of Islay for Clann Domnaill proper.[36] In 1400 Henry IV had dispatched Henry Percy to meet 'John of the Isles lord of Dunyvaig and the Glynns and Donald his brother'. The recognition of his title suggests something of the regard for the power of Clann Eoin Mhóir's founder the new English king felt.[37] In 1403 Eoin Mór entered into indentures with Henry IV at Carrickfergus in which his title to the Glynns received official recognition.[38] Clann Domnaill proper had continued to enjoy civil relations with England through its role in the politics of the western isles; in 1407 and 1408 two missions to the Isles underlined the continuing interest of the English Crown in the region.[39] It was in precisely this period that Edward IV was giving thought to his Ulster lordship, sending a donative to Énrí Ua Neill of Tír Eoghain in the same year as his commissioning of the bishop of Down and Connor.[40] The treaty of Westminster/Ardtornish should be seen in the context of an attempt by the English Crown to stabilise the position of the Anglo-Irish settlement in Ulster. Indeed Edward IV seems to have recognised the integrity of the North Irish Sea region as a unit. An understanding with Clann Eoin Mhóir complimented the tentative *rapprochement* with the Uí Neill by securing the position of the Anglo-Irish settlement in Antrim and Down.

The treaty, which was witnessed by Ragnall Bán as one of the ambassadors of the Isles, is an attempt to ensure that the unique capacity of the MacDomnaill of the Glynns was not exercised in a manner inimical to English interests.[41] Ragnall's apparently peripheral role in purely Hebridean affairs hints that he spent most of his time in Ulster; he appears only once in surviving charters of the Isles.[42] Ragnall and his sons were entirely immersed in the affairs of Ulster; *Sliocht Ragnaill* was worthy of separate genealogical remark and appear in the Annals.[43]

If an improvement in the lot of the Anglo-Irish of Ulster was Edward's goal in 1462 then he achieved a measure of success. As with the Uí Neill, there is no record of Clann Eoin Mhóir attacking the English in the years which follow 1463. Corroborative of this is the breakdown of the customary alliance with Clann Aodha Buidhe which would have drawn the Mac Domnaill into such attacks. Instead in 1465 Clann Aodha Buidhe actually carried out a raid on the Antrim Scots in which Sean mac Alasdair Mac Domnaill and many of his people were killed.[44]

The English king's achievement was short-term and was not followed up by an attempt at a comprehensive re-ordering of political reality in Antrim. For Clann Eoin Mhóir, as for the lords of Tír Eoghain, a lasting redefinition of relations with the English Crown remained an aspiration but little more. A letter from a fearful Anglo-Irish squire in 1474 illustrates the misapprehension and fear which continued to characterise the corporate feeling of English Ireland concerning Clann Eoin Mhóir. The 'xm and more' Scots in Ulster were in this view a miasma, deliberately released by James III, weakening the Anglo-Irish lordship prior to a full scale invasion; the ultimate aim of this operation was 'to subdue al thys land to the obeysaunce of the Kyng of Scottes'.[45] Such an understanding of interaction with the Isles was still coloured by memories of the Bruce Invasion rather than the more imaginative and informed analysis of Edward IV; and a return to the paranoia of the 1420s occured.

Domnall Ballach died late in 1476, probably on Islay; the last reference to him was with John II when he witnessed a charter, in August of that year, as 'Donaldo ballache de Dunnoweg'.[46] The death of Domnall Ballach represents the start of the loss of unity amongst Clann Domnaill, yet until the 1490s, as has been suggested above, the conciliar institution of which Domnall had been so careful a supporter remained workable.[47] His career as a trans-insular lord provided an example which generations of later Mac Domnaill leaders were to endeavour to emulate. With an ability to function on either side of the North Irish Sea, Clann Eoin Mhóir and its descendents, were to continue to baffle and frighten external observers. Ultimately however, without strong lordship which bound the collateral branches and client kindreds of the Clann Domnaill affinity together, the kindred was unable to exploit the ignorance of national governments. Without leadership of the calibre provided by Domnall Ballach, by the early sixteenth century the *anima* of greater Clann Domnaill unity was to suffer the same dislocated fate as Sweeney.

REFERENCES

1. T. Thompson (ed.), *Acts of the Parliament of Scotland (A.P.S.)* (London, 1814), ii., 11, c.18.

2. *Calendar of Close Rolls*, 1429–35 (H.M.S.O., London), p.42.

3. E. Tresham (ed.), *Rotulorum Patentum et Clausorum Cancellariæ Hiberniæ Calendarium (C.C.H.)* (Dublin, 1828), 246, n. 21.

4. *Hugh MacDonald's History of the MacDonalds (Mac. of Sleat)*, in J.R.N. MacPhail (ed.), *Highland Papers*, i, (Scottish History Society, 1914), 44.

5. The translation is from S. Heaney, *Sweeney Astray* (London, 1984), 18.

6. J. Gairdner (ed.), *Letters and Papers, Foreign and Domestic, of the Reign of Henry VIII* (London, 1907) xix, no. 795; H. Wood (ed.), *The Chronicle of Ireland by Sir James Perrott* (Dublin, 1933), 23.

7. J.S. Brewer and W. Bullen (eds.), *Calendar of Carew Manuscripts* (London, 1868), ii, 438, n. 623.

8. This was unanimously regarded as the work of Domnall Ballach, see: W.A. Craigie (ed.), *The Asloan Manuscript(Asloan Ms)* (Scottish Texts Society, 1923 & 1925), i, 221.

9. J. Munro and R.W. Munro (eds.), *The Acts of the Lords of the Isles, 1336 – 1493 (A.L.I.)* (Edinburgh, 1986), Appendix B, 241.

10. *Asloan Ms*, i, 221.

11. *A.L.I.* 68; from Sir James Balfour, *The Annales of Scotland* (Edinburgh, 1824), i, 173.

12. Pitscottie appears to confuse Donald with John as he claims he was both 'Lord of the Illis and Lord Rose'. He does state that it was the same Donald of the Isles who was responsible for the raiding of the west coast in sympathy with the Douglas family after a visit from James Douglas. A.J.G. Mackay (ed.), *The Historie and Cronicles of Scotland...by Robert Lindesay of Pitscottie (Pitscottie)* (Scottish Texts Society, 1899), 123.

13. W. Baillie (ed.), *Ane Breve Cronicle of the Earlis of Ross* with *Ane Brieve Discourse of the Earlis of Ross* (Edinburgh, 1850), 13, He wrote this despite having killed Domnall Ballach off in an earlier section of his account. In *Ane Brieve Discourse of the Earlis of Ross*, an associated record, even greater confusion arises: in a list of the earls of Ross after Alexander comes 'Donald, erll of Ross and Lord of the Iyllis, in the yeir of God 1454,...at last [he] was slaine be ane Irischman, ane clershear, in the yeir of God 1461.' Domnall is obviously being confused with Angus Óg in this entry but it is nevertheless clear that someone of the name was so significant a force in the Isles in the 1450s that outsiders believed him to be in charge – the argument put forward here suggests that he was. ibid, 25.

14. Given the similarity of the Gaelic for Islay (Ile) and the Isles (na h'ile) confusion in the anglicisation of the two words is not surprising. Thus if it was Domnall Ballach in the bond of 1445 his description of himself as 'lord of the Isles' would not have been in opposition to Alexander but merely a clumsy translation of his Gaelic title into English or Scots. Equally the chroniclers from the lowlands may simply be giving him the wrong title. Gregory wrote the confusion off as simple mistakes by later writers: Domnall Ballach's 'celebrity as a warrior, and the high rank he held, have led several historians into the error of calling him Donald, *Lord* of the Isles, a title which he never claimed.' D. Gregory, *History of the Western Highlands and Islands of Scotland from A.D. 1493 to A.D. 1625* (Edinburgh, 1836), 62; The exchequer rolls for the 1440s do hint at the titles Lord of the Isles and Earl of Ross being held by different people; in 1442, for example, letters are borne to the earl of Ross, (indicating that the title was being recognised by the crown). However, two years later Douglas was paid £7 for expenses during his communication with the Lord of the Isles [domino (sic) insularum], J. Stuart, *et al.* (eds.), *The Exchequer Rolls of Scotland* (*E.R.*) (23 vols., Edinburgh, 1878–1908), v, 118 & 166.

15. The *Buke of Howlatt* written in the early 1450s lampoons the Livingstons and their allies on behalf of the Douglas family; amongst those satirised are the Mac Domnaill. The figure used to represent them is a rook which appears at a feast to address the other birds. The character is a 'bard out of Irland' and in what has been read as a satire on Clann Domnaill inauguration ritual it harangues the company with incomprehensible genealogical material. 'The Buke of Howlat', in F. J. Amours (ed.), *Scottish Alliterative Poems* (Scottish Texts Society, 1897), stanza lxii . M. Stewart, 'Holland's 'Howlat' and the fall of the Livingstones', *Innes Review*, .xxvi (1975), 67–79. The rook may simply refer to Irish bardic families like the Mac Mhuirich who were employed by the Lords of the Isles, however there were many lords in Gaelic Scotland who employed such poets and this would hardly be the most significant distinguishing feature of Clann Domnaill. Domnall Ballach with his extensive lands in Antrim had a much more remarkable Irish connection and iy is possibly to it that reference was being made. Circumstantial evidence points to Domnall Ballach's prominence in the acts of the Lords of the Isles also points to him as a possible member of the bond. Finally Domnall was the one lord in the Isles and, arguably, in the kingdom, who could act with impunity: able to retreat to safety if disaster struck. As he had shown after Inverlochy, the Glens of Antrim provided a safe haven beyond the reach of the Scots king; by the 1440s he had an even more secure base with powerful local allies to which he could retreat in Ulster. From 1456 to 1476 Domnall was the chief witness to a series of charters and was evidently the senior member of the council of the Isles, *A.L.I.*, 90–4, 107–9, 111–9, 121–4, 126–9, 141–3, 152–6, 171, 176–8, 233, 241.

16. This is suggested in the account by A. & A. MacDonald but they give no

authority. A.& A. MacDonald, *The Clan Donald* (Inverness, 1896–1904);The relationship between Ragnall and Domnall of Harlaw, second lord of the Isles, in which the former as *Aird Sdiudhor* and experienced leader directed the early steps of the new Lord of the Isles.

17. *A.L.I.*, xxv, 171 [no.107] &.233 [A64].

18. There are twelve charters in which Domnall features as the chief advisor to John.

19. *A.L.I.*, 233, A.64.

20. The description is Hewitt's from 'The Glens' in F. Ormsby (ed.), *The Collected Poems of John Hewitt* (Belfast, 1991), 310; see also the comments of B.S.Turner, 'Distributional aspects of family name study as illustrated in the Glens of Antrim', (Queen's University Belfast, PhD thesis 1974) 138, and further A. Roberts,'Retreat from Kintyre to the Glens :The evidence of family names', in *The Glynns*, xviii (1990), 14–22.

21. Direct involvement by Alexander seems unlikely, not least because there are no records of the campaign from the Scottish side of the North channel which would seem strange if he had initiated it. In any case, having just been released from royal custody, the Lord of the Isles was pursuing an entirely pacific policy.

22. A. Cosgrove, 'Ireland beyond the Pale, 1399 – 1460', in A.Cosgrove (ed.), *A New History of Ireland, Vol. II* (Oxford, 1987, 2nd ed. 1993), 576.

23. MacDonald of Sleat asserts that Eoin Domnall's heir was fruit of the second marriage to 'Counn O'Neill's daughter of the Clan-Buys of Ireland' *Mac. of Sleat*, 44.The genealogy of Fleatha Ó Gnimh however states that it was from the first union that Eoin came, this is apparantly the version of events which Nicholls favours. B. Ó Cuiv,'Some Irish Items Relating to the MacDonnells of Antrim', *Celtica* , xvi (1984), 139–56. K. Nicholls,'Notes on the genealogy of Clann Eoin Mhóir', *West Highland Notes and Queries* , (Nov. 1991), 12.

24. *A.U.* 1488. For Conn see T.C.D. MS. 1366, f.67.

25. *A.U.* 1465.The only bishop who seems, on the basis of his first name, to be a likely candidate is one 'Donald' who was bishop of Derry from 1423 to 1429. P.P.B.Gams, *Series Episcoporum Ecclesiae Catholicae* (Ratisbonae, 1875).

26. M.A. Costello (ed.), *De Annatis Hiberniae – A calendar of the first fruits fees levied on papal appointments to benefices in Ireland, Vol. 1* – *Ulster* (1909), 139; H. McDonnell,'Glenarm friary and the Bissets', *The Glynns*, xv, (1987), 34–49. McDonnell holds to the MacEoin Bisset identification.

27. '*Cathanach*' may simply mean rough, or indeed warlike ['of the battles'?] but circumstantial evidence suggests it refers in Eoin's case to his foster family, see below 91–3;135. It was not unusual for an epithet to be applied on this basis for example Niall Gallda of Clann Aodha Buidhe (Uí Neill Genealogical Table, 22b) who was presumably fostered in Scotland or with the Anglo-Irish.

28. MacUibhilin feud with the Uí Catháin, *A.U.*, 1441; 1472; 1492; 1495.

29. Otway-Ruthven, *Ireland*, 226, 243, 244.

30. ibid., introduction lxx.

31. Nicholson describes it as having 'results serious enough, but hardly comparable to those envisaged in its terms: before it Ross had already behaved in boisterous fashion, and afterwards he merely behaved in a more exaggerated fashion.' Nicholson, *Scotland*, 402.

32. The text of the Treaty is given in full by *A.L.I.*, 111–16.

33. Eoin spent most of his early life in Antrim as far as it is possible to determine.

34. Cited in *A.L.I*, p.114.

35. J.Bain (ed.), *Calendar of Documents Relating to Scotland(C.D.S.)* (Edinburgh, 1881–8), iv, no.1334 .The utility of Irish clergy in negotiations with the Lords of the Isles had been recognised by Henry IV in 1407 and 1408.

36. Eoin Mór styled 'Jehan de Ilys' features in six treaty lists: *Foedera*, vii. 626, 639, 657, 716, 777 & 824.

37. *Rot. Scot.*, ii., 94–5, 153, *A.L.I.*, lxxvi. The order in which the brothers are mentioned is revealing too; Donald was Lord of the Isles and should surely have been listed first in a Scottish document.

38. Eoin Mór in 1403, The College of Arms, Betham's MSS, Repertory to Records of the Excehquer, Henry IV, 33.

39. 1407 mission C.P.R., H.IV, iii. 361; 1408 mission *Foedera*, viii. 527.

40. For the cordial relations between the Uí Neill and the English Crown see, K. Simms,' "The King's Friend": O Neill, The Crown and the Earldom of Ulster' in J. Lydon (ed.), *England and Ireland in the Later Middle Ages* (Dublin, 1981), 214–36.

41. Ragnall was founder of the line of MacDomnaill of Largie in Kintyre. Sleat suggests Ragnall was given these lands for his services to Alexander at Inverlochy: they were not, he says, part of the patrimony of Eoin Mór. This however is contradicted by the testimony of Ragnall Bán's son Domnall who claimed to hold the lands by charter from Domnall Ballach's son, Mac. of S., 47; *A.L.I.*, 296.

42. *A.L.I.*, 123. This suggestion of an Ulster-based career is corroborated by the description of him in the charter as 'brother of the aforementioned Domnall [Ballach]'. Such an allusion suggests his relative lack of prominence in the Isles. The description of him is incidentally interesting because his epithet 'Bán' is rendered into Latin 'albe' suggesting the scribe who wrote it understood Gaelic. As many of the charters of the Isles survive now only as 'processed' by royal scribes when being confirmed by the crown the question of their faithfulness to their original form arises. The fact that the scribe of this 1463 charter was familiar with Gaelic but wrote in Latin suggests either: a) A confirmation that the Lords of the Isles produced charters in Latin, sometimes questioned; or b) That royal scribes understood Gaelic and may

not have altered the form of the original charters to match standard form. If the latter suggestion is the case then it would appear that scribes to the Mac Domnaill adhered to a fairly conventional format in charters. This further deepens the mystery around the 1408 Gaelic charter and its format.

43. Royal Irish Academy, MS. 23 M. 17. *B. of C.*, 303

44. The 'Sean' of AU is the Eoin son of Alasdair Mac Domnaill who is recorded by AFM as having died in like manner in 1465 . The Alasdair in question was another brother of Domnall Ballach and Ragnall Bán. See genealogies attached.

45. Chancery Miscellanea Bundle 10, no. 29, c.14 Ed. IV [C.47/10/29], printed in D.Bryan, *The Great Earl of Kildare* (Dublin, 1933), 18–9.

46. One of the Carew manuscripts gives a date of death see Ó Cuiv above. *A.L.I.*, 178. The MacDonalds state that Domnall died at Loch Gruinard at the end of 1476. This may be either the townland of Gruinart to the south of the Loch or perhaps the area called Leckgruinart on its western shore. A. & A. MacDonald, *Op. Cit.*, 510.

47. Without lords who were able to command the respect of the client kindreds and formulate consensus, however we describe the machinery by which this was achieved, in the Isles as in Ulster centrifugal forces were irresistible.

4

THE CATHOLIC IRISH IN THE WEST OF SCOTLAND: 'A SEPARATE AND DESPISED COMMUNITY'?

Martin J. Mitchell

I

In the early 1790s there were very few Irish immigrants in Scotland. By 1851, however, there were 207,367 people of Irish birth in the country, of whom 135,975 or almost two-thirds of the total lived in the west of Scotland (the counties of Lanarkshire, Ayrshire and Renfrewshire). Furthermore, as large-scale immigration from Ireland had been occurring for over fifty years there were also a considerable number of second and third generation Irish in Scotland by the middle of the nineteenth century.[1]

The bulk of Irish immigrants during this period came from the nine counties of Ulster, and historians have estimated that the Catholics among them amounted to two-thirds or perhaps even three-quarters of the total. This immigration fundamentally altered the pattern of Roman Catholicism in the west of Scotland. In the early 1790s, prior to the arrival of the Irish, there were only between 500 and 600 Catholics in and around Glasgow, of whom most were recent arrivals from the Highlands. Elsewhere in the region Catholicism was all but extinct. From the late 1790s onwards the overwhelming majority of Roman Catholics in the west of Scotland were Irish or of Irish descent.[2]

Most of those who have written extensively or commented on the Irish in nineteenth century Scotland have argued that whereas the Protestant Irish immigrants were, in the main, welcomed and accepted (because they shared the same religion and culture as the Scots) the Catholic Irish were despised by the native population on account of their religion and because they were employed mainly as strike-breakers or low-wage labour.[3] As a result of this widespread hostility the Catholic Irish, it has been argued, were unwilling or unable to participate in strikes, trade unions and political movements with Scottish workers; instead, they formed separate and self-contained communities, centred on their chapels, in the towns in which they settled in significant numbers, and politically were concerned almost exclusively with issues relating to Ireland, Catholics and the Catholic Church.[4] For example, Tom Gallagher, in his major study of the Catholic community in Glasgow during the nineteenth and twentieth centuries, argued that prejudice towards the Catholic Irish was 'endemic throughout society'[5], and as a result they constituted an isolated community which

> preserved its separate identity because it was a form of psychological protection. Priests and other community leaders encouraged what amounted to voluntary segregation in all the big areas of Irish settlement and in many of the smaller ones where the conditions existed for a distinct enclave community.[6]

He also stated:

> Finding religious intolerance and sectarian hate in many areas of nineteenth century Scottish life, the immigrants preferred to remain expatriate Irish rather than strive to make common cause with the Scots in their midst.[7]

T.C. Smout claimed that in the 1830s and 1840s the 'native Lowland Scots despised...the Irish 'Paddy''. As a result:

> The Catholic Irish were...driven...firmly into a ghetto mentality, and clung to the bosom of Mother Church to find some kind of comfort and support in a totally unwelcoming environment.[8]

Callum Brown has argued that 'partly through the use of immigrants as strike-breakers and partly through sectarianism, Catholics [in Scotland] were generally isolated from the trades-union and Labour movements before 1890'.[9] Furthermore, Brown has concluded: 'In the context of a hostile presbyterian reception, the incoming Irish turned to the chapel and its activities for cultural and ethnic identity.'[10]

Recent research, however, has demonstrated that the Catholic Irish in the west of Scotland in the first half of the nineteenth century were not as isolated and despised as these and other historians have claimed.[11] This chapter, therefore, will reassess the Catholic Irish experience in the region during that period. It will not deal with the attitudes of Protestant ministers and the middle classes towards the immigrants as these have been well documented.[12] Nor will the chapter be concerned with Irish agricultural labourers, seasonal harvest workers and navvies (or as Handley once described them, 'Irish migratory labourers'[13]). Instead, it will focus on the Catholic Irish in the major towns in the west of Scotland and their relationship with those whom they lived and laboured beside – the Scottish working class.

II

During the first half of the nineteenth century the Catholic Irish did indeed form distinct communities in those towns in the west of Scotland – such as Glasgow, Paisley, Greenock, Ayr and Kilmarnock – in which they settled in significant numbers. Members of these communities were of Irish birth or descent and were deeply proud of this. For example, in 1829 Bishop Andrew Scott, who became Vicar Apostolic of the Western District of the Catholic Church in Scotland in 1832, informed a colleague that his 'Paddies' in the western lowlands were 'poor, ignorant people, enthusiastically attached to every thing that bears the name of Irish'.[14] In 1844 he told the Poor Law Inquiry that the Catholic Irish in the region 'were very national in their ideas and sentiments – rather too much so in some cases'.[15] The bulk of the politically active Catholic Irish in the west of Scotland idolised Daniel O'Connell, the great political leader of Catholic Ireland, and in the 1840s became enthusiastic supporters of his campaign for the repeal of the Act of Union between Great Britain and Ireland.[16]

Another characteristic which set the Catholic Irish apart from the bulk of the remainder of the population in the region was, of course, their religion. The Catholic Irish, including those who did not attend to their religious duties on a regular basis, were deeply attached to their Church and their faith.[17] Indeed, William Sloan has demonstrated that although non-practising Catholics in Glasgow in the 1830s and 1840s formed the majority of the city's Catholic Irish population, these lapsed individuals

> in their financial support of the Catholic church, in their respect for and deference towards the Catholic clergy, in their unwillingness to forego the Catholic rites of passage, and in their disdain of Protestant proselytism, demonstrated an allegiance and loyalty to Catholicism....[18]

Such people probably sent their children to the Catholic schools which were eventually established in most of the major towns in the region during this period.[19] Moreover, although little research has been undertaken on the subject, it is likely that given their attachment to Catholicism the Catholic Irish did not often intermarry with Protestant Scots or Irish.[20] Other features distinguished the Catholic Irish from the native population. The immigrants and their progeny were overwhelmingly working class and most lived in the worst districts of the towns in which they settled. Such localities, however, were never exclusively inhabited by them.[21] The Catholic Irish assisted one another in times of distress and unemployment,[22] and some also engaged in 'Orange and Green' party disputes with Protestant Irish immigrants.[23] Furthermore, many Protestant clergymen and sections of the middle class despised Catholicism and the Catholic Church and as a result were very hostile towards the Catholic Irish communities. One consequence of this was that Catholic Irish men and women were often discriminated against when they applied for poor relief. Another was that their oaths and evidence were often disregarded in the local courts.[24] Such bigotry undoubtedly reinforced the Catholic Irish population's sense of communal identity. It is therefore evident that distinct Catholic Irish communities existed in the west of Scotland during the first half of the nineteenth century. What now needs to be established is whether or not these communities and their members were despised by the bulk of the native population.

It is indisputable that Irish immigrants were used to break strikes and as a result encountered the hostility of Scottish workers.[25] Most of the evidence for this relates to the mining industries of Lanarkshire and Ayrshire, and mainly from the mid-1830s onwards. Indeed, the introduction of the Irish into the pits often resulted in acts of violence against them by local colliers. Such incidents have been well documented.[26] However, the Irish experience in the mining districts was more complex than some historians have suggested. In many instances Irishmen who were used as strike-breakers were not new to the industry but were already employed in and about the pits as labourers and had apparently lived and worked alongside the Scottish colliers without incident.[27] Campbell has shown that, once part of the mining workforce, most Irish immigrants – whether they had entered the pits as strike-breakers or had been taken on in new works during the general expansion of the coal and iron industries – were unwilling to join district unions, for social, economic and cultural reasons.[28] Yet there is, as Campbell acknowledged, evidence that some Irish colliers and miners participated in strikes to protect or improve their wages and conditions.[29] For example, the manager of William Dixon's Calder Iron Works near Coatbridge stated in 1834 that his Irish employees 'require more looking after…If any thing like a combination gets a footing, they seem more forward and active in taking the lead than the Scotch'.[30] During the great strike of 1842 the miners at a Mr Gordon's pit in the parish of St Quivox in Ayrshire stopped work; most were Irishmen from Connaught and some were involved in an attack on strike-breakers which resulted in the death of one new worker. Moreover, some of the blacklegs, including the murder victim, were Irish.[31] Catholic Irish colliers and miners in Hamilton and in other civil parishes in the middle ward of Lanarkshire participated in the miners' general strike of 1856.[32]

Irish handloom weavers were involved in strikes and trade unions with Scottish workers.[33] Hugh Cogan, a Glasgow cotton manufacturer who employed between 600 and 800 weavers in the city, of whom about one-half were Irish, commented in 1834:

> With regard to combination among the weavers, the Irish are rather urged on by the more acute and thinking among the Scotch; but when the emergency comes the Irish are the more daring spirits; and as they are in themselves less reflective and worse educated, they are more prone to use violence, without regard to consequences.[34]

Of the 1553 members of the weavers' trade unions in and around Glasgow who were supplied with work by the city's Relief Committee during the economic depression of 1837 595, or almost 40 per cent of the total, were born in Ireland.[35] Admittedly, neither of the examples given reveal the religion of the Irish weavers who engaged in collective action. However, it is most unlikely that none were Catholics. After all, the weavers' associations of the first half of the nineteenth century did not seek to exclude Catholic websters.[36] The policy of these unions was to include all weavers who would abide by their rules and regulations; only by doing this could they hope to be effective.[37] As Norman Murray, the historian of the handloom weavers in Scotland has argued, 'the process of undercutting could not be effectively curbed so long as a sizeable portion of the labour force remained unorganised'.[38] By the early 1830s perhaps around one-half of the weavers in and around Glasgow were first or second generation Irish – Catholic and Protestant.[39] It would have been a foolish union which sought to exclude such a large number of Catholic Irish weavers.

The majority of cotton spinners in Glasgow and Paisley during the first four decades of the nineteenth century were Irish or of Irish descent. These workers were the driving force behind the Glasgow Cotton Spinners Association, which from 1816 to 1837 was the most powerful and active workers' organisation in Scotland.[40] For example, in his *Report on the State of the Irish Poor in Great Britain*, published in 1836, George Cornewall Lewis stated:

> In Glasgow and its neighbourhood, the formidable union of the cotton-spinners was first organized by the Irish, who…were at first almost exclusively employed in the cotton factories of Lanarkshire and Renfrewshire.[41]

In the course of his inquiry Lewis was informed by George Miller, the manager of a cotton works at Blantyre, that:

> It is believed…that the union could never have acquired that degree of consistence that it now possesses had it not been for the daring character of the Irish, who scrupled at little in accomplishing their ends, even to the destruction of life and property, of which there are many miserable instances on record.[42]

By the 1830s most spinners were members of the Association. Irishmen continued to play a leading role in its affairs: indeed, in the aftermath of the disastrous spinners' general strike of 1837 a former member of the Association who had participated in the dispute informed the authorities 'That almost all the jobs done in the union…were done or originated by Catholics and Irishmen'.[43] One such Catholic Irishman was Peter Hacket, who at the time of the stoppage was the treasurer of the Association. He was also one of the four committee members of the union convicted for their role in the strike in the famous trial in Edinburgh in January 1838. Hacket had been active in the Association for several years and in the early 1830s was involved in the campaign in Glasgow for reform of conditions in factories.[44] Another Catholic Irish spinner who was prominent in that movement was Patrick McGowan, who spoke at and chaired major meetings of the city's factory reformers.[45] McGowan was a leading figure in the Glasgow Spinners Association during those years. In June 1830 he was one of the Scottish delegates to the conference of the Grand General Union of cotton spinners, held in Ramsay on the Isle of Man. During the remainder of that year McGowan toured the north-west of England promoting both the Grand General Union and John Doherty's general union, the National Association of United Trades for the Protection of Labour. After McGowan returned to Scotland he continued to advocate general unionism.

McGowan was a well-respected figure in the Glasgow labour movement. In May 1832 the newspaper for the city's working classes, the *Trades' Advocate*, stated that McGowan had

> been many years an active, persevering, and deservedly esteemed member and conductor of the cotton-spinners' association. By his brother operatives he has been frequently engaged in missions of great importance, wherein his eloquence and perseverance have proved eminently successful.[46]

A few months later McGowan was dismissed from his position at the Springfield Mill as a result of his prominent role in the movement for factory reform. He soon found employment in the offices of the Trades' Advocate's successor, the *Liberator*, although he continued to act on behalf of the Spinners' Association. For example, he helped negotiate the end of a strike in Houldsworth's Mill at Anderston in November 1832. By 1837 McGowan was again spinning and during the general strike was sent to Lancashire to raise funds for the union.

The Glasgow Spinners' Association, which throughout its existence had a large Irish membership (Catholic and Protestant), was an important part of the labour movement in and around the city. It was represented on the various Trades' Committees during the 1820s and 1830s and was prominent in the working class agitations of those decades. The Association was the driving force behind the campaign in the west of Scotland for a reform of working conditions for all workers in all factories, and appears to have been the principal backer of the *Liberator*.[47]

Members of the Catholic Irish communities in the west of Scotland were also involved in political agitations with Scottish workers.[48] In August and September 1819 Andrew Scott, then the sole priest of the Glasgow Mission, informed the Home Secretary Lord Sidmouth that the secret revolutionary organisation in the city was attempting to recruit into its ranks members of his congregation.[49] Scott later revealed to his superior Bishop Cameron that despite his efforts to dissuade them a number of Irish Catholics had joined the insurrectionary movement.[50]

The radicals in the west of Scotland decided to launch their revolt in April 1820. Part of their strategy involved a successful general strike during which the workers in the region would prepare for the rising, which would occur only when it became apparent that workers in the north of England had taken up arms.[51] The call for a general stoppage was well received in the west of Scotland – indeed, various contemporary accounts stated that all workers in Glasgow and Paisley went on strike in support of the aims of the radicals.[52] This suggests that Irish workers – Protestant and Catholic – took part in the stoppage.[53] The radicals in the region abandoned their plans for revolution when it quickly became apparent that their English counterparts had not rebelled. Once workers in Glasgow and Paisley realised this the general strike was soon over.

Catholic Irish workers participated in the great processions and demonstrations in Glasgow in 1831 and 1832 for the Reform Bills, and in those held to honour the visits to the city of the noted reformers the Earl of Durham and Daniel O'Connell in October 1834 and September 1835 respectively.[54] Moreover, Catholic Irish involvement in these and in other reform activities during this period was not insignificant, but was on such a scale as to be noted and welcomed by Scottish participants,[55] and to be viewed with great alarm by Bishop Andrew Scott. In March 1833 he informed a Cardinal in Rome that in the west of Scotland the Catholic Irish

> have naturally keen dispositions and passions, and since the famous reform bill was mooted, they have all become keen politicians, and without proper management, are in danger of walking in the footsteps of the French Infidels in the first French Revolution, of which I had the misfortune of being a witness.[56]

In June 1844 Charles Bryson, who was a leading figure in the Glasgow Catholic community and had been for over twenty years, proudly recalled that the Catholic Irish in the city had been 'Radical reformers during the agitation of the Reform Bill' and added that in this, 'and in all those other agitations for measures of civil and religious liberty, their behaviour was always worthy of the cause they were connected with'.[57]

Two Catholic Irishmen were particularly prominent in the pre-Chartist reform agitations of the 1830s. Patrick McGowan, the cotton spinners' leader, was in 1832 one of the delegates on the Glasgow Trades Committee, which organised the role of the city's workers in the struggle for the Reform Bills. He was also one of the speakers at probably the most famous reform meeting in Scotland during this period of political agitation, the 'Black Flag' demonstration on Glasgow Green on 12 May 1832. At this meeting a middle class reformer urged the people to tell the intransigent House of Lords: 'It was now the Bill or the Barricades. The Reform Bill must be passed or blood should flow.'[58] McGowan's performance that day was praised by the *Trades' Advocate*, which stated that his speech 'did great credit to the class he belongs to, for the firmness and moderation of its sentiments, under such exciting circumstances as were then presented to a provoked and long-insulted people'.[59] The other Irish Catholic who played a leading role in reform activities in Glasgow during this period was William McGowan, a teacher who in the 1820s was the secretary of the Glasgow Catholic Association, a society involved in the movement for Catholic Emancipation.[60] McGowan was not prominent in the campaign for the Reform Bills, but between 1833 and 1837 he participated in most of the major political meetings in the city.[61] For example, in January 1837 he spoke at the great meeting of Glasgow operatives held to repudiate the Tory sentiments expressed in an address to Sir Robert Peel from the newly established Glasgow Operative Conservative Society. Nine months later McGowan gave a speech on the utility of trade unions at a public meeting which condemned the local authorities for their arrest of the committee of the Glasgow Cotton Spinners' Association.[62]

William McGowan was one of the leading figures behind the establishment in September 1838 of Glasgow's Chartist society, and the following February was a main participant in the meeting at Greenock which resulted in the formation of a Chartist association for that town.[63] Other Irish Catholics played leading roles in the Chartist movement in the west of Scotland between 1838 and 1842, the peak years of the agitation. Thomas H. Donnelly, a surgeon, chaired the February 1839 meeting at Greenock in which William McGowan was involved, and for the next two years was a major figure in the town's Chartist organisation.

Moreover, he addressed Chartist meetings in the west of Scotland and was in demand as a lecturer. For example, in early 1840 he was asked by the Kilmarnock Working Men's Society to visit their town and employ his 'Mellesian brogue' to persuade people to join the campaign for the Charter.

The dominant figure in the Chartist movement in Great Britain was Feargus O'Connor, and two of his leading supporters in Glasgow were Catholic Irishmen, namely Con Murray and Dennis McMillan, who both became prominent in Glasgow Chartism during 1841. In September that year the O'Connorite National Charter Association, the Chartist organisation for England, raised a new National Chartist Petition. This differed from the previous one as it demanded not only the Six Points of the Charter, but also called for a repeal of the Act of Union between Great Britain and Ireland, and a repeal of the English Poor Law Amendment Act. Murray and McMillan quickly became enthusiastic proponents in Glasgow of this new programme. In February 1842 the city's Chartists voted by at least two to one to support the Petition. However, those who opposed it included most of the leading figures in Glasgow Chartism. These men were hostile to the measure because they believed that a Chartist petition should include only the demand for the Six Points and not other issues which received the support of only a section of their movement. Most were also opposed to O'Connor and his dominance of their agitation. Soon afterwards these leaders split from the city's O'Connorites and helped form a Complete Suffrage Association. Complete Suffragism was a recently established movement which aimed to unite the middle and working classes in a campaign for the Six Points. O'Connor and his supporters were vehemently opposed to this agitation which in England, as in Scotland, was supported by many leading Chartists hostile to O'Connor and his policies. In Glasgow the schism within the Chartist movement led to the formation of the Glasgow Charter Association, an organisation dominated by O'Connor's leading supporters in the city such as James Moir, George Ross, John Colquhoun, Dennis McMillan and Con Murray.

There is evidence of a Catholic Irish presence in the rank-and-file of the Chartist movement in Glasgow between 1838 and 1842. Catholic Irish workers participated in the procession and demonstration in Glasgow in May 1838 which launched the campaign in Britain for the Charter, and in those held to honour the visits of John Collins and Feargus O'Connor in September 1840 and October 1841 respectively. Irish Catholics were also present at other Chartist meetings in the city.

However, the bulk of the Catholic Irish community in Glasgow, and probably elsewhere in the region, did not participate in the Chartist movement between 1838 and 1842. Their political idol Daniel O'Connell was hostile to Chartism because it was dominated by O'Connor and his followers who regarded 'the Liberator' as a traitor to the working class. The O'Connorites argued that the use or threat of force to achieve political reform was justifiable; O'Connell maintained that change would come only as a result of peaceful agitation. Moreover, for much of this period O'Connell was convinced that no government would implement the Six Points and so the working class should campaign instead for a more modest programme of reform. He also argued that the Chartists were hostile to Ireland and Irish issues and therefore urged his Catholic Irish followers – the O'Connellites – to eschew involvement in the Chartist movement. In Glasgow, as in most parts of Great Britain with large Catholic Irish communities, the bulk of the O'Connell's supporters followed his advice.

By 1840 Glasgow's Chartist leaders were fully aware that they had failed to gain many recruits for their agitation from the ranks of the city's Catholic Irish community and this concerned them greatly. Between 1840 and 1842 they held meetings and discussions on how to bring the Catholic Irish back into the radical movement and debated the merits of Chartism and of O'Connell with some of his leading supporters in the city. The Chartists also attended O'Connellite meetings to put forward their case. As has been noted, in February 1842 the Glasgow Chartists even voted to include Repeal as part of their programme. Such efforts made little impact. Indeed, by May 1841 a Repeal society had been established in Glasgow and the city's O'Connellites soon became enthusiastic supporters of their leader's movement for an Irish legislature.

This is not to suggest, as some have done, that the bulk of the Catholic Irish community in Glasgow did not share the same political concerns as Scottish workers and were interested almost exclusively in issues relating to Ireland and the Catholic Church. The Catholic Irish Repealers were in favour of the Six Points and hoped that they would soon become law. However, they could not bring themselves to support the movement for the Charter so long as it was dominated by O'Connor and his followers. For example, at a Repeal meeting in the city in February 1842 Charles Bryson stated:

> He was of opinion that it was a pity for any dispute to arise between Irishmen and Chartists. (Hear, hear and approbation). Their object was the same, and he declared he would sign a petition for the Charter the moment it was presented to him. (Cheers.) He was a Chartist out and out, and the reason why he had not hitherto mingled so much amongst them as he would otherwise have done, or induced his countrymen to do so, was not because he had any doubt of the justice of their principles, but because he could not join with some of their leaders. (Applause.)[64]

Indeed, when the Complete Suffrage movement emerged in Glasgow the city's O'Connellites soon became enthusiastic supporters of it. Bryson and three other leading Repealers – Dr John Scanlan, Dr Henry Gribben and Peter McCabe – were elected to the committee of the Glasgow Complete Suffrage Association at its founding meeting in May 1832. Meetings of the city's Repealers passed resolutions in favour of Complete Suffragism. The new movement finally gave Glasgow's O'Connellites an opportunity they could take to participate in a national campaign for the Six Points of the Charter: O'Connor and his supporters were not involved in Complete Suffragism whereas their leading opponents within the Chartist movement were. Charles Bryson declared at a Repeal meeting in June 1842:

> It was now necessary that they should throw aside all minor points of difference, and promote that union amongst Reformers without which no great movement could hope to be successful....It was their interest to embrace into their views all who, in common with themselves, were struggling to get quit of the yoke of their aristocratic oppressors, and the Complete Suffragists, as rational, peaceable, and constitutional reformers, were in every way entitled to their co-operation and assistance.[65]

By the beginning of 1843, however, both the Chartist and Complete Suffrage movements had collapsed and were therefore no longer forces of any great political significance. Over the next few years the O'Connellites in Glasgow and elsewhere in the west of Scotland concentrated on the agitation for Repeal. In spring 1848, almost a year after the death of O'Connell, Repealers in the region joined forces with the resurgent Chartist movement and, in a period of hope and excitement engendered by news of the revolution in Paris, campaigned for Repeal and the Charter. Such a development occurred in a number of towns throughout the United Kingdom. By the end of the summer, however, government repression had crushed both the Repeal and Chartist movements.[66]

From the late 1830s onwards the temperance movement in the west of Scotland expanded rapidly, and many members of the Catholic Irish communities became enthusiastic advocates of total abstinence. For example, in June 1841 it was reported that 18,500 of the 32,000 Catholics in Glasgow had taken the teetotal pledge.[67] The Catholic Irish abstainers in the region, however, were not involved in the temperance societies established by the Scots, but instead supported their own organisation.[68] In Glasgow they even held major demonstrations. On 2 January 1841 between three and four thousand members of the Glasgow Catholic Total Abstinence Association assembled on Glasgow Green and then marched through the principal streets of the city with their bands playing and flags flying. They were led by James Enraght, an Irish priest at St Andrew's chapel who during his stay in Scotland (1840–42) was the dominant figure among Catholic abstainers. The procession and the large crowd which followed it returned to the Green, where Enraght addressed a multitude estimated at around 30,000.[69] On 15 July 1843 a similar procession of Catholic Irish teetotallers took place through the city. As with the previous event, this did not attract any hostility or acts of violence from the native population. Instead, it 'called forth the warm approbation of thousands of spectators'.[70]

Although the Catholic Irish teetotallers in Glasgow had their own organisation they did not, as Sloan has suggested, promote the temperance cause in isolation.[71] The Catholic total abstainers worked closely with their Protestant counterparts. For example, in February 1840 the secretaries of the committee for the various Scottish temperance district committees in the city reported that: 'Though the Catholics have a separate Society, we are united in our efforts....We interchange speakers, and the greatest harmony prevails.'[72] Father Enraght spoke at large teetotal meetings in the City Halls and the Bazaar.[73] The Scottish and Catholic Irish total abstainers in Glasgow also held joint demonstrations. On 17 July 1841 between five and seven thousand of them walked in procession through the city. The Catholic Irish participants, headed by Enraght, were in the majority.[74] The *Scottish Temperance Journal* lavished praise on the event:

> The most kindly feeling pervaded both sides; their opposing creeds were for the time forgotten; and as teetotal brethren, united in one grand moral confederation against the common enemy, they were animated by one spirit, and by one fixed purpose, – the extermination of alcoholic influence. Bigotry had either gone to bed from pure vexation, or was seeking elevation to its sunk spirits in some dark den of inebriation. It dared not show its ill-omened face on such an auspicious occasion....Thousands of our fellow-citizens were spectators in the Green, and as the cavalcade proceeded through the streets; and in no case did we see any other feeling manifested than delight and satisfaction; all looked on with deep interest, and some could not restrain the tear of joy.[75]

On 16 August 1842 members of the Catholic and Protestant temperance societies in and around Glasgow walked in procession and held a demonstration to honour the visit to the city of the renowned Irish temperance advocate Father Theobald Mathew. The procession, which also included total abstainers from surrounding counties, was led by Fathers Mathew and Enraght, who were at the head of the Catholic Irish participants. On their return to Glasgow Green the marchers were welcomed by a crowd which numbered around 50,000. During his three days in the city Mathew administered the teetotal pledge to upwards of 40,000 people.[76]

Indeed, some within the Scottish temperance organisations came to advocate even stronger links with their Catholic Irish allies. In May 1844 the *Scottish Temperance Journal*, the organ of the Western Scottish Temperance Union (which represented almost all the Protestant teetotal societies in the western lowlands), published a report of the soirée held to celebrate the fifth anniversary of the Glasgow Catholic Total Abstinence Association. One of the toasts given at the event was 'The Protestant total abstainers of Glasgow'. The *Journal* commented that

> the enthusiasm with which these sentiments were responded to by the meeting, evidences the willingness of our Catholic brethren to co-operate with us in the great work of moral reformation. We rejoice in the manifestation of such a feeling on their part, and trust that some plan will be speedily adopted which will unite us more closely in the bonds of union and brotherly love, that we may more effectually hasten the downfall of those drinking customs, which still exercise so pernicious an influence over the opinions and practices of our fellow-countrymen.[77]

Such a union, however, was never effected, probably because enthusiasm for the temperance cause soon waned among many within the Catholic Irish community in Glasgow.

Irish Catholics were also involved in riots and disturbances alongside Scots during the period under examination. On 12 July 1831 Scottish and Catholic Irish political reformers in Girvan attempted to prevent Orangemen from parading through the town. Much violence ensued and a special constable was killed by an Orangeman who was soon afterwards convicted and hanged for the crime. During the 'bread riots' in Glasgow in March 1848 sixty-four people were arrested, of whom twenty-six were Roman Catholics.[78]

The Catholic Irish also engaged in other forms of joint action with the native population. In Greenock in 1815 Catholic Irishmen participated in a procession and demonstration of freemasons, despite having been warned not to by their priest. Eighteen years later Scottish reformers and Irish Catholics in the town united in an unsuccessful attempt to prevent an anti-Catholic lecture from taking place.[79]

At the beginning of this chapter it was shown that the prevailing historical view of the Catholic Irish in nineteenth century Scotland is that they were despised by the bulk of the native population and as a result formed separate and isolated communities. Yet this section has demonstrated that during the first half of the nineteenth century members of Catholic Irish communities in the west of Scotland – the region in which the majority of Irish immigrants settled – were involved in strikes, trade unions, trade union campaigns, political agitations, the temperance movement and riots with Scottish workers. Moreover, when the Catholic Irish presence in some of these activities was not as great as was hoped, as for example in the radical agitation of 1819 and in the Chartist movement between 1838 and 1842, native participants actively sought their involvement.

However, not all Scottish workers were strikers, trade unionists, political reformers, temperance advocates or rioters. Perhaps those who participated with the Catholic Irish in collective action were more enlightened and less bigoted than those who did not. The following section will therefore examine the relationship between the Catholic Irish and the rest of the Scottish working class.

III

Some historians have concluded that the strength of opposition in the west of Scotland in early 1829 to the Bill for Catholic Emancipation was mainly a consequence of popular hostility towards the Catholic Irish in the region. For example, the Checklands stated the following:

> The great mass of the petitioners against Catholic emancipation were of the uneducated lower classes, no doubt motivated by fear and distrust of Irish labour, so often used by employers to make effective unionism impossible. Thus the hostility to the Catholics was greatest in the industrial west...[80]

Tom Gallagher argued that:

> Ordinary Glaswegians displayed particular hostility to the act for social as well as religious reasons. Workers and artisans were acutely aware how rapidly the city's Irish community was growing and what the consequences might be for their livelihoods...[81]

Callum Brown and Bruce Lenman have expressed similar views.[82]

There was indeed opposition in the region to Catholic Emancipation but it would appear that its extent has been overstated. The Glasgow petition against the measure contained 36,790 signatures and was completed in ten days.[83] According to the *Glasgow Herald* it was signed solely by 'males above 14 years of age...'.[84] Yet in 1831 there were 54,684 males in Glasgow and suburbs who were 15-years of age and above.[85] This suggests that in 1829 a large number of the city's adult males did not actively oppose Emancipation. Moreover, there were claims that women and children had been allowed to sign the petition and that some schoolboys had repeatedly signed it, while others had put down several different names.[86]

Furthermore, it is by no means certain that all workers in the west of Scotland who protested against Emancipation did so because they were hostile to the Catholic Irish in the region.[87] After all, petitions condemning the Bill were sent to London from all over Scotland, including parts of the country with few or no Irish Catholics.[88] One such area was the far north, where 'a broad belt of strong protest ran from Inverness northwards'.[89] Ian Muirhead examined many of the anti-Catholic petitions and concluded that the principal argument contained in them was that if Catholics were able to enter Parliament and hold high office it would be a 'subversion of the Revolution Settlement, the Treaty of Union and the Protestant Establishment'.[90]

The full extent of popular support in Glasgow for Emancipation was never established, although one attempt was made. On 18 February a shop was opened in the Trongate to receive signatures to a petition in favour of the Bill, and placards announcing this were placed in its window. The shop, however, was situated immediately opposite the Tron Church Session House, one of the places in the city where the anti-Emancipation petition could be signed. After a few hours, at around 6 o'clock, a porter, possibly hired for the purpose, stationed himself outside the shop and urged passers-by to sign the anti-Catholic petition housed across the street. A large mob soon assembled and those who signed the pro-Emancipation petition were verbally abused. Two hours later the police arrived at the scene and closed the shop.[91] The following morning the shop reopened, but closed only a few hours later after a mob had rushed in and destroyed the petition sheets. The next day, 20 February, the shop once again opened, but in the afternoon 'a crowd of blackguard boys' gathered in front of it, 'and hissed, hooted and threw mud at almost every individual who entered or came out'. A party of police soon appeared but was unable to disperse the mob. Eventually the landlord arrived and closed his shop, and announced that it would not be reopened.[92] Although the shop had been open for only a short time, the pro-Emancipation petition received 4,200 signatures.[93]

The actions of the Trongate mob appear to have discouraged those in the city who were pro-Emancipation from raising another general petition in favour of the Bill.[94] (There was also a belief among some reformers that the Glasgow police and magistrates had – perhaps deliberately – not provided sufficient protection for the Trongate shop and for those who signed the petition or who wished to do so.)[95] On 23 February a meeting of middle-class supporters of Emancipation was held in the Tontine Hall at which it was decided to petition Parliament in favour of the measure. Kirkman Finlay, a leading cotton manufacturer and merchant, chaired the event and argued 'that the public generally should not sign the petition..'.

In an obvious reference to the Trongate disturbances he stated that he 'wished…to prevent that irritation which existed in the public mind, and had already shown itself to some extent'. More importantly, however, Finlay was convinced that the petition 'should only have the signatures of those who, from education, subsequent reflection, and habits, had acquired such knowledge as gave them the means of forming an opinion worthy to be attended to…'. Those present agreed and decided that the Committee which organised the meeting should make the arrangements for obtaining support from among the middle classes.[96] The petition eventually received around 300 signatures, mainly those of clergymen, university professors, bankers, merchants and traders.[97]

There is evidence which suggests that at least one group of workers in the west of Scotland was not hostile to the political claims of the Catholics. In March 1829 the handloom weavers in and around Glasgow and Paisley were experiencing severe economic distress as a result of a series of reductions in wage-rates made by manufacturers since the previous December. Meetings of weavers' delegates from the region took place in Glasgow to discuss their plight, and the committee of their Association discussed wages with the employers and the provision of relief work with the local authorities. However, the manufacturers could not (or would not) increase payments and the weavers regarded the relief work given by the city's magistrates as wholly inadequate. Moreover, the distress of the weavers was increasing daily. Eventually, a meeting of weavers' delegates held on 21 March decided that a general meeting on Glasgow Green of members of their trade was needed.[98] It was to be held 'for the purpose of taking into consideration their present destitute and pitiable condition, and adopting such steps as should be deemed advisable for their relief'.[99] This development greatly alarmed the middle classes. Two 'influential gentlemen', one of whom was a member of the Town Council, met the Weavers' Committee to discuss the proposed meeting. They stated that they did not see what good could come from such a gathering and

> were afraid from the excitement of society, relative to the Catholic Question, some unfavourable event might happen. Blackguards might mingle with them, and some such project as breaking the windows of the Catholic chapel might be the result.

They added that a delegation to the local authorities would be just as effective as an aggregate meeting.[100] (Indeed it is probable that the two men had been sent by the Lord Provost and Magistrates.)[101] The Weavers' Committee informed them that it was too late to cancel the event and stated:

With respect to the Catholic question, the committee were not afraid of a disturbance on that account. There was not a weaver around Glasgow, but was glad at the success of the Catholics, for religious liberty, and hoped that by following the same course, they would gain a better remuneration for their labour.[102]

The general meeting, attended by around 12,000 weavers, took place peacefully on the Green on 30 March.[103]

The Catholic Emancipation Act received Royal Assent on 13 April 1829. In August 1835 it was announced that Daniel O'Connell, whose activities had been mainly responsible for the Wellington's decision to introduce the Emancipation Bill, was to visit Glasgow the following month as part of his Scottish tour.[104] His opponents were convinced that he would not be made welcome. For example, the Tory and Orange *Glasgow Courier* stated the following:

We make no surmise as to how Edinburgh may receive him; but we give him this timely warning, that in this Protestant and Covenanting City, it may be dangerous for any bloodthirsty Papist and political agitator, like him, to approach it nearer than Camlachie or Tollcross. We trust this hint will be sufficient, both to the big beggarman and his paltry gang here and hereabouts; for we can assure both that the ancient spirit of the land is not yet dead, nor will any insult upon its religious feelings be tamely submitted to.[105]

Attempts were made to rouse 'Protestant and Covenanting' Glasgow. A short time before O'Connell's visit two itinerant preachers, O'Sullivan and McGhee, appeared in the city and gave lectures against Catholicism and the Catholic Church. Reformers were convinced that these men had been hired by O'Connell's religious and political opponents to stir up popular hostility towards both his visit and the Catholic population of Glasgow.[106] Moreover, the *Reformers' Gazette* claimed that during the two weeks prior to O'Connell's arrival all the Church of Scotland ministers in the city attacked him from their pulpits, and some even threatened 'everlasting woe in the world to come, against all those who took part in the O'Connell Demonstration!!!'[107]

Despite such hostility O'Connell's visit was a tremendous success. When he appeared on the hustings at Glasgow Green he was given a huge ovation. O'Connell then addressed a multitude estimated by some at 100,000 strong and by others at double that amount.[108] At this event he received an address from the Glasgow Trades in which he was described as 'the first man of his age, the representative of wronged Ireland, and the champion of civil and religious liberty over the whole world'.[109] The demonstration and procession in O'Connell's honour were reminiscent of those which took place in 1831 and 1832 for the Reform Bills, and in 1834 for the visit of the Earl of Durham. O'Connell also made successful visits to Edinburgh, Paisley and Greenock in September 1835. His tour of Scotland was not marred by any anti-Catholic riots or disturbances.

The lack of opposition to O'Connell's presence in Scotland appears to have greatly vexed his opponents. A few weeks after his visit to Glasgow a number of Church of Scotland ministers and laymen in the city established a Protestant Association

> for the purpose, by public meetings and the press, of exposing the errors and pernicious tendency of the Popish system, – extensively diffusing information respecting the character and history of the church of Rome, and arousing Protestants to the duties to which they are specially called.[110]

One of the reasons given for the founding of the society was 'the dangers of Popery arising from the accession of Roman Catholics to power in the Legislature of the country'; another was 'the magnitude of the Roman Catholic population in Glasgow…'. The Association organised two courses of anti-Popery lectures in the city during the winters of 1835–6 and 1836–7. Topics included 'Ireland – Popery and Priestcraft, the cause of her misery and crime' and 'The Dangerous Nature of Popery'. The lectures were subsequently published and, according to a leading figure in the society, 'extensively sold and widely circulated'. In addition to these works the Association claimed to have printed around 85,000 pamphlets, lectures and tracts by 1840. It also imported anti-Catholic speakers from England and Ireland to 'enlighten' the citizens.[111] During the second half of the 1830s Church of Scotland ministers at Paisley, Greenock and Airdrie delivered their own No-Popery lectures.[112] There is, however, no evidence that such activities received the support of the bulk of the native working class in the west of Scotland, and the region did not experience any upsurge in hostility towards the Catholic Irish during these years.[113]

Other anti-Catholic organisations made little impact on the native workforce during this period. The Orange Order in Scotland at its peak, in 1848, had less than 700 aherents, most of whom resided in the western lowlands. The bulk of this membership was composed of first and second generation Protestant Irishmen. Indeed, these Orangemen constituted only a very small proportion of the total Protestant Irish male population in the region.[114] The Glasgow Operative Conservative Society was founded in December 1836 'to maintain…the British Constitution as established at the era of the Revolution in 1688…to defend the interests of the Ecclesiastical and Educational Establishments of Scotland…and…to promote the purity of administration…'. It was supported by the Tory press in Glasgow and by the city's Church of Scotland journal the *Scottish Guardian*. However, during the era of radicalism and Chartism the Society was never a force of any great social or political significance, and appears to have disbanded in the summer of 1843.[115]

Moreover, what is striking, given the dominant historical view of the Catholic Irish in the west of Scotland, is that outwith parts of the Ayrshire and Lanarkshire coalfields there is little evidence of popular hostility to their presence. There were no riots or disturbances against the Catholic Irish in these non-mining areas, not even during years of severe economic depression such as 1816–17, 1819–20, 1826, 1829, 1830–32, 1837, 1839–42 and 1847–48, when there could have been a search for scapegoats and a resulting backlash against members of such a distinct community. There are only a few newspaper reports of street brawls between groups of Irish and Scottish workers in the major towns in the region and little is known about these minor incidents, or even whether the Irish participants were always Catholics.[116] Indeed, if the contemporary press was a reliable guide to the immigrant experience it would appear that the Catholic Irish fought more among themselves,[117] or with the Protestant Irish,[118] or with the police,[119] than they did with native workers.

There is in fact evidence which suggests that by the early 1830s, if not before, the Catholic Irish in the major towns in the west of Scotland were not despised by the majority – perhaps even the bulk – of the native population, and that they even associated with Scottish workers in the course of their everyday lives, in some places to a considerable extent. It comes not from an obscure source but from one of the most important and famous parliamentary papers of the nineteenth century, the *Report on the State of the Irish Poor in Great Britain*, published in 1836. This was written by George Cornewall Lewis, who also collected the evidence contained in its appendix during the first four months of 1834. In his statement to Lewis, Bishop Andrew Scott stated:

> the Irish in Glasgow do mix, and are obliged to mix, with the natives in the course of their ordinary employments; and I never observed any disinclination on the part of the Irish to mix with the natives who treat them civilly. I must also observe, that almost all the Irish in this city and neighbourhood come here from the northern counties of Ireland, and there is not much difference between the habits of the northern Irish and the Scotch in the lower classes of life; they do not remain a distinct body from the natives here, but they certainly retain some of their own peculiarities, and all their natural vivacity and quickness of temper.[120]

He remarked, however, that the Catholic Irish experienced hostility from some sections of the Scottish working class.[121] Other witnesses noted that the Irish in the city associated with the Scots to a considerable extent and argued this was a cause – for some the principal cause – of the deterioration in the moral condition of the native population. For example, one businessman maintained that the Irish were

> more addicted to drink, to lying, and to swearing, than the natives; by mixing so much with them, they have lowered the tone of morals among the Scotch, whilst they, the Irish, have been in a greater proportion improved.[122]

Moses Steven Buchanan, the senior surgeon of the Glasgow Royal Infirmary and an Elder and Deacon of St John's Parish, stated that there were no streets or districts in the city exclusively inhabited by the immigrants, who appeared to him 'to be quite amalgamated and mixed up with the poor population…' He added:

> In consequence of the large numbers of Irish who come here, and their great ignorance, both intellectual and religious, their morality is inferior, and this has a tendency to lower the Scotch. You may educate and raise the native population as you will, still there is a constant influx of ignorant and uneducated Irish, who, by their example and association, deteriorate the condition of the natives.[123]

James Wright, a cotton manufacturer, argued that the Irish were

> extremely ignorant, those who come here being generally the lowest of the population, and their mixing with the natives produces a bad moral effect on them, from their want of religious education. Generally I think that the Irish have contributed considerably to demoralize the working classes of Glasgow by their example, arising from the want of religious and moral training, and by evil communication.[124]

On the other hand, Andrew Scott and Henry Houldsworth, one of Scotland's leading cotton manufacturers, contended that the moral condition of some Irish immigrants in Glasgow had declined as a result of their mixing with 'the lower orders' of the Scottish population.[125]

In Ayrshire the relationship between the Catholic Irish and the Scots appears to have been different in its two leading towns. William Thomson, the Catholic priest whose charge covered most of the county, informed Lewis that the Irish in Ayr mixed with the natives and adopted their customs and habits. The Superintendent of the Poor of the town gave similar evidence.[126] Yet in Kilmarnock it was stated that the Irish did not mix much with the Scottish population, although the Session Clerk added that this did 'not hold with regard to the children' of the immigrants and an umbrella-maker stated that 'the more indifferent' natives mixed with the Irish.[127]

Lewis received conflicting evidence concerning the Catholic Irish experience in Greenock and Paisley, the two major towns in Renfrewshire. William Gordon, the Catholic priest of Greenock, stated that the Irish in the town were 'treated…with a kind of exclusive policy, principally by the lower classes…[who] consider them as a distinct class of persons'. He suggested religious prejudice as one probable cause of this, but added that it was 'now fast wearing away'.[128] However, Robert Sinclair, the owner of an engine works, maintained:

> The Irish mix up with the natives after they have been here some time; there appears to be a considerable affinity between the Irish working population and the Scotch: they assimilate themselves very much to them.[129]

John Bremner, the Catholic priest of Paisley, told Lewis that the Catholic Irish in the town

> mix with the natives and in a great measure adopt their habits. They do not remain distinct from the natives by any peculiarities known to me, save the peculiarities of idiom and religion.[130]

A cotton-thread manufacturer stated that the Scots in the town no longer remained aloof from the Irish, but did not 'readily associate' with recently arrived immigrants.[131] Alexander Campbell, the Sheriff Substitute of the county, testified that the Irish were 'accustomed to associate with each other, and not much with the Scots, and for years after coming from Ireland retain their peculiarities',[132] a view shared by two local officials.[133] Campbell, however, added that the children of the Irish became 'assimilated to the Scots', yet retained habits which were 'believed to have had an unfavourable influence upon the Scots with whom they mix'.[134]

Whatever the extent to which the immigrants in Paisley associated with the Scots might have been, it is evident from the *Report on the State of the Irish Poor* and from other sources that the Catholic Irish community in the town was not despised by the bulk of the native population. For example, in May 1841 a severe economic depression began in Paisley and lasted for almost two years. At the height of the crisis, in February 1842, nearly 15,000 people were supported by the town's General Relief Committee. (The population of Paisley and suburbs in the census of 1841 was around 60,500.)[135] By January 1843 12,000 inhabitants were still on relief and 'terrible deprivation' existed.[136] However, the Local Relief Committee, which had taken over the administration of relief to the destitute the previous June, no longer received enough weekly funds to provide all those in need with 'even a bare subsistence…'. It therefore concluded that in order to give some of the distressed adequate assistance it had to strike others off the Relief List.[137] On 6 January 1843 the Committee decided, by 10 votes to 6, to remove from the List 'all the Irish and their families' who had not lived in Paisley for more than ten years.[138] These inhabitants were struck off because they had 'not so strong a claim' upon the Fund as the Scottish poor and because it was believed that under the provisions of the new Irish Poor Law they would obtain relief in any part of their native land.[139] To enable these unfortunate people to return to Ireland the Committee also decided that they should receive their final week's allowance in cash if required.[140] At that time there were 629 'Irish heads of families, men, widows and deserted wives, and destitute females' on the Relief List. It is not known how many dependants they had.[141] The total number of Irish struck off as a result of the resolution of 6 January – heads of families and their dependants – amounted to only 208.[142] Most were members of the town's Catholic community.[143]

The actions of the Relief Committee towards a section of the Irish population caused tremendous outrage in Paisley.[144] For example, a public meeting on the affair was held in the town's Exchange Rooms. Three resolutions were passed unanimously at this event, two of which were the following:

> That this meeting expresses its abhorrence of the inhuman conduct of the Paisley Relief Committee, in excluding from the supply list the unemployed Irish who have not had a residence of ten years in the town.
>
> That this meeting expresses its approbation of the conduct of the unemployed Irish, in common with the rest of our fellow-townsmen, who have borne such extensive and protracted sufferings with becoming fortitude and patience, deeply sympathise with them in their distress, and recommend their case to the friendly consideration of all charitable individuals.[145]

The *Renfrewshire Reformer* described the Committee's decision as 'unpopular' and 'indefensible'.[146]

Those who were struck off the Relief List did not, however, return to Ireland but instead remained in the town. The publicity given to the affair caused uproar and ill-feeling not only in Paisley but also throughout the whole of the United Kingdom, and as a result John Bremner received donations from every quarter, which he distributed to the distressed Irish. Moreover, public indignation and pressure eventually forced the Relief Committee, on 27 March, to rescind the offending resolution. Fortunately, by around that time trade had begun to revive and on 29 April 1843 the Committee was wound up.[147]

Indeed, such was the outcry throughout the British Isles against the 6 January resolution that the Government appointed a Parliamentary Inquiry into the distress in Paisley and the actions of the Relief Committee, and in particular its decision to remove from the Relief List a section of the Irish townspeople.[148] John Bremner was called as a witness and one of the questions he was asked was whether his Catholic Irish congregation had 'lived on good terms with their neighbours' during his time as priest in the town. Bremner answered: 'Always during the last 13 years.'[149] The reactions of the native population to the Relief Committee's treatment of some of the Irish inhabitants of Paisley in early 1843 suggests that Bremner's assessment of the relationship which existed between the Catholic Irish and Protestant Scots in the town was accurate.[150]

IV

It is evident that the extent of popular opposition to the Catholic Irish in the west of Scotland before the 1850s has been greatly exaggerated. Some historians appear to have noted the hostility towards Irish immigrants in some of the mining districts in Lanarkshire and Ayrshire and assumed that Scottish workers elsewhere in the region were equally opposed to the Catholic Irish presence, and for the same reasons. It must be emphasised, however, that the majority of Irish immigrants did not settle in mining areas and were not used to break strikes. Moreover, Handley demonstrated that in the major towns in the west of Scotland most Irish workers – Catholic and Protestant – did not deprive the Scots of employment:[151]

> for much of the labour that they undertook the Irish had no competitors among the native population. As builders' labourers, as stevedores, at the canals and reservoirs, on the railways, in road-making and mending, in pipe-laying, in brick kilns and potteries, at gas-works, in quarries, in sugar refineries, in cotton factories, the Irish had no rivals to dispute their presence, for the native avoided such employment either on the ground that it was too strenuous for him or because it fell below his aspirations.[152]

The only occupation apart from mining in which Irish and Scottish workers were employed in large numbers during this period was handloom weaving. For example, by the mid-1830s perhaps around one-half of the weavers in and around Glasgow were first or second generation Irish and such a presence might have contributed to the decline in wages paid to handloom weavers in the west of Scotland. Yet there was little hostility towards the Irish websters. There were several reasons for this. The Irish did not enter the weaving trade as strike-breakers. Moreover, the large proportion of Irish in the weaving workforce in Glasgow and in other towns in the region was not achieved overnight but after nearly forty years of large-scale immigration. During that time many members of traditional weaving communities abandoned the trade because of the decline in wage-rates and for the same reason did not bring up their children to the loom. In those decades migrants to the towns from the Highlands and rural lowlands became, or already were, handloom weavers. Therefore it was not the case that Irish workers flooded into traditional and stable weaving areas over a very short period of time and deprived members of those communities of employment.[153] Finally, as was shown earlier, once part of the weaving labour force many Irish immigrants became involved in strikes and trade unions alongside their Scottish co-workers.

Although Handley recognised that there was little economic rivalry between Irish immigrants and the Scots he maintained that the Catholic Irish were despised by the bulk of the native population:

> most of all…the Irish were disliked because the religion of the vast majority of them was execrated by the native. In antipathy on this ground almost all heartily joined, though naturally the fires of resentment were stoked chiefly by the official ministers of religion. This enmity was directed against the Irish solely as Catholics. Protestant immigrants from the North were accepted by the Scots as one with themselves, and the distinction has persisted.[154]

Scotland, of course, had a long history of hostility towards the Roman Catholic Church and faith. Indeed, in 1778 – only some twenty years before the beginning of significant Irish immigration – the announcement that the Government intended to introduce a Relief Bill into Parliament which would repeal some of the Penal Laws against Catholics in Scotland aroused fierce opposition throughout the country.[155] Such a measure was regarded as 'highly prejudicial to the interest of the Protestant religion in Scotland, dangerous to our constitution, civil and religious, a direct violation of the treaty of union, inconsistent with the King's honour, and destructive to the peace and security of his best subjects'.[156] In Glasgow, 85 societies hostile to the proposals were quickly formed and soon had a membership of at least 12,000. There were also two major anti-Popery riots in the city during which the houses and property of two Catholics were destroyed. At that time there were perhaps less than two dozen Catholics in Glasgow. The strength of feeling in Scotland against giving relief to Roman Catholics was so intense that in February 1779 the Government abandoned its plans to introduce the bill.[157]

However, neither Handley nor those other historians who maintained that the Catholic Irish immigrants and their progeny were, on account of their religion, loathed by most Scots, produced convincing evidence to support their arguments. There was in fact little open popular hostility towards the Catholic Irish in the major towns in the west of Scotland in the first half of the nineteenth century. Furthermore, while most Scottish workers might have disliked Catholicism as a religion and the Catholic Church as an institution, many did not let their personal religious beliefs prevent them from participating in joint activities or associating with members of the Catholic Irish communities in the region.

This clearly represented a fundamental change in popular attitudes in the west of Scotland to Catholics and Catholicism. Indeed, in March 1835 Henry Cockburn, the former Solicitor-General for Scotland, noted in his journal that 'The toleration of the Catholics by the people is one of striking changes of our time',[158] although he added that there were still 'thousands of worthy people who not only retain all the horror of their ancestors against the professors of this creed, but would like to see them still persecuted. But this weakness is abating'. According to Cockburn:

> Its decline is to be chiefly ascribed to the general improvement of the public mind, but it had its proximate causes here besides. It first begun to relax in Scotland from necessity. Poor Catholics multiplied so fast in Glasgow and the all the west, that it was found absolutely indispensable to educate and civilise them. This familiarised people to their chapels, their schools, and their openly associating; and admitted their priests into measures of public charity....The whole country was overrun by Irish labourers, so that the Presbyterian population learned experimentally that a man might be a Catholic without having the passions or the visible horns of the devil. New chapels have arisen peaceably everywhere; and except their stronger taste for a fight now and then, the Irish have in many places behaved fully as well as our own people. The recent extinction of civil disability on account of their religion removed the legal encouragement of intolerance, and left common-sense some chance; and the mere habit of hating, and of thinking it a duty to act on this feeling, being superseded, Catholics and rational Protestants are more friendly than the different sects of Protestants are.[159]

There is much merit in Cockburn's explanation for the lack of hostility towards the Catholic Irish by the 1830s. It is probable that most of those who protested so vociferously and violently in Glasgow in 1778–9 against the proposals for Catholic Relief had never met or even seen a Roman Catholic. Yet they hated and feared Catholics and Catholicism. As a result of Irish immigration many native workers in the west of Scotland came to realise from experience that Catholic men and women were not evil and did not constitute a threat to Protestantism or to the peace and security of the Kingdom.[160]

Two other developments undoubtedly contributed to the change in popular perceptions of Roman Catholics and their faith. First, from the late eighteenth century onwards rapid urbanisation and industrialisation, along with new political ideas which emanated from the French Revolution and from English radicals during the post-Napoleonic War social unrest, transformed traditional attitudes and relationships in the towns in the west of Scotland, and as a result by the 1830s 'a substantial measure of working-class unity and consciousness' had emerged.[161] Secondly, over the same period the power and influence which Protestant clergymen had over the urban populace declined considerably.[162] For example, during the controversy in 1778–9 over relief for Scottish Catholics the sermons and tracts against the Government's proposals by Church of Scotland ministers 'stirred crowds to massive violence...'.[163] By contrast, the anti-Catholic lectures and sermons of Protestant clergymen in the 1830s made little impact on the native working class, despite the presence of priests, chapels and tens of thousands of Catholics in the region. Indeed, one of the reasons given for the formation of the Glasgow Protestant Association in October 1835 was 'the loose notions of religious principle unhappily prevalent among a large body of Protestants' in the city.[164]

Ever since James Handley's studies of the Irish in Scotland were published in the 1940s historians have accepted without criticism his conclusion that the Catholic Irish immigrants and their descendants were despised by the bulk of the native population.[165] One consequence of this has been that most historians of the Catholic Irish in nineteenth century Scotland have not deemed it necessary to examine the relationship between Scottish and Catholic Irish workers; instead, they have focused on issues such as Catholic Irish political and social movements, the growth and development of the Catholic community, the provision of schools, chapels, priests and voluntary organisations.[166] Much good work has resulted and more detailed examinations of these themes are in fact needed. However, by concentrating on such internal developments these historians have helped to reinforce the thesis, first advanced by Handley, that Catholic Irish communities were separate, self-contained and isolated. This chapter has focused on Scottish-Catholic Irish relations in the west of Scotland during the first half of the nineteenth century and argued that the prevailing view of the Catholic Irish does not for that period carry much conviction. Future studies of Catholic Irish communities in nineteenth century Scotland must, therefore, include an examination of the relationship which existed between their members and the native population.

REFERENCES.

1 . Martin J. Mitchell, 'The Irish in the West of Scotland, 1797–1848: Trade Unions, Strikes and Political Movements' (Ph.D thesis, University of Strathclyde, 1996), 1–3.

2. *Ibid.*, 6.

3. See for example, James Handley, *The Irish in Scotland, 1798–1845* (2nd edition, Cork, 1945), chapter 8; Tom Gallagher, *Glasgow, the Uneasy Peace: Religious Tension in Modern Scotland* (Manchester, 1987), Introduction and Chapter 1; T.C. Smout, *A Century of the Scottish People, 1830–1950* (Pbk. edition, London, 1987), 22–3.

4. For a fuller discussion of historians' views on the Irish in Scotland see Mitchell, 'Irish in the West of Scotland', 7–16.

5. Gallagher, *Glasgow, The Uneasy Peace*, 16.

6. *Ibid.*, 18.

7. *Ibid.*, 32.

8. Smout, *Century of the Scottish People*, 23.

9. Callum G. Brown, *Religion and Society in Scotland since 1707* (Edinburgh, 1997), 120. See also Callum G. Brown, 'Religion, Class and Church Growth', in W. Hamish Fraser and R.J. Morris (eds.), *People and Society in Scotland Volume II, 1830–1914* (Edinburgh, 1990), 322.

10. Brown, *Religion and Society*, p.32. See also Brown, 'Religion, Class and Church Growth', 322; Callum G. Brown, 'Religion and Social Change', in T.M. Devine and Rosalind Mitchison (eds.), *People and Society in Scotland Volume I, 1760–1830* (Edinburgh, 1988), 159.

11. Mitchell, 'Irish in the West of Scotland'.

12. See, for example, Handley, *Irish in Scotland*, chapters 5, 6 and 8; Bernard Aspinwall, 'Popery in Scotland: Image and Reality, 1820–1920', *Records of the Scottish Church History Society*, XXII (1986), 235–57.

13. Handley, *Irish in Scotland*, chapter 3; James Handley, *The Navvy in Scotland* (Cork, 1970).

14. Scottish Catholic Archives [SCA], Blairs Letters, BL5/248/16, Andrew Scott to Alexander Paterson, 23 October 1829.

15. Quoted in Handley, *Irish in Scotland*, 284–5.

16. Mitchell, 'Irish in the West of Scotland', chapters 4–8.

17. William Sloan, 'Religious Affiliation and the Immigrant Experience: Catholic Irish and Protestant Highlanders in Glasgow, 1830–1850', in T.M. Devine (ed.), *Irish Immigrants and Scottish Society in the Nineteenth and Twentieth Centuries* (Edinburgh, 1991), 67–90.

18. *Ibid.*, 85.

19. Handley, *Irish in Scotland*, 279–82.

20. See, for example, Parliamentary Papers [P.P.], 1836 (40), XXXIV, *Report on the State of the Irish Poor in Great Britain*, 138–9.

21. *Ibid.*, 116–18, 135, 145–6; Mary McCarthey, *A Social Geography of Paisley* (Paisley, 1969), 104, 106, 109.

22. *Report on the State of the Irish Poor*, 130–2, 139–40, 144–5.

23. Handley, *Irish in Scotland*, 305–13.

24. *Ibid.*, chapters 5, 6 and 8; *Report on the State of the Irish Poor*, 106; Mitchell, 'Irish in the West of Scotland', 142; Aspinwall, 'Images of Popery', *passim*.

25. For a full discussion of the Irish and trade unions and strikes during this period see Mitchell, 'Irish in the West of Scotland', chapter 1.

26. *Ibid.*, 48–52; Alan B. Campbell, *The Lanarkshire Miners: A Social History of their Trade Unions, 1775–1874* (Edinburgh, 1979), chapter 7.

27. Campbell, *Lanarkshire Miners*, 81, 102, 181.

28. *Ibid.*, 194–201.

29. *Ibid.*, 194–5; Mitchell, 'Irish in the West of Scotland', 54–8.

30. *Report on the State of the Irish Poor*, 115.

31. Mitchell, 'Irish in the West of Scotland', 57–8.

32. Glasgow Archdiocesan Archives, Condon Diaries, Hamilton 1850–1859, 392.

33. Mitchell, 'Irish in the West of Scotland', 58–66.

34. *Report on the State of the Irish Poor*, 109.

35. C.R. Baird, 'Observations upon the Poorest Class of Operatives in Glasgow in 1837', *Journal of the Statistical Society of London Vol. I* (1839), 167–72.

36. See, for example, *Weavers' Journal*, 1 February 1837.

37. Norman Murray, *The Scottish Handloom Weavers, 1790–1850: A Social History, 1790–1850* (Edinburgh, 1978), 196, 200–1; *Glasgow Chronicle*, 9 September 1824; *Articles of the General Union of Weavers in Scotland Instituted 1832* (Paisley, 1834).

38. Murray, *Scottish Handloom Weavers*, 196.

39. Mitchell, 'Irish in the West of Scotland', 59–60.

40. *Ibid.*, 28–37.

41. *Report on the State of the Irish Poor*, p.xxiii.

42. *Ibid.*, 108.

43. West Register House, Lord Advocates' Papers, AD14/37/453, Declaration of Henry Cowan, 15 November 1837.

44. Mitchell, 'Irish in the West of Scotland', 34–5.

45. The discussion of McGowan and his activities is based on *ibid.*, 37–42.

46. Quoted in *Poor Man's Advocate*, 23 June 1832.

47. Mitchell, 'Irish in the West of Scotland', 47–8.

48. For a full discussion of the Irish and political movements in the region see Mitchell, 'Irish in the West of Scotland', chapters 2–8.

49. Scottish Record Office [SRO], Home Office Correspondence, RH2/4/126, Andrew Scott to Lord Sidmouth, 23 August and 22 September 1819.

50. SCA, Blairs Letters, BL5/89/7, Andrew Scott to Alexander Cameron, 13 January 1820. See also BL5/180/1, Andrew Scott to William Reid, 7 February 1825.

51. For an overview of the post-Napoleonic War political agitations see Mitchell, 'Irish in the West of Scotland', 122–8.

52. See, for example, SRO, Home Office Correspondence, RH2/4/31, Henry Monteith to the Lord Advocate, 3 April 1820, enclosed with William Rae to Lord Sidmouth, 4 April 1820; Strathclyde Regional Archives, Monteith Correspondence, G1/2/33, Oliver Jamieson to Henry Monteith, 3 April 1820; *Glasgow Courier*, 4, 6, 8 and 11 April 1820.

53. For a discussion of the role of the Irish in the agitations of 1816–1820 see Mitchell, 'Irish in the West of Scotland', 128–151.

54. *Ibid.*, 203–7.

55. See, for example, *Reformers' Gazette*, 26 December 1835.

56. SCA, Presholme Letters, PL3/234/5, Andrew Scott to James Kyle, 22 March 1833.

57. *Glasgow Saturday Post*, 8 June 1844.

58. Janet Fyfe (ed.), *Autobiography of John McAdam (1806–1883), With Selected Letters* (Edinburgh, 1980), 9.

59. Quoted in *Poor Man's Advocate*, 23 June 1832.

60. For the Glasgow Catholic Association see Mitchell, 'Irish in the West of Scotland', chapter 4.

61. For McGowan's reform activities in the 1830s see *ibid*, 221.

62. *Glasgow Evening Post*, 14 January, 28 October 1837; *Glasgow Courier*, 26 October 1837; *Scots Times*, 28 October 1837.

63. The following discussion of the Catholic Irish in the West of Scotland and Chartism in based on Mitchell, 'Irish in the West of Scotland', chapters 6–7.

64. *Glasgow Saturday Post*, 26 February 1842.

65. *Glasgow Chronicle*, 10 June 1842.

66. Mitchell, 'Irish in the West of Scotland', chapter 8.

67. *Scottish Temperance Journal*, July 1841; *Glasgow Courier*, 19 June 1841.

68. *Scottish Temperance Journal*, March 1840; P.P. 1841, (342), VI, *Reports of the Inspectors of Factories…for the half year ending 30th June 1841*, 9.

69. *Scottish Temperance Journal*, February 1841; *Glasgow Courier*, 5 January 1841.

70. *Scottish Temperance Journal*, August 1843.

71. Sloan, 'Religious Affiliation and the Immigrant Experience', 77.

72. *Scottish Temperance Journal*, March 1840.

73. *Glasgow Courier*, 19 June 1841; *Scottish Temperance Journal*, July 1841, June 1842.

74. *Glasgow Courier*, 20 July 1841; *Northern Star*, 31 July 1841; *Scottish Temperance Journal*, August 1841.

75. *Scottish Temperance Journal*, August 1841.

76. *Glasgow Chronicle*, 15 and 17 August 1842; *Scottish Temperance Journal*, September 1842.

77. *Scottish Temperance Journal*, May 1844.

78. Mitchell, 'Irish in the West of Scotland', 6–7; Alexander Wilson, *The Chartist Movement in Scotland* (Manchester, 1970), 218–21; John F. McCaffrey, 'Irish Immigrants and Radical Movements in the West of Scotland in the Early Nineteenth Century', *Innes Review*, XXXIX (1988), 55–7.

79. SCA, Blairs Letters, BL5/31/2, John Gordon to Alexander Cameron, 19 May 1817; *Glasgow Courier*, 17 October 1835; *Scottish Guardian*, 13 October 1835.

80. Olive and Sydney Checkland, *Industry and Ethos: Scotland 1832–1914* (2nd edition. Edinburgh, 1989), 125.

81. Gallagher, *Glasgow, the Uneasy Peace*, 10.

82. Bruce Lenman, *Integration, Enlightenment and Industrialisation: Scotland 1746–1832* (Edinburgh, 1981), 158; Brown, 'Religion and Social Change', 154.

83. *Glasgow Herald*, 5 March 1829.

84. *Ibid.*, 27 February 1829.

85. James Cleland, *Statistical Facts Descriptive of the Former and Present State of Glasgow* (Glasgow, 1837), 5.

86. Ian A. Muirhead, 'Catholic Emancipation: Scottish Reactions in 1829, part one', *Innes Review*, XXIV (1973), 32–3. See also *Glasgow Herald*, 23 March 1829.

87. This point is made in *Glasgow Herald*, 9 March 1829.

88. Muirhead, 'Scottish Reactions', 27–28. This was also the situation in England. See Linda Colley, *Britons: Forging the Nation, 1707–1837* (Pbk. edition. London, 1994), 330.

89. Muirhead, 'Scottish Reactions', 40.

90. Ian A. Muirhead, 'Catholic Emancipation in Scotland: The Debate and the Aftermath', *Innes Review*, XXIV (1973), 106. See also pp.106–10 for a survey of the petitions.

91. *Glasgow Chronicle*, 20 February; 11, 20 and 23 March 1829; *Glasgow Herald*, 20 February 1829; *Glasgow Courier*, 21 February 1829.

92. *Glasgow Chronicle*, 20 February 1829. See also *Glasgow Courier*, 21 February 1829; *Glasgow Herald*, 23 February 1829.

93. *Glasgow Herald*, 13 March 1829.

94. See, for example, *ibid.*, 9 March 1829.

95. *Glasgow Chronicle*, 20 and 23 February, 20 March 1829; *Glasgow Herald*, 13 March 1829.

96. *Glasgow Herald*, 27 February 1829.

97. Presenting the petition to the House of Commons Sir James MacKintosh observed 'that there were some occasions when petitioners should be weighed, not numbered. The Catholic question was of all others that upon which well-educated and intelligent men were most likely to form a correct opinion…' *Ibid.*, 9 March 1829.

98. *Glasgow Chronicle*, 11, 16 and 23 March; 6, 10 and 17 April 1829; *Glasgow Herald*, 20 March 1829.

99. *Scots Times*, 4 April 1829. See also *Glasgow Chronicle*, 11 March 1829.

100. *Glasgow Chronicle*, 27 March 1829.

101. For example, earlier that month the weavers had decided to call a general meeting on the Green. During a meeting of weavers' delegates held on 10 March to arrange the event, the Procurator-Fiscal arrived 'by order of the Sheriff of Lanarkshire, and the Lord Provost and Magistrates of Glasgow'. He warned against the aggregate meeting for much the same reasons as the 'two influential gentlemen' a fortnight later. The weavers cancelled the proposed meeting after assurances were given that they would be provided with adequate relief work. *Ibid.*, 11 March 1829.

102. *Ibid.*, 27 March 1829.

103. *Ibid.*, 30 March 1829; *Scots Times*, 4 April 1829.

104. For O'Connell's tour of Scotland see Handley, *Irish in Scotland*, 319–22.

105. *Glasgow Courier*, 12 September 1835.

106. *Reformers' Gazette*, 26 September, 26 December 1835.

107. *Ibid*, 26 September 1835.

108. *Glasgow Evening Post*, 26 September 1835; *Reformers' Gazette*, 26 September 1835.

109. *Glasgow Evening Post*, 26 September 1835.

110. *New Statistical Account, Vol. VI, Lanark* (Edinburgh, 1845), p.901. See also *Reformers' Gazette*, 31 October 1835.

111. *N.S.A., Lanark*, pp.901–2. See also Handley, *Irish in Scotland*, 298–303. The activities of the Glasgow Protestant Association can be followed in the pages of the *Scottish Guardian*.

112. Handley, *Irish in Scotland*, 301.

113. Handley claimed that as a result of such activities 'Hostility towards the immigrants in workshop and factory increased', but he did not provide any evidence to demonstrate this. *Ibid.*, 302.

114. For Orangeism in Scotland during this period see Elaine McFarland, *Protestants First: Orangeism in Nineteenth Century Scotland* (Edinburgh, 1990), chapter 4.

115. J.T. Ward, 'Some Aspects of Working-Class Conservatism in the Nineteenth Century', in John Butt and J.T. Ward (eds.), *Scottish Themes: Essays in Honour of Professor S.G.E. Lythe* (Edinburgh, 1976), 147–151. See also the *Scottish Guardian* and *Glasgow Courier* of the period.

116. *Glasgow Chronicle*, 22 June 1829, 27 August 1841; *Glasgow Herald*, 5 September 1831; *Glasgow Courier*, 16 May 1833.

117. *Glasgow Chronicle*, 31 May 1827, 28 December 1829; *Glasgow Courier*, 14 July 1831, 14 December 1837; *Glasgow Evening Post*, 27 July 1831, 15 March 1834.

118. *Glasgow Courier*, 16 and 19 July, 15 October 1831; 27 July 1833; 16 July 1835; 23 March 1841; *Glasgow Chronicle*, 13 July 1827, 15 July 1829, 25 July 1842; *Glasgow Saturday Post*, 19 August 1843. In early 1834 the Superintendent of the Police of the Gorbals stated: 'The Irish fight both in the streets and in the houses, generally with their fists, and only occasionally with weapons....The Scotch mix occasionally in these affrays, but the rows of the Irish are chiefly among themselves, betwixt the Catholics and Protestants.' He added that most of these brawls occurred on Saturday night or Sunday morning. The Superintendent of the Police of Calton and Mile-End gave similar evidence. *Report on the State of the Irish Poor*, 120.

119. *Scotch Reformers' Gazette*, 28 August, 13 November 1841; *Glasgow Courier*, 20 July, 12 August 1841; *Glasgow Chronicle*, 7 and 10 October 1842.

120. *Report on the State of the Irish Poor*, 105.

121. *Ibid.*, 106.

122. *Ibid.*, 112. See also 116–17.

123. *Ibid.*, 118.

124. *Ibid.*, 110.

125. *Ibid.*, 105–7.

126. *Ibid.*, 147, 158.

127. *Ibid.*, 143–5.

128. *Ibid.*, 139.

129. *Ibid.*, 141.

130. *Ibid.*, 131.

131. *Ibid.*, 133.

132. *Ibid.*, 130.

133. *Ibid.*, 132.

134. *Ibid.*, 130.

135. For the Paisley depression of 1841–3 see T.C. Smout, 'The Strange Intervention of Edward Twistleton: Paisley in Depression, 1841–3', in T.C. Smout (ed.), *The Search for Wealth and Stability* (London, 1979), 218–43. See also P.P., 1843 (115), *Select Committee on Distress in Paisley*; Tony Clarke and Tony Dickson, 'Social Concern and Social Control in Nineteenth Century Scotland: Paisley 1841–1843', *Scottish Historical Review*, LXV (1986), 48–60.

136. Smout, 'Paisley in Depression', 239.

137. *Glasgow Chronicle*, 3 April 1843. See also *Select Committee on Distress*, 94.

138. *Select Committee on Distress*, 31.

139. This was provided they could demonstrate to those who administered relief that they were destitute and willing to work. *Ibid.*, 31, 95; *Glasgow Chronicle*, 3 April 1843.

140. *Select Committee on Distress*, 31.

141. *Ibid.*

142. According to Alexander Campbell, Sheriff-Substitute of Renfrewshire and member of the Relief Committee, the number affected by the decision 'was unexpectedly small; we thought it would have been larger. If I had supposed the number struck off would have amounted only to 208, I never would have interfered about it…'. John Bremner, the town's Catholic priest, stated that the Committee had expected that between 1000 and 1500 people would be struck off. *Select Committee on Distress*, 96, 121.

143. *Ibid.*, 121, 123.

144. *Ibid.*, 21; *Glasgow Chronicle*, 3 April 1843.

145. *Glasgow Chronicle*, 6 March 1843; *Paisley Advertiser*, 4 March 1843.

146. Quoted in *Glasgow Chronicle*, 6 March 1843.

147. *Select Committee on Distress*, 108, 122; *Glasgow Chronicle*, 6 March 1843; *Glasgow Saturday Post*, 1 April 1843; *Paisley Advertiser*, 15 and 29 April 1843.

148. *Glasgow Chronicle*, 6 March, 3 April 1843.

149. *Select Committee on Distress*, 122.

150. Bremner was also asked the following: 'Have they [the Scots and the Catholic Irish] mutually exchanged kindness towards each other?' He answered: 'Always, so far as I have known.' *Ibid.*

151. Handley, *Irish in Scotland*, chapter 4.

152. *Ibid.*, 142.

153. Murray, *Scottish Handloom Weavers*, 31–5; *Report on the State of the Irish Poor*, 109–11.

154. Handley, *Irish in Scotland*, 287.

155. *Ibid*, 288–290; Robert Kent Donovan, 'Voices of Distrust: The Expression of Anti-Catholic Feeling in Scotland, 1778–1781', *Innes Review*, XXX (1979), 62–76; Michael Fry, *The Dundas Despotism* (Edinburgh, 1992), 70–7.

156. Quoted in Brown, 'Religion and Social change', 154.

157. A Catholic Relief Act for Scotland was finally passed in June 1793.

158. *The Journal of Henry Cockburn, 1831–54: Volume I* (Edinburgh, 1874), 83.

159. *Ibid.*, 84–5.

160. Such a feeling might have intensified after 1815. Linda Colley argued that by 1829: 'Toleration was growing. Victory at Waterloo, and the onset of peace with dominance, meant that Britons were less likely to associate the Catholic presence at home with a military threat from abroad.' Colley, *Britons*, 332. See also *Glasgow Free Press*, 26 March 1825.

161. Tony Clarke and Tony Dickson, 'The Birth of Class?', in Devine and Mitchison (eds.), *People and Society, Volume I*, 304–5.

162. For the problems faced by Protestant churches in Scotland during that period see Brown, 'Religion and Social Change', 153–60.

163. Donovan, 'Voices of Distrust', 75.

164. *N.S.A., Lanark*, 901.

165. In addition to *The Irish in Scotland, 1798–1845*, Handley also wrote *The Irish in Modern Scotland* (Cork, 1947), which covered the period from 1845–1945.

166. See, for example, Bernard Aspinwall, 'Children of the Dead End: the Formation of the Modern Archdiocese of Glasgow, 1815–1914', *Innes Review*, XLIII (1992), 119–144; Bernard Aspinwall, 'The Making of the Modern Diocese of Galloway', in Raymond McCluskey (ed.), *The See of Ninian: A History of the Medieval Diocese of Whithorn and the Diocese of Galloway in Modern Times* (Ayr, 1997), 81–187; Raymond McCluskey, *St Joseph's Kilmarnock, 1847–1997: A Portrait of a Parish Community* (Kilmarnock, 1997); William Sloan, 'Aspects of the Assimilation of Highland and Irish Migrants in Glasgow, 1830–1870' (M.Phil thesis, University of Strathclyde, 1987). John McCaffrey, however, discussed links which existed between Scottish and Catholic Irish radicals and reformers. See his 'Irish Immigrants and Radical Movements', 46–60 and 'Irish Issues in the Nineteenth and Twentieth Century: Radicalism in a Scottish Context', in Devine (ed.), *Irish Immigrants*, 116–37.

5

'GLASGOW'S GREATEST IRISHMAN': JOHN FERGUSON 1836–1906

Elaine W. McFarland

John Ferguson attracted soubriquets with ease. Hailed by his many friends as 'Celt of the Celts', 'the Lion of Benburb' and 'Philosopher John', his political career spanned over forty years: from the Home Rule Association of Isaac Butt to the Irish Parliamentary Party of John Redmond; from the Reform League of Bradlaugh and Beales to the Liberalism of Asquith and Lloyd George. It was a record which astonished contemporaries.[2] Ferguson, it seems, was acquainted with almost every leading figure in the nationalist and progressive politics of his era: Davitt, Parnell, Dillon, O'Brien, Dilke, Henry George, Hyndman, and Keir Hardie. His geographical range was also impressive. He showed a remarkable facility in being present at key moments of British, Irish and Scottish political history, including the formation of Reform League in London in 1865, the meeting which launched the Irish Land League at Irishtown, County Mayo in 1878, and the inauguration of the Scottish Labour Party in Glasgow in 1888.[3]

Yet, it is not John Ferguson's ubiquity which lends him interest, nor the fact that his biography can be employed in the conventional sense as a mirror to 'great events'. Instead, Ferguson is the figure who shatters the stereotypes of the Irish in Scotland. His career is one of apparent contradictions and departures, emphasising both the fluidity of late nineteenth century political alignments and the intricacies of the interface between nationalist and indigenous politics. It stands as a corrective to the traditional view that the Irish were an inevitable barrier to the development of a unified working class consciousness and political practice in Scotland, or indeed that they were set on an equally pre-ordained pathway to independent nationhood.[4] Political debate was vehement in these years precisely because so many outcomes seemed possible and participants like Ferguson tried accordingly to bend the course of history.

Here was an Ulster Protestant who was Irish nationalism's most prominent exponent in Scotland; an Irish nationalist whose politics were not contained by ethnic consciousness, but who was also driven to embrace the struggles for independent working class representation and for radical land reform, in both Ireland and Great Britain. Ferguson was at the same time an Irish nationalist and a British democrat, a pragmatic political activist and a self-made radical intellectual. Indeed, his own political principles were dominated by a dynamic combination of two narratives: the unfolding destiny of the Irish nation and the progress of humanity, the exact emphasis between them varying during his lifetime. Throughout his career, moreover, he was to represent a personal junction point for the politics of nationalism and radicalism in his city of adoption, attempting to convince his allies that they too should share a similar generous, non-sectarian outlook.

The present chapter does not attempt a detailed chronological account of Ferguson's extensive political career: already by 1894, by his own estimate he had produced some 1200 platform addresses in England and Scotland and over 1400 articles and letters on economic and political questions. [5] Instead it concentrates on the *making* of this very public man, on the man behind the speeches. It suggests that this making was not simply the product of Ferguson's own direct experiences, but also reflected what was available to him in terms of the ideological forces and social languages of his day, the most crucial of these being nationalism, social reform and self-improvement. We begin by tracing his early life and move on to examine themes in his later writing and politics.

Early Life

Important barriers exist in tracking John Ferguson's roots and formative development. One practical problem is presented by the lack of information on births, deaths and marriages in Ireland. Registration of civil and non-Roman Catholic marriages only took effect from 1845 and Church of Ireland records are notoriously imperfect. [6] Even more challenging is the active part which Ferguson himself played in the construction of his own public image. Before entering the public domain, Ferguson had to 're-make' himself, in other words renegotiate his ethnic and political identity as an Irish Protestant. This process was to continue throughout his lifetime and indeed one of his most striking features was to be the way in which his public identity was to remain marginal and decentred. The effusive obituaries at the close of his lengthy political career suggest, for example, how his audience were able to interpret the themes of his life in line with their own priorities. While in Ireland there seemed little difficulty in hailing Ferguson's combined contribution to the causes of 'Ireland and suffering humanity' or 'nationality and social progress', in the Scottish context at least two Ferguson's emerge.[7] For allies in the democratic movement he was 'not an Irish extremist', but a 'notable social reformer', and 'an advanced Liberal, with latterly pronounced leanings towards labourism'.[8] The image of Ferguson as a firebrand tempered by his involvement in Scottish politics was a recurrent one. As Lord Provost Bilsland expressed it:

> The Town Council of Glasgow exercised a wholesome influence on the whole man, and improved him by toning him down, but whether this was the mellowing effect of age or a sense of responsibility it was difficult to determine for those who had long known him.[9]

In contrast, for the nationalist press Ferguson was a talisman of continuity. He had provided a living link with the heroic days of struggle – a 'lisping infant' in the days of Daniel O'Connell, he was 'in virile manhood when the men of '67 fought and suffered for Ireland...whilst at a riper age, side by side with Parnell and Redmond, he was the glory and the pride of the intellectual and political life of Ireland...'.[10] His own politics remained constant. Although he championed 'great democratic causes', he remained 'an Irishman first and always' and 'always a nationalist in the truest sense':

> The John Ferguson of the latter years was the John Ferguson of all his days. Other men changed, changed their politics, changed their creed. John Ferguson stood firm as a rock. The passing of the years, the changing of men affected him not a hair's breadth. What he was in the eyes of Isaac Butt, so he was in the eyes of Parnell and John Redmond – a man in a thousand. His character bears comparison with any of the great patriots Ireland has produced. That is great praise, for no country has produced nobler or more unselfish patriots.[11]

For all this insistence on constancy, it was precisely Ferguson's mobile quality which was useful in an era of unpredictable and open-ended political and social change. Here is perhaps an initial clue to his political longevity. His receptiveness to new conditions, plus a visionary and iconoclastic element in his make-up, gave him a dynamic edge even when he eventually buried himself in the minutiae of local taxation issues.

Who then was the 'real' John Ferguson? He was born in Belfast on 15 April 1836. Understandably contemporaries and subsequent historians have often assumed that Ferguson was an Ulster Presbyterian, drawing on that denomination's traditions of libertarianism and independence of thought. The *Weekly News,* for example, pictured him gaining an informal education, 'in the libraries of the Presbyterian manses where the theories of Wolfe Tone and his companions had not yet been exploded'.[12] In fact, his family background was much less straightforward, illustrating rather the complexities of denominational and political allegiances in Ulster during the course of the nineteenth century. His grandfather had been a Presbyterian radical in 1790s and a kinsman of the United Irishman William Orr, hanged at Carrickfergus in 1797. Already by the time of Ferguson's birth, however, the historic realignment of Presbyterians behind the Union was underway and his father, a Belfast provision merchant, was a staunch Presbyterian conservative.[13] Ferguson was, moreover, the product of a 'mixed marriage' in an Ulster Protestant sense. His mother was an Episcopalian from an Antrim farming family and, after his father's early death, it was in this tradition, surrounded by Orange yeoman symbols and mythology, that Ferguson was raised. The other Ireland, Catholic Ireland, barely impinged and like his peers he learned of the 1641 Rebellion when, 'fifty thousand Protestant men, women and children lay in blood in Ulster.[14] His mother even shielded him from knowledge of his own family's radical Presbyterian past. It was only after he had begun to establish his career in nationalist politics that, vexed at his arraigning the Protestants of Ireland for treason to their country, she disclosed the 'rebel blood in [his] veins'. A delighted Ferguson then proceeded to weave this image into his emerging public persona.

This was hardly a propitious start for a nineteenth century Irish nationalist. One can compare, for example, the rich migrant culture of Mayo which sustained Ferguson's great ally Michael Davitt in his boyhood in Lancashire or the collective remembrance of dispossession and famine which was to embitter Tim Healy's politics and drive him in his enthusiasm for proprietorial conservatism.[15] Ferguson's settled rural boyhood in County Antrim may have bequeathed a lasting belief in the redemptive power of land and a pronounced anti-urbanism in later life, but his conversion to nationalism was to be accomplished only once he had left his accustomed surroundings.

Ferguson next began a conventional commercial career in Belfast where he was apprenticed to the stationery trade. In the 1850s, burgeoning Belfast acted as a magnet for the surrounding rural counties.[16] It was a city proud of rampant utilitarianism: or as W. B. Yeats summed it up: ' "the man who sells a cow cheaply goes to hell" is the religion of Belfast'. It was amid this atmosphere of commercial smugness that Ferguson's self education and questioning of received wisdom began and where we can begin to see the foundations of the later public man. He was obsessively determined to complete his education and in true mid-Victorian style devised a personal system of study. He attended extra-mural lectures and became an omnivorous reader of history, logic, English literature and political economy, a particular influence being exercised by T. E. Cliffe Leslie, Professor of Jurisprudence and Political Economy at Queen's University, who awakened a lifelong passion for land reform. [17] Ferguson was now discreetly, beginning to mark himself out from his Protestant conservative peers by the very breadth and tolerance of his reading material, but for the moment he avoided John Dillon's dilemma of 'two altars' set up in his heart, 'on the one is enthroned knowledge, on the other duty and my country'. [18] Rather, he displayed the incredible eclecticism of the autodidact and his drive for self improvement lacked a sense of purpose.

This changed with his arrival in Scotland. This was a major milestone in the politicisation of Ferguson and his is a case which should sensitise us to the diversity of the Irish migrant experience. Ferguson migrated from a position of strength. He settled in 1860 and shortly afterwards became a traveller with the publishing firm of the Glasgow radical and land agitator, Duncan Cameron. [19] Established in the 1850s, this was already a thriving business and as it expanded in the new decade so did Ferguson's fortunes. By 1867 he had become a partner and within a few years had moved his family from Tradeston to the new suburb of Lenzie. [20]

This material advance concealed underlying weaknesses in Ferguson's position. He had moved from being a member of the dominant commercial class in Belfast to an initially more marginal status in Glasgow, and significantly he clung to the familiar fellowship of an Irish Protestant circle on first arrival. [21] Yet, it was in Scotland by his own admission that he 'became an Irishman'. Scottish sympathisers later assumed that it was the more liberal, enabling environment of Scotland which allowed him to flourish. [22] His own account is more precise and revealing as to the pervasiveness of anti-Irish hostility in literate Scottish opinion in the 1860s, even before the onset of the Fenian panic in the middle of the decade.

The number of Irish-born residents in Scotland remained virtually static at around 207,000, between the 1851 and 1871, but this population was grouped in recognisably distinct communities in many Scottish towns and cities including Glasgow. [23] In addition, their over-representation in the poorest wards and in the casual labour market made them symbolic for some observers of contemporary urban 'social evils'. [24] Indistinguishable to potential employers from their Catholic counterparts, many Irish Protestants consequently struggled to maximise their social and economic position, using local systems of influence, such as Orange lodge membership.

Ferguson's journey was in a contrary direction. He had been struggling for some time to decide between the stirrings of nationalist sentiment and the dictates of his social and business connections. In Belfast he had painstakingly built up an intellectual infrastructure and in Glasgow he received the emotional impetus to act on 'those principles which were calculated to destroy the conservative notions of his family surroundings'. [25]

In the end he portrayed his conversion as a Damascus-type experience. He had attended a meeting in the Eclectic Hall, in Nelson Street in Glasgow. The principal subjects that evening were 'Popery' and 'Ireland''

> Having little knowledge of the Catholic Church, Mr Ferguson contented himself with being a silent listener to the progress of the discussion, but when the turn of Ireland came and the usual Scotch and English views were ventilated and defended he plunged into the thick of the fight, espousing the Irish side with pluck and energy. He retired to use his own words 'completely beaten', not that he lacked ability in putting his case, but because his information on that subject was defective.[26]

This was Ferguson's first public appearance. Henceforth, he determined, he must master Irish history as deeply as he had liberal political economy.

This latest stage in his self-education was was more than simply an acquisition of factual ammunition, although throughout his career contemporaries were in awe of 'his capacity for remembering facts and rendering them subservient to an argumentative purpose that overbore all contentions of opponents'.[27] Instead, his developing personal and political identity became increasingly sustained by an identification with the romantic narrative of sufferings of the Irish people through seven hundred years of history, a birthright which he believed laid the basis of claims for nationhood. The new 'nationalist Ferguson' threw himself into the narrative. He was 'an Irishman and a Protestant strong in both by politics and my ethics', but he rejected 'the planter curse' which swept the six counties clear of 'the gallant clansman who had so long maintained the independence of Ulster'.[28] By-passing the Plantation, he proclaimed his lineage from 'the very oldest tribe of [the] Irish race', a descendent of Fergus, High King of Ireland who had founded the Scottish monarchy.[29]

It was not only in the context of Irish nationalism that Ferguson placed himself in a great historical scheme. He continued to read deeply into the liberal canon in the 1860s and 70s and shared its confidence in the triumph of reasoning humanity. It was from Bright, Cobden, but particularly from John Stuart Mill and Herbert Spencer, that he began to develop his political credo. Mill's attraction is easy to grasp. His writings on the Irish land system in *Principles of Political Economy* (1848–65) and in his pamphlet *England and Ireland* (1868) stated the historicist case for reform and were to be drawn heavily on by the Irish Land League.[30] His view that, 'no nation, however benevolent its intention, can rule another country as that other could rule itself' also became a guiding principle for Ferguson.[31] Yet, Mill also appealed to his wider intellectual curiosity. The philosopher's social science method, inverse, deductive and historical, suited his own explanatory and analytical bent, while his attacks on religious intolerance and his demarcation of individual liberty which stressed that true beliefs gain vigour in the face of opposition were similarly congenial.

As to why a young radical like Ferguson found intellectual excitement in Spencer is perhaps initially more difficult to determine, yet the answer goes to the heart of his intellectual and personal development. Although Spencer's evolutionary philosophy as set out in *First Principles* (1862) is now often dismissed as a polemic of nineteenth century individualism, he was one of most respected and influential thinkers of the Victorian age.[32] He presented a detailed organic analogy of society and a visible theory of social change by 'revealing' fundamental laws of nature and society which seemed to offer absolute faith that truth and progress were attainable. More specific to Ferguson's case, Spencer's unrestrained individualism still had a radical component in the 1860s, being especially attractive to figures like Ferguson who had left the functional dependence of the home setting for a new beginning. His biography also suggested various parallels to Ferguson's own experience: his iconoclasm and determination to ignore pressure from traditional authorities; his provincialism and liminal status; and most notably in his self education and his sometimes awkward attempts to work things out for himself when reliance on received wisdom might have produced a more convincing, and certainly smoother, account of the world.

Essentially, Ferguson's obsessive pursuit of knowledge as a young man did not serve merely as the passive intellectual background to his political activities. He was not an original thinker, but showed an impressive ability in linking into the prevailing intellectual forces of his day and in assimilating, using and popularising new ideas. Despite his own insistence on 'eternal verities', his political and and social thought was to undergo continuous development throughout his career.[33] The radical land ownership doctrines of Henry George, for example, gained him elevation to Ferguson's intellectual pantheon in the early 1880s and by 1900 he was criticising the hardening of Mill's and Spencer's principles into creeds when 'there is no finality in nature'.[34] Above all the wellspring of Ferguson's activism was the message that the existing order *could* be changed, whether the challenge be urban poverty or Ireland's position in the Empire: in his own words: 'It is within human power to make conditions in which all men can have opportunities of lives worth living'.[35]

Writing and Politics

The historical narratives of human and national progress find continued expression in Ferguson's writing and his politics. He wrote in florid, pungent prose studded with organic metaphors, typically proclaiming that:

In the existing social organism the vast mass of mankind constitute a sort of human manure, out of which a few cultivated superior forms are developed at the expense of all the others, and they are resolved to have their fair share of the conditions of a higher life.[36]

His arguments were also buttressed by a wealth of international examples form Basle to Toronto and by appeals to an impressive array of authorities, 'the highest in economic science and continental philosophy', including Marx, Smith, Ricardo, Malthus, Hegel, Voltaire, Ruskin, Keating, Lecky, Cardinal Manning, Pope Leo XIII, Gibbon, Thiers, Allison, Hume, Hallam, Thorold Rodgers, Milton, Locke, Kay, Mons, Laveleye and Lavergne.[37]

Immediately striking in his work is a continuing emphasis on reconciling apparent dichotomies, analogous perhaps with his own position as a bridge between Irish Protestantism and nationalism. His ultimate goal was a bloodless 'Social Revolution' which in turn would lead to 'that final conclusion which is its ultimate destiny: "The greatest happiness of the greatest number with the least suffering to any".'[38]

This approach had three main elements. First, the issue of Ireland was consciously embedded in broader social and economic questions of reform. What is good for Ireland, suggested Ferguson, is good both for British commerce and the British working man. The Irish land struggle from the late 1870s offered a wider clarion call beyond national boundaries, lifting the 'banner of rights of man' and turning arid economic doctrines into real political issues.[39] Indeed, it was not Ferguson's purpose to 'raise national or religious hatreds':

I prefer to tell how Saxon Protestant peers robbed Saxon Protestant peasants; I prefer to show how England is dying, like Ireland, from the same cause. I hold humanity to be above the nation. I teach nineteenth century philosophy in alliance with the old world doctrine that all men are brethren.[40]

Nor was separatism his solution for Ireland. Not only could she could enjoy 'a higher social condition' within the Empire, if only her national parliament were restored, but such an outcome also ran contrary to his vision of human development:

...we have now reached a stage of the social evolution when the individual, the family, the tribe or clan, the nation or empire, each marking a distinct stage and each entitled to certain inalienable rights, must all recognise that they are but the organs of a greater social organism in which the sublime ethical truth which the Christian age has taught us will obtain more and more, 'the Fatherhood of God and the brotherhood of humanity'.[41]

Secondly, the key role of 'humanity' in Ferguson's thought was evident in his refusal to let social revolution degrade into strife of class. Instead a constant appeal was made to capital and labour as natural allies. An artificial and unnatural system had organised them into hostile camps which placed the country and the whole social edifice in danger, when, in fact, the real social division was between wealth producers and speculators – or, as Ferguson preferred to label the latter: 'loafers'.[42] Again, the message was one of constructive cooperation in line with benevolent evolutionism:

> It is a revolution of the brain, not of the barricade; it is a revolution in which Radicalism and Religion join, and the weapons of their warfare are passive resistance to tyranny and the ballot for reform. Its soldiers shoot ideas into men not bullets; its seeks to expand men's brains, not to scatter them…[43]

Finally, following Cobden, Ferguson rejected any opposition between the interests of town and country. Land reform was essential for the well-being of both and their fates were intimately connected. The crux of his argument was that by the early 1880s Britain was paying the price for the historic monopoly on land enjoyed by an economically useless class. This had led to the undervaluing of her productive agricultural population which was now diminishing and with it the home market for British goods; migration had taken place to the towns, but in the longer term the industrial labour supply would also be exhausted 'as man deteriorates under urban conditions of life'.[44] This basic task of rallying the urban masses to reclaim their lost heritage was to underpin Ferguson's later espousal of the taxation of land values.

The bold and expansive spirit of his writings was carried into Ferguson's practical political activity, and indeed was much needed in the often fractious world of Home Rule and progressive politics in Glasgow. According to his own, often unreliable, chronology, he served his political apprenticeship among the ranks of the British radicals beginning around 1864, attending the inaugural meeting of the Reform League in the spring of 1865 and enjoying the excitement of the Hyde Park 'riot' in July 1866.[45] By 1869 or 1870, he had become publicly involved in Irish political affairs for the first time as one of the young men drawn to Isaac Butt's scheme of self government.[46] A central link here was Ferguson's fascination with the land question, originally stimulated during his Belfast days. Land reform was an important element of British radicalism and Ferguson's hero Mill was the author of its programme and leader of its most influential organisation, the Land Tenure Reform Association.[47] As Davitt reminds us, Butt too was, 'a land reformer as much as a home ruler and Ferguson was to prove himself as a key advisor on this issue.[48]

Ferguson's subsequent career falls basically into two broad phases, with the early 1880s marking an important shift in emphasis. In the first, Home Rule issues dominate, although Ferguson characteristically also found time to attempt the foundation of a Republican Society in Glasgow.[49] In the second, while nationalist priorities are by no means eclipsed, Ferguson's parallel interest in land reform and in broader social questions develops and matures.

Of course, the political organisation of the Irish in Glasgow did not begin and end with the conversion of John Ferguson to the cause. Paralleling Ferguson's own journey towards self worth and identity, was a wider search for national regeneration and community advancement on the part of Irish Catholics.[50] This had assisted the rise of Fenianism in the 1860s and the determined and independent spirit of that movement continued to influence the Home Rule movement in the city in succeeding decades.[51] Ferguson's relationship with Fenianism was typically ambiguous, and stimulated debate amongst his obituarists.[52] According to his own testimony he never became a sworn member of the Irish Republican Brotherhood, yet his reputation for being 'of the advanced party' was to assist his attempts to reshape Irish political activity to meet the new realities of the 1870s.

It was Ferguson who chaired the meeting addressed by Issac Butt on 14 November 1871 which prompted the formation of the Home Government Association in Glasgow.[53] However, in pursuing their goal of 'fair play and justice for Ireland', the Irish in Britain faced a series of well-documented electoral and social barriers, including a restrictive franchise and insufficient residential concentration in individual constituencies.[54] Less thoroughly researched has been the contested terrain of their own politics, where ideological and tactical tensions between 'advanced' and 'whig' home rulers were complemented by sporadic rivalry between the main centres of Irish settlement. In Scotland these surfaced in an undignified tug-of-war between Home Rulers in Dundee and the West of Scotland over Butt's tour in 1873.[55] In addition, British-based activists in the 1870's suffered the handicap of distain from the old guard in the Dublin leadership who were suspicious of any attempt to 'dictate to Irish Home Rulers'.[56]

Amidst these difficulties, Ferguson appeared well placed to forge a strategy of organisation, education and persuasion. First, as he began to establish himself in Glasgow, his rising social status and successful business background were of great practical advantage to the Home Rule movement during the 1870s and beyond. This was a commercial city where politics were run on business lines.[57] Ferguson thus not only had a point of connection with the political managers of the Liberal party who were the most likely allies for the Irish, he also brought his energy and communication skills to bear on Home Rule politics. The estimation and management of the Irish vote, however, proved a challenge despite his best efforts. In 1871, amidst an initial burst of optimism, he had reckoned on 15,000 potential Irish voters in Glasgow, a figure he believed capable of delivering half a dozen seats in the Town Council and an MP, but after almost a decade of registration work, he could claim an electoral block of only 8,000.[58] The comparative solidarity of both Tories and Liberals before the first Home Rule crisis also undermined his attempts to use this block to gain leverage for the Irish community's demands. This was illustrated by Ferguson's ill-fated attempts to influence the election of a new Liberal MP for Glasgow in 1879 when his advocacy of tactical voting in the Tory interest aroused the sarcasm of his political opponents.[59]

Besides this direct approach, Ferguson led a broader campaign of education and propaganda in order to convince the major parties, Irish-based Home Rulers and, not, least the Glasgow Irish that they were more than an insignificant provincial auxiliary. From the 1870s, Ferguson advocated the use of elaborate public demonstrations which would claim a place for the Irish in the mainstream of Scottish society by their display of numerical strength, respectability and seriousness of purpose.[60] Ironically, this use of 'public rituals' paralleled not only the attempts of Irish Americans to use St Patrick's Day as an expression of community power, but also those of Scottish Orangemen in the same decade to remould their Twelfth July parades to gain political clout.[61] Ferguson also organised and chaired a series of large public meetings which featured platform visits from leading Home Rule figures such as Butt, Parnell and Davitt, simultaneously integrating local efforts with the wider Irish national movement and attracting the attention of potential Scottish sympathisers.[62]

Ferguson's final contribution was a more symbolic one. His Protestantism may, as Wood suggests, have help defused suspicions of Home Rule alliances in the context of early Scottish labour politics, but it also had a wider resonance for the Irish in Scotland.[63] He was a *Protestant* nationalist and it was this conversion, frequently referred in his oratory, which helped convince them of the justice of his own cause.[64] Here was a man who had seen the light and had exiled himself from his 'own sort', finding refuge in the arms of a just cause and a righteous people. The public image which shone through was that of 'Honest John Ferguson'. In his platform appearances it was this personal sincerity, which, allied to a commanding physical presence, inspired confidence.[65]

Despite his impeccable bourgeois credentials there was something of the older 'gentleman leader' tradition in Ferguson, akin to O'Connell or indeed Parnell.[66] Yet, as Parnell was to discover there were dangers too in this in that selflessness could be defined as opportunism when times became hard for the Home Rule cause. The 1870s were pioneering years when initially Ferguson's Protestantism promoted a non-confessional dimension for Home Rule claims, but already by the middle of the decade his religion had become a more controversial issue. Following disputes over the celebration of the O'Connell centenary in 1875, opposition arose from sections of the Catholic clergy who were determined to retain their hegemony among the Irish community. Ferguson, who had wanted to use the day as a political demonstration in favour of the amnesty movement, now faced charges that he was a 'Protestant adventurer', using patriotism for profit and exploiting Home Rule in the interests of his publishing company.[67] By 1877, in some exasperation, he was already counselling the Glasgow Irish of the need to break out of ethnic isolation and participate in Scottish political issues or, he threatened, he himself would serve the cause of Ireland from the ranks of 'his old friends the British radicals'.[68]

In the event, however, it was not frustrations with local nationalist politics, but ultimately developments within the parliamentary-based movement which edged Ferguson out of the leadership of the political section of the Glasgow Irish and drove him to seek new avenues for his activism.[69] Although he had been originally instrumental in Parnell's rise to power, Ferguson became increasingly alienated from a party under his imperious leadership which by the early 1880s seemed to view aggression in Westminster as a substitute for nationalist agitation at home and which was turning decisively away from radicalism on the land issue.[70] He also resented the growth of centralisation and the blotting out of local distinctions in the interests of the national cause. New men, such as Owen Kiernen, who were willing to bow to the will of Parnell, were entering the political scene and beginning to hold important positions in Scotland.[71] Most importantly, with the backing of leading parliamentary figures, they were hostile or at best indifferent to the growing radical element in local politics which Ferguson believed could be usefully cultivated.[72] Since his business interests would not allow him to become an MP and challenge these developments at source, in 1884 Ferguson resigned as Honorary President of the Home Government Association Branch of the National League in Glasgow and announced his 'retiral' from politics.[73]

This was indeed a strange retiral. In fact, this decision marks the final stage in the making of Ferguson and sets the keynote for the rest of his political career. Like his friend and collaborator Michael Davitt he now became a 'freelance' nationalist, with the advantages of a natural constituency among the Glasgow Irish but without the constraints of party – unless, of course, party directives suited him. He was also led further into alliances which were consistent with his core beliefs grounded in radical philosophy and political economy. It was the land reform platform which allowed him to develop his ideas and associations and above all urban land issues which became his political battleground, reflecting Ferguson's pragmatic grasp of the rise in urban tenures. His social and economic emphasis on the land question had long marked him out from the more political calculations of the Irish Land League leadership and he had been one of a handful of 'prominent Britishers' selected by Henry George to receive an 'Author's Edition' of *Poverty and Progress* in 1880.[74] After a year of ostensibly withdrawing from politics, he was campaigning to swing the Irish vote behind candidates of the Georgite Scottish Land Restoration League at the 1885 General Election, thus linking Irish Home Rule with Scottish rural unrest and urban dissatisfactions.[75] While his efforts in defiance of Parnell's electoral manifesto earned him the censure of the Executive of the Irish National League, his enduring local prestige was reflected in the backing the Glasgow Home Government Branch.[76]

Ferguson displayed the same independent spirit as a pioneer of labour representation. Again, the claims of labour and of Ireland were fundamentally intertwined in his worldview. Home Rule, he believed had gained a new lease of life when it called up 'economic and democratic forces', sweeping the Irish masses and gaining the support of the British working man'. Labour in turn would support Home Rule 'as a first measure to clear the way for the labour and land reform it demands'.[77] When translated into actual electoral tactics, however, this vision gave way to pragmatic and sometimes contradictory positions. Despite supporting Keir Hardie in the 1888 Mid-Lanark by-election and acting as a founding Honorary Vice-President of the Scottish Labour Party, Ferguson was a lifelong Liberal. Like Davitt, he showed a preference for working with the established Liberal alliance to deliver Home Rule, although he believed that the future belonged to the emerging forces of Labour.[78] This was to lead to some painful dilemmas as at a further by-election in the Mid-Lanark constituency in 1894 when Ferguson was forced to back a lacklustre Liberal over the Labour candidate Robert Smillie, 'an honest Home Ruler'.[79]

By the 1890s, the vacuum in nationalist politics following the Parnell split gave further impetus to Ferguson's strategy of expanding 'Irish issues' from the ideological and constitutional to the material. Municipal politics not only avoided some of the strains of the Irish-Labour alliance at national level, but also offered the ideal forum for implementing his 'civic gospel' of cross-class collaboration in the interests of social progress. From his entry into the Glasgow Corporation in 1893 on a Progressive and Irish Nationalist ticket, he was one of a group of Labour 'Stalwarts', guiding Glasgow into the vanguard of the struggle for the taxation of land values as a practical solution to poverty and exploitation. Under his tenacious leadership the city was to sponsor a series of national land values conferences and parliamentary bills, promoting the municipalisation of land within the city's parameters.[80] Ferguson's unexpected death in 1906 came at the height of these campaigns and indeed at the very culmination of his career.

This very public man was given a private, unpretentious funeral at Kirkintilloch on 26 April 1906.[81] Although he was widely mourned, there was no 'cult' of Ferguson following his death. The causes he fought for, radical liberalism and constitutional nationalism, were short-circuited by the Great War and his role in independent labour representation was eclipsed by others like John Wheatley. Yet, John Ferguson was an abiding presence amid Irish and progressive politics during their formative period of development in Scotland. This was a complex and rewarding figure who deserves understanding and attention, not least for his creative and inclusive approach towards the causes he united for over forty years. As Baillie David Wilson wrote in an elegy for his municipal colleague:

> Who shall my emerald banner bear
> So proud in battle's van,
> When leaguered oppression seeks to rear
> Her standard on the rights of man?
>
> Let History enrol his name
> Among her heroes past and gone,
> And future ages swell the fame
> Of Lion-Hearted FERGUSON.[82]

REFERENCES

1. Thanks are due to Marianna Birkeland and Jim Whiston for invaluable assistance during the fieldwork for this paper.

2. For example, *Glasgow Star and Examiner* 28 April 1906; *Glasgow Observer* 28 April 1906.

3. *Glasgow Echo* 1 September 1894; *Parnell Special Commission Act 1888, Report of Proceedings before the Commissioners,* (London, 1890) Vol 3, 284; J. Stewart, *J. Keir Hardie,* (London, 1921), 44.

4. For useful reappraisals see, I. S. Wood, 'Irish Immigrants and Scottish Radicalism' in *Essays in Scottish Labour History*, ed. I. Macdougall (Edinburgh 1978) 65–89; J. F. McCaffrey, 'Irish Issues in the Nineteenth and Twentieth Century: Radicalism in a Scottish Context', in *Irish Immigrants in Scottish*

Society in the Nineteenth and Twentieth Century, ed. T. M. Devine (Edinburgh, 1991), 116–137.

5.   *Glasgow Echo* 1 September 1894.

6.   For similar problems in the case of one of Ferguson's contemporaries see, T. Bowman, *Peoples' Champion. The Life of Alexander Bowman, Pioneer of Labour Politics in Ireland.* (Belfast, 1997), 4–6.

7.   *Irish News* 4 May 1906.

8.   *Daily Record* 24 April 1906'; *Evening News* 24 April 1906.

9.   *Kirkintilloch Herald* 2 May 1906.

10. *Irish News* 4 May 1906: 'Report of the Memorial Meeting of the Home Government Branch at the Albion Halls, Glasgow'. Note also Michael Davitt's inclusion of Ferguson in the role call of Protestant Nationalist heroes: *The Fall of Feudalism in Ireland: or the Story of the Land League Revolution,* (London and New York, 1904), 714.

11. *Glasgow Star* 28 April 1906.

12. *Weekly News* April 28 1906; *Daily Record* 24 April 1906.

13. *A Brief Account of the Trial and Execution of William Orr* (Dublin, 1797); *Glasgow Observer* 28 April 1906.

14. J. Ferguson, *Three Centuries of Irish History. From the Reign of Mary the Catholic to that of Victoria the Protestant. An Unbroken Record of Confiscation and Persecution, Mixed with Massacre, and Terminating in Extermination by Unjust and Ruinous Taxation,* (Glasgow [c.1898]), 1–2.

15. Moody, *Davitt,* 12–14; F. Callanan, *T. M. Healy* (Cork, 1996), 4–5.

16. Its population grew from 75,000 in 1941 to 119,000 in 1861: L. A. Clarkson, 'Population Change and Urbanisation 1821–1911', in *An Economic History of Ulster 1820–1939,* eds L. Kennedy and P. Ollerenshaw (Manchester 1985), 138–9.

17. See, T. E. Cliffe Leslie, *On the Self-Dependence of the Working Classes under the Law of Competition* (Dublin, 1851); *Inquiry into Mechanics and Literary Institutes* (Dublin, 1852).

18. F. S. L. Lyons, *John Dillon. A Biography,* (Chicago 1968), 13.

19. *Parnell Special Commission,* vol 3, 285. For Cameron see, *North British Daily Mail* 15 September 1873.

20. *Glasgow Directory 1867;* Valuation Roll 1876–7: Cadder Parish, Scottish Register Office.

21. *Glasgow Observer* 28 April 1906.

22. *Glasgow Echo* 1 September 1894.

23. B. Collins, 'The Origins of Irish Immigration into Scotland' in *Irish Immigrants,* ed. Devine, 11; C. Pooley, 'Segregation or Integration? The Residential

Experience of the Irish in Mid-Victorian Britain', in *The Irish in Britain, 1815–1939,* ed. R. Swift and S. Gilley, (London, 1989), 63.

24. 'Shadow', *Midnight Scenes and Social Photographs: Being Sketches in the Streets and Wynds and Dens of Glasgow* (Glasgow, 1858), 124–5. The overwhelmingly working class nature of the community was still evident in the 1911 Census: J. Smyth, 'Labour and Socialism in Glasgow 1880–1914', PhD thesis, University of Edinburgh, 1987, 157–9.

25. *Glasgow Echo* 1 September 1894.

26. *Glasgow Star* 28 April 1906.

27. *Weekly News* April 28 1906.

28. Ferguson, *Three Centuries of Irish History.* 5–6.

29. *Glasgow Star* 28 April 1906; J. Denvir, *The Life Story of an Old Rebel,* (Dublin, 1910), 176. Fergus Mac Erc, Prince of Dalriada in North Antrim who had crossed to Scotland and founded the Gaelic kingdom there in AD 470. 'Ferguson' is generally accepted to be a Scottish name and numerous in the North East counties of Ireland: E MacLysaght, *More Irish Families* (Dublin 1982), 98–9.

30. Moody, *Davitt,* 37–8.

31. Ferguson, *Three Centuries of Irish History.* 122.

32. D. Macrae, *The Man and the State* (Harmonsworth 1968); see, for example, *Diary of Beatrice Webb,* vol. 1 ed. N. J. Mackenzie (London 1982), 8. She considered Spencer 'the touchstone of intellectual honesty'.

33. For his colleagues, this phrase was indeed Ferguson's trademark: W. O'Brien, *Recollections* (London 1905), 140.

34. *Glasgow Herald* 18 March 1882 for Henry George's visit to Glasgow'; J. Ferguson, *Glasgow City of Progress,* (Glasgow 1900), 9.

35. Ferguson, *Glasgow,* 7.

36. J. Ferguson, *The Taxation of Land Values. A Retrospect and a Forecast.* (Glasgow 1906), 14.

37. J. Ferguson, *The Land for the People. An Appeal to all who Work by Brain or Hand,* (Glasgow 1881).

38. Ferguson, *Taxation,* 19; *Land for the People,* 31.

39. Ferguson, *Land for the People,* 17.

40. Ferguson, *Land for the People,* 20.

41. Ferguson, *Three Centuries of Irish History.* 135.

42. Ferguson, *Taxation,* 6–10.

43. Ferguson, *Land for the People,* 31.

44. Ferguson, *Land for the People,* 5; *Glasgow,* 8–10.

45. Ferguson, *Three Centuries of Irish History.* 68. For background see, D. Bell, 'The Reform League from its Origins to 1867', D. Phil., University of Oxford, 1961, 79–87.

46. *Parnell Special Commission,* vol 3, 285; Denvir, *Life Story,* 12–29.

47. R. Harrison, *Before the Socialists,* (London 1994), 210–46.

48. *Fall of Feudalism,* 85; *Glasgow Observer* 27 June 1891; see also J. Ferguson to I Butt, 2 March 1876, Butt Ms. 8698, National Library of Ireland (N.L.I.).

49. *Glasgow Herald* 9 December 1871.

50. E. W. McFarland,' "A Reality and yet Impalpable" :The Fenian Panic in Mid-Victorian Scotland', *Scottish Historical Review,* forthcoming 1998.

51. P. W. Morris, 'The Irish in Glasgow and the Labour Movement 1891–22', B.Phil. University of Oxford, 1989.

52. *Parnell Special Commission,* vol 3, 285; see *Glasgow Star* 28 April 1906.

53. *Glasgow Herald* 15 November 1871.

54. I. G. C. Hutchison, 'Politics and Society in MidVictorian Glasgow 1846–86', Ph.D. University of Edinburgh, 1975, 475; A. O'Day, 'The Political Organisation of the Irish in Britain 1867–1890' in *The Irish in Britain,* ed. R. Swift and S. Gilley, 186.

55. J. Ferguson to I. Butt, 9 December 1873, Butt Ms.8695, N.L.I.

56. *The Nation* 26 October 1878.

57. J. McCaffrey, 'The 1885 General Election in Glasgow', PhD thesis University of Glasgow, 1970, 308.

58. *Nation* 3 June 1871; *Glasgow Herald* 31 December 1871; *Glasgow Herald* 31 July 1879.

59. *Glasgow Herald* 14 July 1879; 4 August 1879; see *The Bailie's* profile 6 August 1879.

60. *Glasgow Echo* 1 September 1894; *Glasgow News* 30 July 1874.

61. S. A. Marston, 'Public Rituals and Community Power: St Patrick's Day Parades in Lowell, Massachusetts, 1841–74' *Political Geography Quarterly,* 8/3, July 1989, .255–69; E. W. McFarland, 'Marching from the Margins: Twelfth July Parades in Scotland 1820–1914,' in *We'll Follow the Drum: The Irish Parading Tradition,* ed. T. Fraser . (London 1998).

62. For Butt see J. Ferguson to I. Butt, 1 September 1873; 6 March 1876, Butt Ms.8695; 8697, N.L.I : Ferguson had particular hopes of the 1876 tour attracting 'a large Scottish Liberal presence'. For examples of Parnell's impact see *Glasgow Herald* 29 May 1877; 13 June 1881 ; for Davitt's 1882 Scottish Tour see, Diary Entries 24 October – 11 November 1882, Davitt Papers, Ms. 9535 Trinity College Dublin (T.C.D.).

63. Wood, 'Irish Immigrants', ed. Macdougall, 65.

64. *Freeman's Journal* 22 November 1873.

65. *Glasgow Herald* 24 April 1906.

66. See P. Joyce, *Democratic Subjects* (Cambridge, 1994), pp. 214–5.

67. *North British Daily Mail* 7, 9, 16, 17, 19, 20, 21 August 1875 for Ferguson's correspondence with Father Tracy.

68. *North British Daily Mail* 19 August 1875.

69. *Glasgow Herald* 27 March 1882.

70. Moody, *Davitt,* 545–554; M. Davitt to J. Ferguson 25 June 1884, Davitt Ms. 9375, TCD. For Ferguson's role in promoting Parnell see *Glasgow Herald* 29 May 1877.

71. Kiernan had the full support of the National League Executive and was appointed organiser for the northern district in the Summer of 1885, further splitting the Glasgow Irish: *Glasgow Observer* 7 October 1885.

72. *Glasgow Observer* 30 May 1885 for Joseph Biggar's speech in Glasgow condemning the land restoration movement.

73. *Exile* 25 August 1884; *Freeman's Journal* 26 August 1884; *Evening Citizen* 19 September 1884.

74. P. Bew, *Land and the National Question in Ireland,* (Dublin, 1980), 38–45; Ferguson, *Taxation of Land Values.* 2; E. P. Lawrence, *Henry George in the British Isles,* (Michegan 1957), 7.

75. *Glasgow Observer* 21 November 1885.

76. *Glasgow Observer* 5 December 1885.

77. *Glasgow Observer* 9 January 1892.

78. Smyth, 'Labour and Socialism', p. 318.

79. Diary entries 31 March to April 5, Davitt Papers 9555, TCD.

80. *Glasgow Herald* 5 December 1902; *The County and Municipal Record* 6 February 1904.

81. *Kirkintilloch Gazette* 27 April 1906.

82. *Glasgow Star* 28 April 1906.

6

IN SEARCH OF A CHRISTIAN SOCIAL ORDER: THE IMPACT OF SOCIAL CATHOLICISM IN IRELAND

Finín O Driscoll

Historical Background

Within the general configuration of nineteenth century European developments among Catholics, Irish Catholics did not face the same problems as their continental counterparts. Whereas continental Catholics had built up extensive and often elaborate practical and intellectual frameworks for the Christian reorganisation of society, Irish Catholics had not. The political aspirations of the Catholic Church were intertwined with the aspirations of the Home Rule/Irish Parliamentary party.[1] This negated any need for a separate Catholic political party. The social question had still not arisen as a topic for discussion on the social democratic agenda. Ireland was predominantly an agricultural-producing country with a rural-based social structure. The effects of economic liberalism were seen to minimal effect in the main urban centres in the island.[2]

By the turn of the century this picture had changed significantly. The growth of urbanisation in Belfast, Dublin and Cork had brought with it an intensification of modern urban social problems. Housing conditions, poor sanitation, poor conditions of employment were considered comparable to the situation in Britain's main urban centres by many contemporary policy-makers.[3] This expansion of the social question was to dominate the urban social democratic discussion in Ireland for the first two decades of the new century. Moreover, despite the large Land-Purchase schemes introduced by the British administration in the 1880s and 1890s, the economic life of the small farm-holder in the more remote regions of the west, south-west, and north-west tended to be just as precarious as it had been in the past. The turn of the century saw the increasing marginalistion of the small farmer in rural Ireland.[4] Within these new developments in Irish social conditions, the Irish churches now found themselves having to face the same problems as their continental counterparts had faced a century before.

Commentators at the turn of the century highlighted the need for the church to direct its attention to the growing social problem in Ireland. Filson Young in his study *Ireland at the Cross-Roads*, held the Catholic Church responsible for 'a large proportion of the present misery of Ireland' with the view that the tall spires acted as wasteful 'conductors of the people's energies.'[5] Sir Horace Plunkett, the Unionist MP for South Dublin and founder of the Irish Co-operative movement, made the same criticism of the Irish church in his controversial work *Ireland in the New Century* stating that the Church presided over 'an entire lack of serious thought on public questions; a listlessness and apathy in regard to economic improvement which amount to a form of fatalism'.[6]

Contemporary historians have followed the same line of criticism. John Whyte argued that Irish Catholicism at the beginning of the twentieth century, 'contrasted with many areas of the continent, where Catholics had developed a network of organisations with a social purpose: co-operatives, friendly societies, farmers' organisations, youth movements, adult education movements, trade unions.'[7] Emmet Larkin remarked that it was 'ill-equipped, institutionally and intellectually, to meet the growing complexities of a rapidly changing society to which it was being introduced.'[8]

The Emergence of a Catholic Social Awareness, 1895 to 1916

The majority of the clergy and hierarchy may have been ignorant of the plight of the less well off members of their flock. However, William Ryan, editor of *The Irish Peasant*, noted in 1912 that there were those among the younger clergy whose instinct was 'to help the poor to raise their character, brighten their environment, and widen the opportunities of their children.'[9] Among these influential clerics, there were growing attempts to create more open-mindedness to the changes in Irish society and to foster, first, a social consciousness among the clergy, and then an actual social movement. Dr Walter McDonald, Professor of Theology at Maynooth (1854–1920) was one of the main profagonists in this call for a redirection.[10] In Maynooth, he had formed a small group of like-minded clerics, such as Fr. Michael O'Hickey and Dr William Moran, around him. They were prepared to admit that in the rapidly changing political and social structures of the modern Ireland, the priest would have to retain the recognition of his leadership role within the community on merit. Furthermore, they recognised that with the gradual growth of urban centres in Ireland, new social problems would emerge. Rather than acting on these problems through social–charitable works, they instead urged more practical measures in ameliorating the social problem be initiated by the clergy.[11]

In 1895, McDonald attempted to rectify these deficiencies when he called for 'the necessity of some intellectual progress within the body of the Irish clergy'. To McDonald this made necessary the establishment of a proper union for graduates of the national seminary with the presentation of papers annually relating to the leading social and political problems of the day. Acting on McDonald's proposal, a resolution was passed unanimously by the Maynooth college staff to establish a proper form of a Maynooth Union of Past Seminarians in 1896.[12][13] From 1896 onwards there was a steady stream of papers advocating the implementation of more socially progressive ideas and projects. In 1897 the Bishop of Clonfert, Dr John Healy, delivered a paper entitled 'The Priest in Politics'.[14] Revd Michael O'Hickey, a member of McDonald's 'little circle' attacked the inadequacy of clerical education in Ireland with a paper entitled 'The Old Order Changeth' in the same year. Hickey warned that the role of the priest was fast being undermined by the advance of third-level education and secularism.[15] In 1899 the Jesuit Tom Finlay delivered a paper on 'The Church and the Co-operative Movement'[16] in which he implored his fellow-clergymen to abandon their preconceived notions of co-operation as an instrument of the 'British policy of Killing Home Rule with Kindness'. Instead it was the duty of the Irish clergy to offer the alternative of the developing co-operative movement which would act as an important force for positive change, in improving the condition of the rural and urban working-class.[17] In 1900 a young enthusiastic priest from Galway, Fr. John O'Donovan in the keynote paper saw the role of the priest as being paramount to the industrial development of Ireland.[18] O'Donovan argued for a form of corporatism derived from Leo XIII's social encyclicals where 'the first duty of the priest will be to help in the organisation of the people into societies for agricultural and industrial purposes.'[19]

The growing sense of social responsibility and awareness among the clergy was not confined to the intellectual sphere. The establishment of the Catholic Truth Society of Ireland in 1900 was a direct result of Rev Michael O'Riordan's recommendation to the Maynooth Union for the need of an organisation dedicated to the publication of Catholic literature to 'meet fire with fire' against 'the enormous quantity of literature…of a questionably bad character' imported from England.[20] The rise of the Irish Co-operative Movement between 1890 and 1910, saw an increased participation of some members of the clergy, most prominently the Jesuit

Tom Finlay.[21] Revd Michael O'Riordan, the vice-rector of the Irish College in Rome, in his *Catholicity and Progress in Ireland*, observed that some of his fellow-clergy had redirected their energies in the social sphere through the 600 co-operative societies supported by priests 'identifying themselves with nearly all the industrial technical work done in the cities and towns.'[22] Following on from their success with the Maynooth Union, Walter McDonald and his small circle established *The Irish Theological Quarterly* in 1907. The journal's editorial board was forced to steer a judicious and unexperimental course through Catholic theology. Despite these restrictions, the journal covered a range of topics and interests outside the theological sphere.[23]

The 1912 Lockout and its Impact on Catholic Social Awareness

Paradoxically, the Irish clergy paid very little attention to the plight of their urban flock. The main national force for change in urban Ireland was the nascent Irish Labour movement. The Irish Trades Congress, founded in 1894, counted 70,000 members by 1910. The two main leaders within the movement were James Larkin and James Connolly who founded the Irish Trade and General Workers Union in 1908. Between 1909 and 1914, Connolly and Larkin highlighted the profound need for the Irish social conscience to awaken to the developing problem of urban poverty.[24] However, the majority of the clergy and hierarchy reacted with hostility to the demands made by the Irish Labour Movement. In 1910, Fr. Robert Kane SJ claimed in a series of Lenten lectures that Socialism destroyed the fundamental Christian foundations of society and brought nothing but social and economic misery. Rather, Kane argued, the welfare of the poor should be left to the charity of their better-off neighbours.[25] James Connolly challenged Kane in his pamphlet *Labour, Nationality and Religion*, where he maintained that what the Jesuit had said was not only irrelevant but an appeal to the fear and prejudice of those who knew little or nothing about the aims of the Labour Movement.[26]

For the next decade the Irish labour movement was to force the Irish Catholic social conscience to question the fundamental precepts upon which it was based. McDonald's protégé, Dr M. J. O'Donnell, reflecteing on the impact of the rise of Labour on the Irish Catholic psyche in 1916, observed that it brought 'the ordinary man to realise that something was wrong with the social fabric' but that it also brought 'men back to a just, and Catholic viewpoint.'[27]

The growing industrial unrest experienced in urban centres culminated with the 1913 Lock-Out. This saw renewed attempts on the part of various

Catholic social thinkers to advance the social Catholic viewpoint. At the Maynooth Union in July 1912, M. J. O'Donnell defended the workers and their cause, stating that it was not the agitator who made the trouble in Ireland, but rather that the agitator was the result of the wretched Irish social conditions.[28] Cardinal Logue in the ensuing discussion urged that some new direction on the part of Irish Catholicism was necessary and that 'if [social Catholic] principles were thoroughly studied the priests of the country would be able to advise the people, and I think it would do a great deal towards keeping them correct and properly safeguarded against the danger of being carried away by agitators.'[29] However, such a favourable attitude to the workers' cause was not shared by all members of the clergy. At the CTSI Annual conference in 1912, Fr. Robert Fullerton attacked the lifestyle of the typical Labour leader 'coming forth sleek and well-shaven, well-fed and well-groomed, with his fine black coat flaunting a button-hole to harangue the workers on the crimes of the capitalists'.[30]

By January 1914 the Lock-Out was effectively over. Its main impact was to highlight the 'dividing line between all social, political and ideological forces' within Irish society[31] 'Our contribution', as Peter McKevitt observed, 'to the development of Catholic social doctrine might be described as less than meagre...the defensive mentality was allowed to silence the voice of justice.'[32] Walter McDonald reflected that the issue of the signing of the agreement to return to work, and the support of the clergy for it, was a damning indictment: 'Does it mean that the clergy, to a man, approve of forcing labourers to work in these conditions?'[33] The bishop of Cork, Cornelius Lucey commented, as late as 1949, that 'the Big Strike shocked the Irish people to the consciousness that they had a social as well as a national problem to solve.'[34]

Such sentiments were translated into practical efforts on the part of Catholic commentators. The hierarchy in their joint Lenten Pastoral on February 22, 1914 stated that there was 'a necessity for improved education for the labourer, skilled and unskilled' and recommended 'circles for social study, debate and work.'[35] At the following CTSI conference in 1913 a series of papers indicative of the growing new mood within Catholic circles were delivered: Dr John. R. O'Connell on 'The Catholic Church and the Housing of the Poor'; George Milligan on the 'Rights of Man from a Catholic Standpoint'; Fr. Timothy Corcoran, SJ, 'The Need for Organised Study among Irish Catholics'[36] The Jesuit-run Irish Messenger Office published a series of lectures in its *Social Action Series* throughout 1914. This series had begun earlier in 1913 but was largely confined to pamphlets on temperance and the co-operative movement. By 1918, the series included 28 pamphlets concerned with Catholic social teaching.[37] The series was at once more successful than previous attempts to popularise Catholic social teaching. The pamphlets were priced at one penny and were distributed widely. One of the most prolific and sophisticated writers in the series was the young Jesuit scholar Lambert McKenna[38] whose titles sold over 16,000 copies. In the concluding part of the series, *The Church and Social Work*, McKenna came out with his strongest demand for concerted social action among Irish Catholics. He highlighted the obligation for Catholics to come to grips with the fact that charity was no longer a viable solution to the problems encountered in modern society. Now McKenna maintained that the emphasis of the Church's social endeavours and actions centred on the need to 'reconstitute the diseased and weakened organisms of society, the family, the city, the state.'[39]

This new view of the necessity for social action was further emphasised by the publication of Charles Plater's work *The Priest and Social Action*.[40] In this small essay on the need for social action among priests, Plater identified the essential difference between charity and social action. He stressed this fundamental point of distinction in the case of Irish Catholicism. He remarked that 'it is fast becoming recognised among the Irish clergy themselves that the vast amount of almsgiving charity, for which Ireland is renowned, needs to be supplemented by constructive effort which will aim at preventing destitution, organising labour on sound lines, providing economic security, and in short carrying out the programme of Leo XIII.'[41]

The impact of these works was two-fold. It confirmed what the social-minded clergy had been arguing all along. It added further weight to their call for a new direction in social action. Furthermore, it provided a proper *textbook* of the means to attain some form of practical social action. The painstaking search that had begun in 1909 had now overcome its first obstacle. It marked the foundation of the proper basis for Irish Social Catholicism. The certainty of the belief that social problems could be solved by mere charitable endeavour may have persisted in certain circles.

Nonetheless, the new social Catholicism differed sharply from the traditional response to social problems, namely the provision of charity. It concerned itself, in its technical sense, with the consequences of industrial problems and urbanisation. It represented the belief that it was possible and a matter of moral obligation to improve the social structure as well as to bring charitable relief to the victims of industrial society. There was no fatalism inherent in this new sense of Catholicism. Instead, it believed in the possibility of consciously-directed change, though the kind of change desired might be more backward-looking than forward-looking.

Catholic social commentators also began to see the social question intertwined with the developing nationalist question. The Catholic middle class and clergy saw in Vatican social teaching a viable alternative to the radical social demands of labour and firm security against the rise of an anti-clerical form of socialism among the working classes in Ireland. The young Edward Coyne stated in an essay entitled 'The Necessity for Social Education for Irishmen' in 1918[42] that with the resolution of the Home Rule question, the new 'Parliament on College Green would introduce Catholic laws for a Catholic people.'[43] In April 1919 Rev Myles Ronan noted[44] in an article entitled 'Citizenship in the Irish State' that 'Irish Catholics must necessarily apply Catholic principles to the Labour programme' in an attempt to improve the social problem.[45]

Social Catholicism and the War of Independence

These views were more developed by the Maynooth group. Fr. Peter Coffey, professor of philosophy, and Fr. William Moran, professor of theology, initiated a debate on the merits of what they termed the Distributist solution to the Irish social problem in 1919. For Coffey and Moran and other Catholic social commentators the creation of a new state and self-government allowed scope for social and economic experimentation along Catholic lines.

In essence, they proposed a third way between capitalism and socialism, and defined it as Distributism. Coffey put the press of the Catholic Truth Society to use to publish two pamphlets on this 'third way' in November 1920. Much of what he had written had appeared in a series of articles that he had written earlier for *The Leader*. The first collective work was entitled *Between Capitalism and Socialism* and was an attempt to broaden the appeal of Distributism to the general public. It dealt with the Catholic doctrine of property, capitalism and socialism. Coffey began his defence of Catholic social principles by stating that social Catholic teaching had a positive contribution to make to Irish society through advocating 'the diffusion of small ownership in land and capital; the encouragement of joint ownership and of co-operation in production and distribution'.[46] He maintained that the state had a number of duties: it had the right to control the economic forces of production and distribution; it had the right to supervise and direct so that it be exercised for the common good. Coffey argued that the capitalist system was in need of reform. The inequality of the capitalist economy was impermissible. State intervention was necessary to rectify this state of affairs. The redistribution of property would be achieved through means of state intervention. The state would take over any particular form or excessive quantity of productive wealth from its private owners. The private owner would in turn be compensated with real capital value in government stock or bonds. This system of state intervention would also involve allowing the workers/ farmers to borrow from the state to buy out companies/property and thus establish co-operative ownership. He used the example of the massive Land-Purchase schemes introduced into Ireland at the close of the nineteenth century as existing proof that such a system of recompensation would work. Furthermore, this would not be a rapid system of confiscation. Instead it would be 'a peaceful and orderly expropriation or confiscation of the surplus productive wealth that is held in the control of the few, and its gradual effective redistribution among the many – in other words, a policy of economic readjustment by gradual diffusion of moderate private proprietorship (through co-operative or group guild ownership, or by a variety of other reasonable devices.)'[47] He presumed that this policy of state intervention would bring about a new order in Church-State relations. The Church would be the moral arbiter of such intervention since 'the moral teaching of the Church will always be available to help them [the state].'[48]

William Moran, Coffey's colleague, also developed a theological defence of state intervention in the *Irish Theological Quarterly* to further the Distributist case. In a series of articles entitled 'Social Reconstruction in an Irish State' he reiterated Coffey's main argument. [Surprisingly, these articles did not run foul of either the Archdiocesan censor or Dublin Castle.] Like Coffey, he dealt with the three areas of capitalism, socialism and the state. Moran considered first the question of capitalism. Its historical basis lay in the Reformation, the French Revolution and the Industrial Revolution, all of which introduced the 'principle of unfettered individualism'. The Church however, had stood firm throughout in its demand for the dignity and respect of all individuals. This 'unfettered individualism' led to the justification of the right to excessive property-ownership in the capitalist state. The right to private property must not, he argued, run against the common good since 'the individual's right to live implies, in ordinary circumstances, a right to the field of Labour, from which none can lawfully exclude him. This right to exploit by his Labour the bounty of nature is limited by the necessity of conceding a like right to his fellow-men.'[49] The conditions for the Distributive state were already in existence. Ireland, he remarked, had as of yet undeveloped resources, and the tradition of holding property was still strong among the people. He assumed that since 'such a frame of mind among the Irish workers is a condition of prime importance for the Irish social reformer of the future; it makes a settlement on the basis of diffused ownership a feasible proposition.' Moran continued:

The Irish state must, of course, be the reformer; and the process of repossession or redistribution – in so far as the redistribution may be necessary – will be its most serious problem. Catholic theology recognises in the state a power called the *altum dominium*; and if our main contention throughout this paper is well-founded, the Irish state will possess in its *altum dominium* sufficient authority for any reforms that may be necessary for the establishment of a Distributive State.[50]

Moran ended the series with a warning to those involved in social reform. He urged caution and saw the need for social study among both clerics and laity to resolve the problems of society on Catholic lines. More importantly he believed that the implementation of such proposals could only come about when 'we get our own Government, since the alien Government will always exercise its *altum dominium*, not for the good of Ireland, but of England. If on the other hand, the Capitalistic system is allowed to become part of the constitution of a free Irish state, the difficulty of curbing the moneyed interests afterwards will be immensely increased. It follows that Irish social reformers, and the wage-earners of Ireland in particular, should so educate, organise and discipline their forces, as to be able to make social reconstruction on Catholic lines one of the chief planks in the platform of the first Irish Government'.[51] Coffey and Moran continued to publicise their ideas on Distributism through the *Catholic Bulletin*, and the *Irish Ecclesiastical Record* and the *Irish Theological Quarterly*.[52]

Another attempt to see Catholic social teaching attached to the new nationalist agenda came from direct contact with the Sinn Féin movement. In the early summer of 1920, a small circle of priests and educationalists discussed introducing a scheme of lectures to highlight in more detail the aims of Sinn Féin. The project was endorsed by the publicity office of Sinn Féin and became known as *Cumann Léigheacht an Phobail*. The series covered the area of economics, industrial development, the social problem, history, biography and art: the Jesuit Fr. Edward Coyne on 'Inland transport' (it was the topic for his MA dissertation); Revd Michael O'Flanagan, on 'Co-operation'. Kelleher of the Maynooth group presented one paper on Labour in which he asserted 'that when our national struggle is decided the problem of Labour will demand an immediate settlement.'[53]

Social Catholicism in the New Free State

The 1921 Treaty with Britain secured the right to independent government or dominion status for the Irish Free state. Accepted by the Dáil on October 25 1922, the Treaty was opposed by Éamon De Valera and a remnant of Sinn Féin. Civil war marred the first two years of the new state's existence.

Victory was achieved with the loss of over 600 lives, with about 4,000 casualties overall and widespread destruction of property.[54] The legacy of Civil War was a deep division in Irish society and an enduring bitterness between the two sides. Éamon De Valera and many of his political associates had been arrested in 1923 and had remained in prison until 1924. The new government had the immense and unenviable task of attempting to administer a country on the brink of lawlessness and conflict.[55] The social question took a secondary place in this climate to law and order considerations. Reflecting on the post civil-war era in 1938, Professor George O Brien wrote: 'The anti-treaty party has certainly made the Free State safe for the bourgeoisie.'[56] The Irish hierarchy had taken the side of the government during the civil war. The bishops found that they had come to enjoy a position of privilege and influence in post-independent Ireland. However they were determined to ensure that social radicalism would not spring from the ranks of the clergy. At the same time, the new government did not intend to involve themselves in social experimentation; the Vice-President and Minister for Justice, Kevin O'Higgins stated 'we are the most conservative revolutionaries in history.'

Coffey had established a small study-group early in 1922 consisting of Moran from Maynooth and Fr. O'Flanagan of Marlboro St, Dublin; Mr Frank Sweeney; and Seamus Hughes, a former member of the ITGWU. This group had already declared their ideas in a small booklet entitled *An Economic Programme for the Irish Free State.*[57] That September Coffey published their monetary proposals in *The Irish Times* under the pseudonym 'Scrutator'.[58] The articles were a synopsis of the ideas already presented in the *Irish Theological Quarterly*, and argued that the government should take over the effective control of the nation's credit, so as to 'exploit the national credit for the benefit of the Irish people'[59]; to introduce a financial policy aimed at gradual deflation; to move away from the gold standard; to 'fix the values of the currency upon as many items and goods as possible'.

Later on, in October 1992, Coffey wrote directly to President Cosgrave to state their intentions [60] and he stressed that the existing system of interest-earned income was economically and socially unjust. He advised Cosgrave to establish a commission of inquiry 'to investigate the whole question of the principles and policy of credit-issue, currency and price-fixing, in its relation to the primary purpose of industry.'[61] On 25 October, Coffey presented 'A practical scheme for using the nation's credit to advantage' to Cosgrave whereby the government could utilise the nation's credit to raise money for public work schemes such as housing. The returns —interest free— would then be reinvested in more public schemes.[62] Even though the scheme was intended to solving the housing problem, the authors envisaged it would: a) save the industry of the country enormous tolls of interest; b) encourage industries whose advance is demanded in the national interest; c) offset as required, at least to a large extent, the expansion or contraction of credit caused by the other banks; d) finance consumption as well as production, if it should be necessary in time of crisis.[63]

Cosgrave replied to Coffey that he 'need not refer to the fact that your scheme would require some detailed criticism. If I might say so without offence, it is the scheme of an amateur.'[64] Instead Cosgrave believed that *'these are times when people should at least pay something for the advantages they derive from the change of government'*.[65] [my italics].

Coffey replied to Cosgrave's criticisms on 31 October:

> It comes to this in a nutshell: Will you make the Irish people as a whole pay what the parties intended to be benefited by the National Credit actually receive (National Financing), or will you make them pay double and treble as much over again (in interest charges) to a section who monopolise the issue of the financial credit which enables the Nation to use its Real Credit?[66]

Cosgrave chose the latter course of action. This was the view of the civil servants in the Department of Finance too when Cosgrave circulated the memo. Patrick Hyland in a memo to Cosgrave warned 'in this transition period, and until we have made up accounts with England, I take it that our policy should be to proceed on conservative well-established lines; for one thing we cannot afford to frighten English finance'.[67]

Thus, any attempts to see the new state entertain any radical alternatives to the existing system were met with stiff and conservative opposition both from the Cosgrave government and the civil service. The hierarchy too did not entertain such radical adventurism. It was claimed by William O'Brien, the socialist leader, that Coffey's favourable article on James Connolly prevented him being made a bishop.[68] Furthermore, his efforts to persuade Cosgrave resulted in his being officially silenced by the Hierarchy and the *Irish Theological Quarterly* was discontinued in 1922.

Attempts to Establish a Populist Form of Catholic Action

Central to the pontificate of Pius XI [elected in 1922] was the idea of bringing Catholicism into a more active role in society. In 1925, he published the social encyclical, *Quas Primas* in which he maintained that it was only the Church that could supply the principles and inspiration required for a just settlement of the social, political and economic problems that were besetting nations over the world.[69] In short, the true goal of the church was the establishment of the 'Kingship of Christ on Earth'. Interpreted in an Irish context, Catholics were encouraged to overcome the divisions of the civil war and unite under the one banner in order to achieve the goal of complete and unfettered national sovereignty through the leadership of the Kingship of Christ.

A provisional Catholic Action movement along these lines was founded in the summer of 1925 under the direction of Fr. Edward Cahill, SJ, professor of Church History and Lecturer in Sociology at Milltown.[70] Cahill belonged to the generation which was formed in the years after the fall of Parnell. Like their contemporaries in Europe, this generation were exposed to the same forces and expressions of *Fin De Siècle* Europe with its sense that civilisation was coming to an end and a growing scepticism about the desirability of mass democracy. Nationalistic and anti–modernist romanticism expressed itself in the rise of movements such as the Gaelic League. Cahill remained throughout his life a strong nationalist and Irish speaker.[71] Cahill also devoted himself to the exposure of perceived Jewish/ Freemason/Communist conspiracies in Ireland which were traceable to Freemason Halls in Dublin.

On April 29 1926 the group of around forty lay and clerical figures came together in Dublin to discuss the definite formation of such a movement.[72] Those present at the meeting included some members of Fianna Fáil such as Éamon De Valera, Sean Brady, Eoin O'Keefe. The meeting also included members of Saint Vincent de Paul: George Gavan Duffy, a leading Dublin barrister and future high-court judge, Arthur Clery and Sir Joseph Glynn. Fr. William Keane, a curate from Dublin, [he preferred the Irish name O Catháin] proposed at the meeting that a Catholic Action club be formed. O Catháin was seconded by De Valera. Subsequently a draft programme was drawn up. The organisation would be known as *An Cumann Caitliceach Náisiúnta* – The Catholic National Society. Its aims were: 1. To stimulate an intelligent interest in Irish problems; social, economic and political from a Catholic standpoint and with particular reference to the papal encyclicals; 2. To refute the fallacious systems of Communism, Capitalism and their attendant creed, and to advocate the application of Catholic social principles; 3. To further the idea of a unified and independent Ireland.[73] Membership was only open to students of UCD so as to ensure that no graduates of the 'godless colleges' be allowed join.[74]

De Valera's involvement in the establishment of An Ríoghacht is a point of interest. It is widely accepted by historians that de Valera was a devout Catholic being 'both patriotic and loyally Roman Catholic but in a very independent way.'[75] De Valera's attendance at the meeting was principally due to his friendship with Cahill.[76] However, this friendship was not based on any desire on de Valera's part to establish a Catholic social order in Ireland but rather out of an ulterior motive. The Fianna Fáil party had been formed on May 16 1926 at the La Scala Theatre in Dublin and four years outside of mainstream politics had highlighted to some in the leadership that the party needed to acquire political skills and ideas. De Valera wished to learn more Catholic teaching on political and social issues and the study-circle concept appealed as the best way to learn and allowed him to 'draw upon the resources of the Irish intellectual elite'.[77] For the others who attended, according to John Waldron, himself present, 'The Civil War had ended, leaving an aftermath of disillusionment. Minds which might have become cynical were attracted by the high ideals placed before them by Father Cahill, who was thus able to bring together on a common platform, men and women who had been in opposite camps in the Civil War.'[78]

The meetings of the *ad hoc* group continued for another six months. Eventually agreement on a common aim was found (without O Catháin or De Valera) and An Ríoghacht was established on 31 October 1926, the first feast-day of the Kingship of Christ. At the first meeting, at the Ierne Hall, Parnell Square, Dublin, it was proposed by Eoin O'Keefe to form a definite Catholic Action society. Its main objects were:

a) To propagate among Irish Catholics a better knowledge of Catholic social principles.
b) To strive for the effective recognition of these principles in Irish public life.
c) To promote Catholic social action.[79]

The main objective of An Ríoghacht – to study Catholic social principles – was strictly adhered to. Nevertheless Cahill and the Ard-Comhairle of An Ríoghacht had drawn up *Notes on the Projected National Programme*.[80] The movement argued that a number of areas such as forestry, fishing, manufacturing industry and the control of credit and currency were in need of careful and detailed economic planning to bring about the resurrection of the Irish state and the solving of the social problem. Education, however, was singled out as an area that needed fostering especially against statism. It demanded that the State should have no control of the educational system. The Programme envisaged that the new Catholic order would 'safeguard the inalienable rights of the parents to control the education of their children, subject in moral and religious matters to the guidance of the Church.'[81] Public morality would also come under the strict supervision of the Catholic State. Irreligious and indecent literature would be banned from importation and the State would ensure 'a strict limitation and control of such public activities as tend to foster and promote an excessive craze after dissipation and excitement; such as the undue multiplication of race-meetings, cinema-shows, dancing houses, commercialised sports meetings etc.'[82]

The Economic Programme of the League stressed the importance of self-sufficiency. It also showed that the ideas of Coffey and Moran had been taken up by some Catholic commentators. Its principal aim was to ensure that there be 'the widest possible diffusion of capital; the abolition of capitalistic monopolies especially the monopoly of credit, the curtailment of undue capitalistic control of industries and credit; and the gradual conversion of our present class of small independent owners of capital, especially of land.'[83] There would be a complete ban on the export of Irish financial credit. This was to be followed by a ban on the 'undue expenditure of the energies and capital of the nation on unproductive and harmful activities such as racing, cinema shows, commercialised sports.' The importation of luxuries would only be allowed in return for the exchange exportation of Irish food.[84]

A second popular Catholic thinker in the 1920s, Fr. Denis Fahey, was a close confidant of Cahill's and shared some of his more extreme ideas.[85] Initially Fahey avoided any involvement in Catholic groups – though he did promote the work of An Ríoghacht on occasions – and it was not until 1945 that he established his own group, *Maria Duce*. Fahey's main concern was an attempt to explain the reasons for the breakdown of moral and spiritual order in contemporary society. His thinking was rooted in Thomistic philosophy where there was one true order – the Supernatural Way given by God. This was under constant threat from the forces of naturalism and evil – Satan. Fahey identified the enemies of this true order in the following sequence: Satan; the leaders of the Jews; rank and file Jews; Gentiles; Pilate; and so forth all culminating in the International Communist Movement of the twentieth century. This final enemy was a carefully orchestrated movement, directed by Jewish financiers and Freemasons. Fahey was even ready to accept the authenticity of *The Protocols of the Elders of Zion* as a true historical document long after it had been discounted.

Vocationalism in 1930s Ireland

The social Catholic lobby continued to gather momentum in Irish politics during the 1930s. Perturbed by Mussolini's adoption of the term 'corporatism' to describe the new Italian economic model, Irish social Catholics coined their own phrase 'vocationalism'. However, the pursuit of a vocational order was in stark contrast to the conservative stance of the Irish hierarchy. The bishops concentrated more on the protection of the

Catholic population against the evils of the decadent, modern world. Ireland was a Catholic state where the church had secured a privileged position during the first decade of its existence. The development of popular political Catholicism would only have undermined the power of the bishops.[86] Nonetheless, the Irish hierarchy did have to show cause, if not sympathy, with the efforts of the vocationalist lobby on a few occasions.

The publication of *Quadragesimo Anno* in 1931 gave new impetus to the international Catholic social movement and that militancy spread to Ireland at a time when the political future of the Cumann na nGaedheal government seemed uncertain. The following decade witnessed a vigorous growth of clerical and lay interest in various Irish adaptations of Catholic Action. Journals such as *Catholic Bulletin*, *Catholic Mind*, and *Irish Monthly* redirected their editorial emphasis and disseminated the ideas of Catholic social teaching. The emergence of new magazines in the first half of the 1930s further reflected the growing importance of that movement; the magazine *Outlook* was founded in 1932, *Up and Doing* in 1934, and *Prosperity* in 1935. *Hibernia* was taken over by the Knights of Columbanus in 1936 with the assistance of Denis Fahey and converted into a mouthpiece for Catholic Action. Neo-corporatist ideas were accepted in Irish universities. There was also a proliferation of organisations such as Frank Duff's Legion of Mary and the rural-based Muintir na Tíre. It was also a time that saw short-lived ginger groups such as the League of St Patrick in 1934 and the Irish Christian Front flirt with corporatist ideals but to no avail.[87]

The advocates of a vocationalist order saw the 1932 election of Fianna Fáil, and particularly De Valera, to government as a step towards a new social order. De Valera and Fianna Fáil were not slow to harness Catholic social ideas in their political programme. This pro-Catholic ideology, coupled with a militant nationalism gave the impression to many that Fianna Fáil would attempt a social reconstruction along papal social lines. C. S. Andrews, a founding member of Fianna Fáil, observed that 'many of them [Free Staters] to our satisfaction succumbed to drink, debt and fornication' while Seán T. O'Kelly, the Vice President of Fianna Fáil, stated that 'our policy was the policy of Pope Pius XI.'[88] Shortly after the 1932 election, Seán MacEntee, De Valera's Minister for Finance, declared that Fianna Fáil had won the Catholic vote.[89] When De Valera entered office one Catholic weekly commented that 'this is the day of Catholic Action and it is up to the government of a Catholic country to be a Catholic Actionist Government in every sense of the word.'[90]

De Valera's Fianna Fáil party were given a further encouragement to masquerade as the real and true Catholic political party with the

International Eucharistic Congress held in Dublin in 1932. The preparations for the event covered the whole month of June and a wave of popular piety spread throughout the country. There were special candlelit masses held in the Phoenix Park and general communion services for men and women throughout the country. Four thousand people were received at a State Reception in St Patrick's Hall in Dublin Castle and 20,000 people attended a garden party in the grounds of Blackrock College at the invitation of the Irish hierarchy.[91] The whole events of the week culminated in the celebration of mass in the Phoenix Park with an estimated 1 million participants. In short the event transcended the religious celebration to become a manifestation of Irish Catholic nationalism.

Following this wave of popular Catholic sentiment, Fianna Fáil proceeded to utilise the power of the State in safeguarding Catholic moral standards. In the budget of 1933, a tax was placed on imported daily newspapers. In 1935, the government introduced the Criminal Law Amendment Act, section 17 which prohibited the sale and importation of contraceptives.[92] Furthermore, de Valera, more out of intellectual curiosity, asked a prominent civil servant, Thomas J. Kiernan, to furnish him with a study of how corporatism could be applied to Ireland. Kiernan reported on 29 March 1933 to Seán Moynihan, secretary to the Department of the President.[93] Kiernan's memorandum argued that the entire aim of the corporatist system was 'to prevent exploitation, to give an incentive to initiative and to create an organism in which all working citizens find their place in the economic organisation of the nation.' The Kiernan model was never taken up.

Finally, de Valera's 1937 Constitution contained much reference to Catholicism but not to Catholic social teaching. Articles 40 to 44 on fundamental rights drew heavily on Catholic social teaching in relation to the rights of the family and women. Article 43 reiterated Catholic social teaching on the rights to private property. However overall there was very little which can be claimed to be vocationalist in its outlook and the Constitution did not set out any attempts to reconstruct the Irish state in any radical manner. De Valera had inherited a constitutional situation which he regarded as wholly unsatisfactory. But his concern was much more preoccupied with attempting to break the link with Britain than with restructuring Irish society according to the thinking of Fr. Edward Cahill and those who thought like him.

Despite the early radicalism of the newly elected Fianna Fáil government, the enthusiasts were to be disappointed. The desire to change Irish society into one where 'the people valued material wealth only as a basis of right living', was paid scant attention to by Fianna Fáil. Nevertheless the social Catholic lobby did bring pressure to bear on the government in the area of banking, currency and credit reform.

Social Catholicism and the 1934 – 1938 Banking Commission

A number of government commissions were appointed during the 1930s in order to examine Irish financial and administrative policy and investigated a wide-range of areas such as tillage, emigration and unemployment, vocational organisation. Each commission received evidence submitted by Catholic social commentators and various other lobbies. However, the final reports of the Commission on Banking, Currency and Credit saw the most serious attempt made by a radical vocationalist group, headed by Fr. Edward Cahill, to see Catholic social principles implemented in the nation's financial system.

Fianna Fáil main economic policy objective was to make the Free State self-sufficient. Seán MacEntee, the Minister for Finance had mentioned in March 1932 in a conversation with Joseph Brennan, a department of Finance civil servant and chairman of the Currency Commission that the government was interested in establishing a commission to enquire into the existing currency and banking situation in the Free State. There were several reasons why Fianna Fáil intended to establish such a commission. First, a First Banking Commission in 1927 had stated that its findings should be reviewed within ten years. Furthermore, it corresponded to Fianna Fáil's stated economic policy of striving for more financial and economic self-sufficiency. Besides, the idea of establishing a Central Bank was very much on the international economic agenda during the 1930s – especially among many of the Commonwealth countries such as Canada and New Zealand.[94]

The commission was appointed by McEntee on 20 November 1934 to 'examine and report on the system in Saorstát Éireann of currency, banking, credit, public borrowing and lending' and 'to consider and Report what changes, if any, are necessary or desirable to promote the social and economic welfare of the community and the interests of agriculture and industry.[95] De Valera had worked closely with MacEntee in the selection of the other members. He himself wanted a commission that would incorporate a wide cross-section of Irish society. De Valera and MacEntee included one bishop, four University Professors, two trade unionists, one farmer, and one industrialist. The four university Professors appointed were John Busteed, Professor of Economics and Commerce at University College Cork; Professor Alfred O'Rahilly, Professor of Mathematical Physics, University College Cork; George A. Duncan, Professor of Political

Economy at Trinity College Dublin; and George O'Brien, Professor of Economics at University College Dublin. William O'Brien, General Secretary of the Irish Transport and General Workers' Union, and Séan P. Campbell, Honorary Treasurer of the Irish Trade Union Congress, represented the trade unions. John C.M. Eason, Director of the Eason firm, and John O'Neill, Director of John O'Neill Motors, were representative of the 'industrialist lobby'. Peadar O' Loghlen, a Fianna Fáil local politician from Ballyvaughan, Co. Clare was appointed to represent the rural community. He had the highest record of attendance, excluding the chairman. Despite this he remained a passive member throughout all the meetings of the commission. However, it was to transpire that his role was to hold a watching brief for those outside the commission including De Valera himself.

The Economist admired the selection of such a diverse range.[96] Bishop William McNeely of Raphoe was invited to join the commission. He himself was surprised at his selection. During lunch after the first meeting of the commission, McNeely explained to Per Jacobsson that 'he had been somewhat surprised when he had been asked to sit on the commission as he was no expert in these matters.' According to Jacobsson, De Valera had told him that he wanted a commission which represented different interests to make proposals on different subjects. Furthermore the Bishop approached the Papal Nuncio, Dr Paschal Robinson, who had replied 'that the Catholic Church would not have sought to get a member on the commission but having been asked it could not refuse.'[97]

Outside of the commission, public interest had grown. Apart from the commercial financial groups that gave evidence there were other numerous groups and individuals who presented evidence. The Irish adherents of the Major Douglas Social Credit Scheme, under the auspices of the Financial Freedom Federation, gave evidence.[98] The economic theories of the Italian economist Silvio Gesell were also represented in the evidence.[99] There were two submissions calling for the immediate implementation of Catholic-inspired economic reforms. This was a feature of the commission that was noted by Per Jacobsson, one of the outside members of the commission and head of the International Bank for Resettlements, who commented on this in his diaries with some surprise.[100]

Though no actual group were named on the submissions, Fr. Edward Cahill and the Ard-Comhairle of An Ríoghacht were clearly involved in drawing up these memoranda. Cahill himself did not appear before the commission since his Provincial had warned him that it was out of the question that 'one of Ours appear before the banking Commission.'[101] Instead the task was taken up by Mrs B. Berthon Waters, an economics graduate and member of An Ríoghacht; Mr Cox Gordon, a member of An Ríoghacht; Brian J. McCaffery and James O'Rourke, both members of An Ríoghacht's Ard-Comhairle. They presented evidence on three different occasions in 1935 – May 26, June 6 and October 16. In essence, all three memorandums were condensed denunciations of the existing economic system in the Saorstát. [102] Instead they urged the establishment of 'a Department comparable in integrity and detachment to the Judiciary'[103] that would have the right to issue credit to private and public ventures. All attacked the interest-rate system used by the banks as 'usury' and as harmful to agricultural activity. They called for the promotion of 'rural reconstruction on a national scale through afforestation, draining and reclamation of land and the multiplication of rural homes.'[104] They argued that 'a new orientation of the whole social and economic structure of the country is needed if it is to be brought into harmony with the people's needs and ideals. Such a re-orientation is synonymous with an open application of Catholic principles not merely in the political sphere but also in the sphere of economics'.[105]

These memoranda were dismissed by most members of the Commission as simplifications of Catholic social teaching. They earned particular criticisms from George O'Brien and Bishop McNeely. McNeely singled out the term 'from a Catholic standpoint' used in Water's memorandum and stated that he would 'not like the commission to get the impression that all this scheme of yours is based on Catholic social teaching.'[106]

Members of An Ríoghacht felt that the submission of evidence to the commission had not been successful. They also felt that public opinion needed to be informed on the commission and this could, it was hoped, in turn lead to their proposals being seriously considered. The move to sway public opinion in favour of social Catholic teaching came in the winter of 1935 when a new journal appeared in Dublin entitled *Prosperity*. It was published under the auspices of a new society, the League Against Poverty, the main aim of which was to see the potential for economic development in Ireland used to the full.[107] It called for the shedding of the old economic theories handed down by the British administration and the introduction of new versatile ones. Though the League Against Poverty had no formal committee, they used an office at Room 15, Exchequer Chambers to complete the arrangement of the monthly journal. Funding for the journal came from Lord Monteagle Foynes, Frank Hugh O'Donnell and Pat MacCartan, the ubiquitous Republican who alternated between New York and Ireland, and who was involved in the famous Russian Crown Jewels case.[108] The journal was managed by Fred Johnson, son of the Labour veteran leader Tom Johnson. It managed, according to a Garda Special

Branch Report, to sustain a monthly circulation of 300.[109] However copies were sent free to the hierarchy and prominent members of the clergy. The noted republican, Bulmer Hobson, was the editor of the magazine.[110]

Hobson managed the journal single-handed with contributions from B. Berthon Waters. He later wrote that what was 'required was a bold national policy of reconstruction, utilising our own resources and suited to our own needs.' He castigated the 'British-trained civil service [and] politicians [who] were unable or unwilling to think of any other system save the one they inherited'.[111]

The League's journal reflected much of these economic Sinn Féin attitudes. In the first issue, Hobson called for the implementation of a national monetary policy. It centred on the solving of the unemployment problem. The solution lay, he felt, in the creation of new money.[112] *Prosperity* mainly covered the social encyclicals. It also proposed a practical policy in the area of financing its proposed economic reconstruction. Under the heading 'A Practical Policy' it called for the establishment of an Economic Development Commission. Its main objective would be 'the progressive raising of the standards of economic life in Saorstát Éireann'. Its functions would be flexible and activity would increase and decrease with the rise and fall of unemployment. The Currency Commission would be 'invested with the power to issue legal tender notes to the Economic Development Commission who would in turn be permitted to use this available credit for 'payment of the expenses of the Economic Development Commission, and the financing of schemes of works of national advantage, to be carried out by or for the Commission.'[113] The practical policy also envisaged that the fixed exchange rate link with Sterling would be broken. This in turn would ensure the complete financial independence of the Irish economic system.[114]

MacEntee was perturbed at the criticisms that were being levelled against his party's financial policy by the League. He requested that the Department of Justice identify the group behind the League Against Poverty. In turn Garda Special Branch were requested to ascertain who was involved in the society.[115] Special Branch made a number of enquiries and reported back on the 23 April with a full dossier on the group. It does appear that the Special Branch missed the pivotal figure in the group – Bulmer Hobson. The Department of Justice file continued to be open until 1938.

In early 1936, Hobson, Cahill and Berthon Waters had come together to establish some form of a group to bring the Banking Commission onto the public agenda. Hobson was of the view that the commission 'was heavily loaded with partisans of the existing order.'[116] Thus between July 1936 and October 1938, the three set about with the view to changing the direction of the Banking Commission. In August 1936, the League Against Poverty became known as the League for Social Justice.[117] The League was officially launched in the month's issue of *Prosperity* and its manifesto published. It aimed to create a social order that would be 'far better able to provide abundant wealth for the whole community'.[118] The League was not affiliated with any particular party but 'composed of people of all parties, or of none, who wish to see the social and economic teaching of the Papal Encyclicals given practical effect in Saorstát Éireann.'[119] It reiterated previous proposals for implementing a new national monetary policy.[120]

Meanwhile by December 1936 Hobson, Cahill and Waters had been occupied with the writing of a memorandum that they intended be submitted to the commission. It was completed in the New Year and subsequently sent to the commission on January 14, 1937. However the commission had concluded hearing oral evidence and the League was not invited to give evidence. The memorandum itself ran to 16 pages and was a more detailed exposition of the ideas given in *Social Justice*.[121] In order to correct any deficiencies in the memorandum, Hobson sent the it to two economists in England [122] — the Dublin-educated Professor John G. Smith, Professor of Finance and Dean of the Faculty of Commerce at the University of Birmingham[123] and James E. Meade, a Fellow and lecturer of Economics at Hertford College, Oxford and a future Nobel Prize Winner.[124] Both were critical of certain aspects of the memorandum but were positive overall.

De Valera received copies of these criticisms from Cahill. In September 1937, he received the draft heads of the 'report' that Cahill, Hobson and Waters had written. In a cover note on the Draft, they stated that it was a 'first and tentative draft of the form which a Minority Report might possibly take. It was written some weeks ago; the writers had access to such parts of the Majority Report as were then completed in typescript, but the Majority Report was not finished, nor was it in its final form.'[125] The Draft Heads corresponded to the proposals given in the original League for Social Justice memorandum. Cahill, who already had been in contact with de Valera concerning the drafting of the Constitution, stated that the submitted 'report' 'will enable the Government to give effect to the social aims announced in the Constitution'.[126]

In effect, Cahill Hobson and Waters were attempting to persuade De Valera that there was room for a Minority Report that would differ substantially from the Majority recommendations. Eoin O'Keeffe, a personal friend of De Valera, had an informal discussion with the Fianna Fáil leader in which he 'expressed misgivings that the report of the commission would merely endorse the existing fiscal theory.' O'Keeffe was told by DeValera that those members of the commission who favoured an alternative approach to financial policy should produce such a report.[127] DeValera was attempting to ensure that the more radical element within Fianna Fáil could find solace in one of the Minority Reports and that those elements could not accuse him of losing the ideology of self-sufficiency that brought Fianna Fáil to power. Therefore, after the O'Keefe meeting the race to produce a Minority Report picked up speed when O'Loghlen contacted Cahill.[128] O'Loghlen also warned that McNeeley and George O'Brien 'have analysed memorandums submitted on the question of reconstructing the Social Order…This analysis is to be reproduced in the from of an Appendix to the Report, but it has not, so far been laid before the commission.'[129] Alfred O'Rahilly was approached to join the group but he declined, opting to produce his won report in the end.

The final Reports of the Banking Commission were signed on the 23 March 1938. They were not presented to Seán MacEntee until 4 April 1938. The Majority Report was signed by the chairman and fifteen other members. It consisted of almost two volumes, four addenda, one note and two notes of reservations. There was a total of 32 appendices covering a wide range of areas. The essential feature of the Majority Report, as James Meenan has stated, 'may be summarised as a recommendation to leave things as they were.'[130]

The Cahill, Hobson and Waters report was presented as a Third Minority Report, and signed by O'Loghlen. It began with an examination of the social and economic principles that governed the main text.[131] The Report continued with an elucidation of the Social Encyclicals and took selected quotes from *Rerum Novarum, Divini Redemptoris* and *Quadragesimo Anno.* It argued that the essential duty of the State was to provide for social justice and safeguard the common good. The Report cited the duties in Article 45 which stated the right to private property and safe-guarded the 'concentration of ownership or control of essential commodities in a few individuals to the common detriment.'[132] The Report concluded that this combination of Papal teaching and Constitutional duties had to be implemented by the Irish Government.[133] The Report believed that in Ireland state intervention in the economic system and the attainment of full employment were possible if the government invested in reproductive works of 'a soundly economic character' such as afforestation. This would 'lay the foundations for the future growth of new industries and lead to the rapid development of secondary industry.'[134]

The implementation of these proposals would be seen through by a proposed Economic Development Commission. As was stated in previous

League for Social Justice publications, the activities of the Economic Development Commission would increase or decrease with any rise or fall in the numbers of unemployed. The Economic Development Commission would receive all credit it required for these public schemes from the Currency Commission. This money would be repaid to the Currency Commission through two methods. First 'by the use of all funds resulting from the works undertaken.' Second, these repayments could 'be supplemented, to whatever extent is necessary, out of the Exchequer.'[135]

Finally, the Report recommended that the exchange rate parity with Sterling should be relieved. The Report felt that 'the external value of the Irish currency should not be held arbitrarily at any level which may be determined by circumstances in another country.'[136] It recommended that a Foreign Exchange Committee be established which would 'periodically fix the rates of foreign exchange in such a manner as to even out fluctuations, so that changes of rates should occur as seldom, and when necessary, be as gradual as possible.'[137]

The reaction of the chairman, Joseph Brennan, to O'Loghlen's Third Minority Report was one of incredulity and hostility. The department of Finance immediately set about an attempt to discredit the intellectual origins of the Third Minority report.[138] The reaction was to become more hostile in the following months. One month after the Reports were presented to the Minister for Finance, interest in the final Reports began to be raised within Catholic circles. A short article in the *Irish Ecclesiastical Record*, written by Eoin O Caoímh [Eoin O'Keefe], raised the question of how the commission responded to the promotion of 'the social and economic welfare of the community and the interests of agriculture and industry.'[139] and it hoped that 'all the Reports will be in harmony with Catholic social philosophy.'[140] Denis Fahey wrote on the Banking Commission Report in the May issue of *Hibernia*.[141]

On 8 August 1938, the Banking Commission Reports were published in full. The publication of all the reports immediately attracted comment from a number of Catholic commentators. The September issue of *Hibernia* ran its editorial on the Banking Commission Reports. It lauded the First and Third Minority Reports for being 'of paramount interest to Catholics in Ireland and abroad, who are genuinely interested in establishing a Christian social order.'[142] The Majority Report was censured for its conservative, 'Manchester economics'. The vocationalist, Edward Coyne, SJ, [author of the Report on the Commission for Vocational Organisation 1943] criticised the Majority Report for ignoring the work of an economist such as John Maynard Keynes'[143] Edward Cahill also became involved in the post–publication debate when he denounced the Majority

Report for failing to cover the area of social justice.[144] Instead, unsurprisingly, he applauded the Third Minority Report. Cahill was subsequently silenced by the Provincial on the 25 October. The Provincial stated that Cahill's views on the banking commission 'will injure our work as Jesuits if allowed to continue'. The Provincial concluded by censoring *all* Cahill's public statements.[145] Public interest in the Banking Commission Reports was not confined to clerical commentators. A resolution was put to the Fianna Fáil Ard Fheis on 22 November 1938 on the subject of a national monetary authority. Arising from this Séan O'Grady communicated to MacEntee that a motion be placed on the agenda of the next party meeting urging the convening of a special party meeting 'to consider the Reports of the Banking Commission.'[146]

At the same time, 2000 copies of the Third Minority Report were published by the Three Candles Press in September on orders from Eoin O'Keefe.[147] Copies were sent to various ecclesiastical and political figures with a cover letter from O'Loghlen that stated 'his views were those of the rural population'. Authorities in the Department of Finance became more alarmed at the growing public interest in the Banking Commission Report. Some of the officials within the Department acted in a questionable manner when an unsuccessful attempt was made to gain an injunction against the printing company Sign of the Three Candles through the Chief Solicitor's Office. McElligott, Department of Finance secretary, informed MacEntee that O'Loghlen submitted his report on 'the day of the last meeting of that body…and that even then he would not allow any discussion to take place on it. In the covering letter[148] Maurice Moynihan, future chairman of the Central Bank stated that:

> it is remarkable that Mr O'Loghlen who was strangely silent for three and a half years has been since the report appeared one of the most vocal of our public men. Doubts have been raised as to the authorship of the document but no proof of one way or another have been forthcoming.[149]

Later in December, McEntee sought further reassurance from his staff. McElligott wrote to the minister that he was of the opinion that 'public opinion in regard to the Reports has been founded not on careful reading and study of the Reports themselves.' McElligott laid the blame firmly at the door of what he considered 'partisans with a strong bias in favour of the Minority Reports.'[150] Despite these assurances to their minister, the Department continued to develop an extended tabular comparison on the Third Minority Report. This time, it purported to show the similarity of the two reports to the Labour party Programme and the proposals of the

IRA. [Incidentally, the author of this memo was the young T. K. Whitaker who had just joined the Department of Finance].[151]

In February 1939 in *The Irish Monthly*, Coyne wrote on the papal encyclicals and their relation to the Banking Commission. He[152] accepted the good intentions of the Third Report but warned that this 'certain type of earnest, zealous Catholic'[153] only led to 'an injury to the Church and a serious danger to the whole cause of Catholic social reform'.[154] Coyne denounced all the recommendations of the Report and concluded that such a move would in effect give the Economic Development commission 'dictatorial powers (i) to make new offences, (ii) to judge about these offences, and (iii) to punish these offences. These sweeping powers were never endorsed by any of the teaching of the social encyclicals'.[155] The significance of Coyne's demolition of the Third Minority Report only served to highlight the fact that Irish social Catholicism was not the homogenous force it appeared to be. Rather, the Catholic social movement was a disparate and divided group, with no single world view. The 'problem' of the Third Minority Report passed from the public agenda quickly. The Catholic social movement had by now effectively run out of the momentum that had been created at the start of the decade. To many the appeal of economic experimentation had worn off after the failure of the Fianna Fáil economic 'miracle'. Vocationalism too had lost support with its association with the authoritarian regimes of Salazar in Portugal, Franco in Spain and Mussolini in Italy. The vast majority of Irish people maintained their support for the major political parties which reflected the dominant Catholic values and culture of the time.[156]

Conclusion

The Irish Catholic social movement was thus more developed than used to be thought. The concentration on credit, currency and fiscal reform by Irish commentators was unique among their European counterparts. The British social Catholics, in particular the Distributists, never went so far as to draw up a detailed programme on monetary reform. There is no evidence, apart from the English case, to suggest that other European Catholic social movements believed that currency reform was one basic key to reconstructing society along Catholic lines. Furthermore the Irish Catholic social movement was singular in its attempt to see that the social question be properly addressed. Only the Irish labour movement, which had effectively been politically marginalised in the aftermath of the 1913 Lock-out, also addressed the social question in post-independence Ireland.

In summing up, it must be admitted that the Irish Catholic social movement made its own positive contribution to the debate on the social question during the first decades of independence. It challenged the existing views on how best to solve the social question and took away the emphasis on individual self-help and placed more emphasis on the collective role of the community. The movement also managed to apply its principles to Irish economic and social conditions and to make its proposals part of the public discourse on the social question.

Despite this the Catholic social movement failed in its aim to construct the true Christian state in Ireland. John Whyte has argued that 'one might have thought that a movement appealing to Catholic principles would have been kicking at an open door.' Yet the door had been firmly shut. The state —government and civil service— had no desire to embrace the radical transformations that were proposed by the Catholic social movement. The main political parties were by their very nature confessional. The civil service was intellectually conservative and more concerned with proper administration. The official church itself had arrived at a satisfactory relationship with the state and complemented this by firmly ensuring that clerical radicalism did not disrupt the valuable consensus between the two. As it had been for the last century, the political culture of the newly independent Ireland was confessional not clerical.

A more adroit description of the Ireland at the time is given by the Cork poet Seán Ó Riordáin writing in 1949 on the eve of his sister's emigration to England:

> Mé sa bhaile inniu. 'The Child' ag dul go Sasana amáireach. An cailín bocht. Agus na heaspaig agus na dochtúitrí agus na hollúin agus na lucht díolta gluaistéin ag fanúint sa bhaile. 'A thousand thousand slimy things…"[157]

REFERENCES

1. Dermot Keogh, *The Vatican, the Bishops and Irish Politics, 1919–1939* (Cambridge, 1986); Emmet Larkin, *The Roman Catholic Church and the Home Rule Movement in Ireland, 1870–1874*, (Dublin, 1990); David Miller, *Church, State and Nation in Ireland, 1898–1921*, (Dublin, 1973).

2. Louis Cullen, *An Economic History of Ireland since 1660*, (London, 1972); Maura Murphy, 'The Economic and Social Structure of Nineteenth Century Cork', in David Harkness and Mary O'Dowd, *The Town in Ireland*, (Belfast, 1982).

3. See for example, *Minority Report to Royal Commission on the Poor Laws. Report on Ireland*. [cd. 4630], 1909.

4. Cullen, *Economic History*, 134–171.

5. *Ibid.*, 75.

6. *Ibid.*

7. John H. Whyte, *Church and State in Modern Ireland, 1923–1979*, (Dublin, 1980), 62–64.

8. Emmet Larkin, 'Socialism and Catholicism in Ireland', *Studies*, Vol. 73, (Spring 1985), 87–88.

9. William P. Ryan, *The Pope's Green Isle*, (London, 1912), 278.

10. A native of Kilkenny who, after a brief spell teaching at St Kieran's College there, was appointed professor of Dogmatic Theology at Maynooth in 1881. His subsequent career at Maynooth was marked by controversy and confrontation with his superiors. His first major publication *Motion, Its Origin and Conservation*, in which he examined the relationship between theology and science, was condemned by Rome for being in conflict with the doctrine of free will and placed on the *Index Librorum*. All other subsequent theological works were refused the *imprimatur* by the Irish hierarchy. 10 In 1890 he supported Parnell and disagreed publicly with the hierarchy's condemnation after the split in the Irish Parliamentary Party. He was an ardent supporter of freedom in education. In Maynooth he pressed for the appointment of professors by open competition. He championed the cause of his colleague Fr. Michael O'Hickey who was dismissed in 1909 from his teaching post in Maynooth. McDonald again provoked the wrath of his superiors in 1902 when he unequivocally supported the right of Catholics to enter Trinity College, Dublin.

11. Walter McDonald, *Reminiscences of a Maynooth Professor*, (Dublin, 1925), 100–125.

12. *Ibid.*, 24–26. After initial disagreement between McDonald and Dr Daniel Mannix, the President of Maynooth, an official constitution was agreed on. Membership would be open to all graduates of the national seminary; meetings of the union would be held annually over a weekend basis; papers would be invited from all members of the clergy.

13. *Record of the Maynooth Union, 1896–1897*, (Dublin, 1897), 43. The final figure for attendance was put at 300.

14. 'The Priest in Politics', *Record of the Maynooth Union, 1897–1898*, (Dublin, 1898), 14–20.

15. Michael P. O'Hickey, 'The Old Order Changeth', *Record of the Maynooth Union, 1898–1899*, (Dublin, 1899), 23–24.

16. Tom Finlay, 'The Church and the Co-operative Movement', *Record of the Maynooth Union, 1899–1900*, (Dublin, 1900), 25–32. Finlay (1848–1940) was at the forefront of Jesuit educational endeavor in Dublin. He was Rector of Belvedere College from 1882–1887 and then was appointed, along with his brother Peter, as Professor of Mental and Moral Philosophy at University

College. He was founder-editor of both *Lyceum* (1887–1894) and *The Irish Monthly*. He played an active role in the foundation of the Irish Co-operative Movement and combined his efforts as Vice-President of the Irish Agricultural Organisation Society and editor of *The Irish Homestead*.

17. *Ibid.*, 30.

18. O'Donovan had already earned the praise of Horace Plunkett for his work with the co-operative movement in his own parish of Loughrea in County Galway. Horace Plunkett, *Ireland in the New Century*, 3rd Edition (London, 1905), 119.

19. *Ibid.*, 42. McDonald and the Union committee were impressed by the content of his paper and re-invited the young priest to deliver the main paper for the next year.

20. Michael O'Riordan, 'The Need for a Catholic Publishing Society', Ibid., 44.

21. *The Messenger*, New York, December, 1903. Quoted from Charles Plater, *The Priest and Social Action*, (London, 1914), 112.

22. Michael O'Riordan, *Catholicity and Progress in Ireland*, (Dublin, 1903), 201.

23. McDonald, *Reminiscences*, 158–163. Initially there was little support from the hierarchy who feared, understandably, that a journal under the editorial command of McDonald may attract suspicion from the 'anti-modernist' group in Rome and thus bring interference from the Vatican. However, McDonald won the right to establish the journal but with a cost to editorial licence.

24. Dermot Keogh, *The Rise of the Irish Working Class*, (Belfast, 1982); Emmet Larkin, *James Larkin, Irish Labour Leader, 1876–1947*, (London, 1965).

25. Quoted from James Connolly, *Labour, Nationality and Religion*, (Dublin, 1910); no exact transcript of Kane's Lenten lectures exist but Connolly's quotations are allegedly accurate.

26. *Ibid.*

27. Michael O'Donnell, Review of 'A Catechism of Social Principles' in *Irish Theological Quarterly*, Vol. 11, 4, (December, 1916), 415–416.

28. Michael O'Donnell, 'On Strikes', *Record of the Maynooth Union, 1911–1912*, (Dublin, 1912), 19.

29. *Ibid.*, 27–28.

30. *Freeman's Journal*, October 11, 1912.

31. Goldring, *Pleasant the Scholar's Life*, 98–99.

32. Peter McKevitt, 'Epilogue: Modern Ireland', in Patrick Corish (ed.), *A History of Irish Catholicism, Volume V*, (Dublin, 1970), 8.

33. Walter McDonald, 'How I Studied', 727. McDonald continued :'To me an interested and unprejudiced onlooker, it seemed that, if the men's case was

good in the main, they injured it in several ways; though I also thought that many of their opponents – manufacturers, shopkeepers, farmers, and others – had grown fat on methods which they now pronounced almost demonical, when turned by the labourers against themselves. It was comical to hear a farmer rage against a combination to boycott blacklegs, as if he had not had his own rent reduced, or even purchased his holding as a result of a similar combination – against land-grabbers.'

34.   Cornelius Lucey, *Catholic Truth Society of Ireland, The First Fifty Years*, (Dublin, 1949), 76.

35.   *Irish Catholic*, February 28, 1914.

36.   *Freeman's Journal*, October 17, 1913.

37.   See for example, E. Boyd Barrett, *Our Schools and Social Work*, (Dublin, 1914); John McDonnell, *Socialism and the Working Man*, (Dublin, 1913).

38.   Born in 1870, he entered the Society of Jesus in 1886 and studied in Dublin, Jersey and Louvain. His main area of interest was in the revival of the Irish Language and he kept in close contact with the work of Padraig Pearse. After the publication of his work *The Social Teachings of James Connolly*, (a work which won the praise of many in the Irish Labour Movement) McKenna concentrated more on his Irish language interests and his teaching duties at Belvedere College. He published minor articles on socialism and communism in the 1920s, which often showed a detached and critical view which singled him out from many of his clerical peers. He died in Dublin in 1956.

39.   *Ibid.*

40.   Plater's work was one of the most influential essays on Catholic social action published in the Anglophone world. It was also to be one of the most influential works for all future Catholic organisations in Ireland. His contribution to the nascent social movement in Britain was held in high regard by many of his contemporaries. He was a co-founder of the English Catholic Social Guild; a strong advocate of workers' education and the inspiration behind the Catholic Workers' College in Oxford. Denis Meadows, a student of his, wrote of him as ' not the sort of man who loves bluebooks and statistical surveys for their own sake.... What Fr. Plater did to awaken our minds and emotions about the social implications of Christianity went far beyond whatever he gave us as a teacher of psychology.' Denis Meadows, *Obedient Men*, (London, 1955), 176–178. According to his fellow Jesuit and colleague, Charles C. Martindale, it was Plater who had the most impact on the development of the English social movement. In recognition of his contribution to the British Catholic Social Guild, the Catholic Workers' College in Oxford was dedicated as a 'monument' to Plater in 1921, shortly after his untimely death. Charles Martindale, *Charles Dominic Plater, SJ*, (London, 1922); Jon. M. Cleary, *Catholic Social Action in Britain, 1909–1959*, (Oxford, 1961).

41. *Ibid.*, 120.

42. Edward Coyne, 'The Necessity for Social Education for Irishmen', *The Clongowes Annual*, 1914.

43. *Ibid.*, 26.

44. Myles Ronan, 'Catholic Action in France, Germany, Switzerland, Italy (and Ireland?)', *Irish Ecclesiastical Record*, Vol. 13 , (April, 1919), 276–289.

45. *Ibid.*, 289–290.

46. Peter Coffey, *Between Capitalism and Socialism*, (Dublin, 1920), 5–6.

47. *Ibid.* 14–15.

48. *Ibid.*

49. William Moran, 'Social Reconstruction in an Irish State – I', *Irish Theological Quarterly*, Vol. 15, (January, 1920), 3–5.

50. *Ibid.* 108–109.

51. *Ibid.*, 260.

52. Peter Coffey, 'An Injustice of the Capitalist System: Its Monopoly of Financial Credit', *Irish Theological Quarterly*, Vol. 16, (January, 1921), 38–40.

53. Sean O Ceileachair, *The Labour Problem*, (Dublin, 1921), 10.

54. See, notably : Charles Townshend, *Political Violence in Ireland*, (Oxford, 1983); John Joseph Lee, *Ireland, 1912–1985*, (Cambridge, 1989), 56–59. In regard to the reaction of the Bishops to the Civil War see, Keogh, *The Vatican and the Bishops.*

55. An amusing anecdote is recounted by the poet Patrick Kavanagh in his autobiography *The Green Fool*, (Dublin, 1971); he recalls how he joined the local IRA and assisted in a 'telephone wire-cutting operation' and also went salmon-poaching, all in the cause of the Republic. A more sober account of Civil War experiences is given by Ernie O'Malley, *The Singing Flame*, (Dublin, 1978).

56. George O' Brien, *The Four Green Fields* (Dublin and Cork, 1936), 100–101. (A neglected work that contains many interesting observations on Irish politics and nationalism.)

57. I have been unable to find an existing copy of this work. It is referred to in D/Fin, 519, Department of Finance, National Archives, Dublin.

58. *Irish Times*, September 23, 1922.

59. *Ibid.*, September 30, 1922.

60. Peter Coffey to W.T. Cosgrave, 1922, D/Fin, 519, Department of Finance, National Archives, Dublin.

61. *Ibid.*

62. Peter Coffey to W.T. Cosgrave, 25 October 1922, D/Fin, 519, Department of Finance, National Archives, Dublin.

63. *Ibid.*

64. W.T. Cosgrave to Peter Coffey, 27 October 1922, D/Fin, 519, Department of Finance, National Archives, Dublin.

65. *Ibid.*

66. Peter Coffey to W.T. Cosgrave, 31 October 1922, D/Fin, 519, Department of Finance, National Archives, Dublin.

67. P. Hyland to W.T Cosgrave, 5 December 1922, D/Fin, 519, Department of Finance, National Archives, Dublin.

68. This allegation was made in William O'Brien's *Diary*. See, O'Brien Mss., 15712(14), National Library of Ireland, Dublin.

69. *Quas Primas*, quoted from *The Irish Ecclesiastical Record*, Vol. 28, (October, 1925).

70. Cahill was the most important and prolific member of the *Irish Catholic Social Movement*. Born in Callow, Co. Limerick, 1868, he received his secondary education at Mungret College, Co. Limerick and three years of theological training at Maynooth. He entered the Society of Jesus on 8 June 1891 and was ordained to the priesthood six years later. His career in teaching took him first back to his *alma mater* at Mungret but he moved to Milltown Park in Dublin in 1924 as Professor of Church History, Lecturer in Sociology and later as spiritual director.

71. For a more detailed discussion of this period in Irish intellectual history, see in particular : T. Garvin, *Nationalist Revolutionaries in Ireland, 1858 – 1928* (Oxford, 1987).

72. *Notes on the Formation of An Ríoghacht*, Cahill Papers, Jesuit Archives, Dublin.

73. *Formation of An Ríoghacht.*

74. *Formation of An Ríoghacht.*

75. Dermot Keogh, 'Church, State and Society', in Brian Farrell (ed.), *De Valera's Constitution and Ours*, (Dublin, 1988), 106; see also *The Vatican*, 208–209.

76. The two men, according to Professor Dermot Keogh, may have known each other from cultural-nationalist circles since both were dedicated to the revival of the Irish language. See Dermot Keogh, 'The Jesuits and the 1937 Constitution', *Studies*, Vol. 78, (Spring, 1989), 94.

77. Keogh, 'Church, State and Nation', 108. See also Robert Briscoe, *For the Life of Me*, (London, 1959), 237. Robert Briscoe, one of the more colourful founding members of Fianna Fáil described the early days of Fianna Fáil:

    'De Valera appeared quite happy to lead the Opposition for the time being. He realised that we, who had so long been outside the law, needed training in the science of government before we accepted its responsibilities. Like the schoolmaster he once had been, he set us hard at work learning our trade with himself as our headmaster.'

78. Waldron, 'An Ríoghacht', 275.

79. *An Ríoghacht Constitution*, Cahill Papers, Jesuit Archives, Dublin.

80. *Notes on the Projected National Programme*, Cahill Papers, Jesuit Archives, Dublin.

81. National Programme.

82. National Programme.

83. National Programme.

84. National Programme.

85. Born in 1883 in Kilmore, County Tipperary, he attended the Holy Ghost-run Rockwell College between 1895 and 1900. At the turn of the century, Fahey entered the novitiate of the Holy Ghost Congregation in France. Returning to Ireland for study, he made his final vows in 1907. Later, he travelled to Rome to study in the Gregorian and the Angelicum, taking doctorates in theology from both institutions. Ordained in Rome in 1911, Fahey returned to Ireland in 1912 and took up a teaching post at the Holy Ghost-run school Blackrock College as Professor of Moral Theology. Fahey's intellectual formation is best understood in the context of his early years spent during his novitiate in France and Rome. Though similar to that of his contemporaries such as Cahill, Fahey was more exposed to the extreme conservative elements within continental Catholicism. In France, he was exposed to the anti-Semitism prevalent in French Catholic society at the time of the Dreyfus Affair. He admitted later that he was influenced by the Holy Ghost Father, Henri Le Floch. and the Jesuit Louis Cardinal Billot. Both were leading advocates of the condemned *Action Française* Movement.

86. Keogh, *The Vatican, the Bishops* , Chapter 6 & 7.

87. League of St Patrick and ICF Files, Department of Justice, National Archives, Dublin. The Special Branch force kept files on a large number of societies and organisations in the 1930s. The Unemployed Workers Movement, the Catholic Unemployed Workers Movement, the Irish Christian Front are examples of the extent to which the Special Branch maintained surveillance.

88. C.S. Andrews, *Man of No Property*, (Dublin & Cork, 1982), 50.

89. *Irish Independent*, February 22 1932.

90. *The Assisi Irish Franciscan Monthly*, May, 1932.

91. Keogh, *The Vatican*, 188–196.

92. *Ibid.*, 49–52; Michael Nolan, 'The Influence of Catholic Nationalism on the Legislature of the Irish Free State', *The Irish Jurist*, Vol. 10., 1975, 128–167.

93. Department of the Taoiseach, S10183, National Archives, Dublin.

94. *Ibid.*

95. Commission of Inquiry into Banking, Currency and Credit – Reports and Minutes of Evidence, (Dublin: Government Stationery Office, 1938).

96. *The Economist*, 13 August, 1938.

97. Per Jacobsson Diaries, (7.12.34), quoted in Jucker-Fleetwood,'Per Jacobsson', 73.

98. Commission of Inquiry into Banking, Currency and Credit – Majority Report, 468–496.

99. *Ibid.*, 497–501.

100. Jucker-Fleetwood, 'Per Jacobsson'.

101. Provincial to Edward Cahill, April 6 1935, Edward Cahill Papers, Jesuit Archives, Dublin.

102. Commission of Inquiry into banking, Currency and Credit – Memoranda and Evidence, (Dublin: Government Stationery Office, 1938), 310–311.

103. *Ibid.*, 560.

104. *Ibid.*, 565–566.

105. *Ibid.*, 918.

106. *Ibid.*, par. 4321.

107. *Prosperity*, No. 1, (November 1935), 1.

108. The Russian Crown Jewels case centred around the acceptance by the first Dáil of part of the Crown Jewels as collateral for an interest free loan of $25,000 to the Soviet Union. MacCartan brought the jewels to America in 1920 when Eamon de Valera advanced the loan to communist representatives in Washington.

109. D 14/36, Department of Justice, National Archives, Dublin.

110. Hobson is better remembered for his involvement in the founding of various republican movements in the early decades of the century. He was a co-founder of Na Fianna Éireann in 1903, the Dungannon Clubs in 1905, and he played a major role in the formation of the Irish volunteers. Hobson, though, fell foul of the more extreme members of the IRB in the lead-up to the 1916 Rising and subsequently retired from public life after the War of Independence. He took up a minor civil service post in the Department of Finance which he held until his retirement in 1948. Hobson had experience of editing and managing newspapers before he became involved in *Prosperity*. In 1906, he founded and edited *The Republic* and also worked on *The Peasant*. He also founded the Republican paper *Irish Freedom* in 1910. Hobson was one of the pioneers of the economic Sinn Féin ideal and was Vice-President of Sinn Féin in 1907. In the 1920s he had printed a small pamphlet entitled *National Economic Recovery* that resurrected the debate concerning economic self-sufficiency. Hobson did not put his name to this work, but it was privately printed and distributed by him.

111. Bulmer Hobson, *Ireland, Yesterday and Tommorrow*, (Tralee, 1968), 112–113 and 171. Hobson was an intellectually vain man. His autobiography is often marred by inaccuracies.

112. *Prosperity*, No.. 3, (November, 1935), 3.

113. *Ibid.*, 6.

114. *Ibid.*

115. D 14/36, Department of Justice, National Archives, Dublin.

116. Hobson, *Ireland*, 171.

117. *Social Justice*, No., (September, 1936), 83.

118. *Ibid.*, No.10, (August, 1936), 73.

119. *Ibid.*, 74.

120. *Ibid.*, 76.

121. The League for Social Justice, *Memorandum from the League for Social Justice; Submitted to the Commission of Inquiry into Banking, Currency and Credit,* (Dublin, 1937), 2.

122. Bulmer Hobson to Edward Cahill, 9 June 1937, Department of Taoiseach, S12293, National Archives, Dublin.

123. J.G. Smith to Bulmer Hobson, 4 May 1937, Department of Taoiseach, S12293, National Archives, Dublin.

124. J.E Meade to Glynn, 27 May 1937, Department of Taoiseach, S12293, National Archives, Dublin.

125. Edward Cahill to Eamonn De Valera, 8 September 1937, Department of Taoiseach, S12293, National Archives, Dublin.

126. *Ibid.*

127. J.Anthony Gaughan, *Alfred O'Rahilly, Vol. 2, Public Figure*, (Tralee, 1989), 307–309.

128. Peadar O'Loghlen to Edward Cahill, 8 December 1937, Cahill Papers, Jesuit Archives, Dublin.

129. *Ibid.*

130. James Meenan, *The Irish Economy since 1922*, (Liverpool, 1970), 221.

131. Peadar O'Loghlen, *Commission of Inquiry into Banking Currency and Credit, 1938 – Minority Report No. III*, (Dublin, 1938), 4. This report was printed privately (see above) and all quotations come from this edition.

132. *Ibid.*, 5–9.

133. *Ibid.*, 7.

134. *Ibid.*, 39–43.

135. *Ibid.*, 44–46.

136. *Ibid.*, 46–47.

137. *Ibid.*

138. Department of Finance, D F 9/18/38, National Archives, Dublin.

139. Eoin O Cáoimh, 'The Banking Commission', *The Irish Ecclesiastical Record*, Vol. LL, No. 5, (May, 1938), 499–500.

140. *Ibid.*, 503.

141. Denis Fahey, 'The Report of our Private Banking Commission', *Hibernia*, May 1938, 9.

142. *Hibernia*, September 1938.

143. Edward Coyne, 'Report of the Banking Commission', Studies, Vol. 26, (September 1938), 395.

144. *The Standard*, October 21, 1938.

145. Provincial to Cahill, 25 October 1938, Edward Cahill Papers, Jesuit Archives, Dublin.

146. Department of Finance, D F 9/18/38, National Archives, Dublin.

147. *Ibid.*

148. *Ibid.*

149. Department of Finance, D F 9/18/38, National Archives, Dublin.

150. *Ibid.*

151. *Ibid.*

152. Edward Coyne, 'The Papal Encyclicals and the Banking Commission', *The Irish Monthly*, Vol. LXVII, No. 2, (February 1939), 76.

153. *Ibid.*, 77–78.

154. *Ibid.*, 79.

155. *Ibid.*

156. Keogh, *The Vatican*, 145

157. From Seán Ó Coileáin, *Seán Ó Riordáin – Beatha agus Saothar*, (Baile Atha Cliath, 1982), 269. Translated: 'At home today.' The child' going to Scotland tomorrow. The poor girl. And the bishops and the doctors and the professors and the motor car salesmen staying at home. 'A thousand thousand slimy things…'

7

THE IRISH REPUBLICAN BROTHERHOOD IN SCOTLAND: THE UNTOLD STORIES OF ANDREW FAGEN AND MICHAEL O'CARROLL

John Cooney

'Twas on the 4th of May boys, in 1921,
That the news ran thru auld Scotland,
That a daring deed was done,
Done by a band of heroes,
To release an Irishman,
They assembled in the High Street,
And they smashed the prison van.

(From *The Smashing of the Van*, a street ballad of the Glasgow Irish.)[1]

James Handley, the author of the classic book, *The Irish in Modern Scotland*, claimed a significant role for this doughty immigrant community in the struggle for Ireland's national independence from Britain in 1921. 'A certain amount of gun-running was carried on before 1916 and a considerable number of men and women volunteers went to Dublin for the Easter Rising', Handley wrote. 'But it was not until guerilla fighting broke out in Ireland that sympathisers in Scotland had an opportunity of rendering effective service. That service in money and materials was given so generously that the contribution of Scotland to the *Sinn Fein* campaign far exceeded that of any other country, including Ireland, and was, in the opinion of Mr de Valera, the chief factor in its success.'[2]

Other historians have echoed Handley's judgement. Dr Tom Gallagher, for instance, has argued that the Irish on Clydeside made 'a substantial contribution to the achievement of self-government in Ireland by providing money and military supplies to keep the war effort going back home and safe houses for IRA men on the run from British or Irish gaols.'[3]

A more sceptical viewpoint, however, has been presented by Dr Iain

D.Patterson, who concludes that the share of the victory contributed by Scotland to Irish freedom was 'slight', and that 'the successes, both political and military, of the IRA were won overwhelmingly by the actions of their members and supporters in Ireland.'[4]

Patterson has begun to lift the lid on a sensitive subject which was left alone after Ireland was partitioned. While Patterson's account brings to the fore tensions between the IRA and the IRB as an organisation within an organisation, he reflects the views of Cathal Brugha, who used alleged maladministration in the Scottish Brigade of the IRA for his personality vendetta against Michael Collins.[5] Overall Patterson's approach is unsympathetic. More research needs to be done before the pendulum settles, closer, I suspect to Handley than to Patterson.

As a contribution to this important but neglected debate, this essay will highlight the activites of two principal participants in the Irish republican movement in Scotland: Andrew Fagan (1884–1975) and Michael O'Carroll, (1901–1989). Both were involved in the unsuccessful gun-battle to release a prominent Irish republican from custody in a police van in Glasgow – the 'Smashing of the Van' incident of May 4, 1921.[6] Fagan was earlier involved in the Bothwell raid of October 1920, the other recorded shooting involving Irish republican militants during that turbulent period when the authorities in London feared a conspiratorial confluence of the red and the green on Clydeside.[7]

Before telling their stories, let me digress, briefly, on my chance meeting with O'Carroll, then a sprightly octogenarian, in the County Sligo village of Easkey in August 1985. We talked about Scotland and he asked where I came from. When I said Blantyre, he whispered that he was there often when he was 'in the movement'. Following-up the reference to the Old IRA, I asked if he had known my grand uncle, Andy Fagan. It transpired that not only had O'Carroll known Fagan, he had worked with him and had stayed in his home.

O'Carroll agreed to be interviewed. We met in various places, including Lurganboy, County Leitrim, where he lived. I arranged a reunion in Ireland between O'Carroll and Fagan's daughter, Cathie Callaghan, who remembered the visits of the handsome young Irishman. On a visit to Scotland, O'Carroll returned to the scene of the 'Smashing of the Van' in the re-landscaped Rottenrow district, adjoining Strathclyde University and Glasgow Cathedral. O'Carroll was photographed placing his hand in the bullet hole left in the wall of old Duke Street prison which the late Jack House described as the most popular attraction for tourists to Glasgow.[8]

Out of these meetings also came further information from the late Mrs Callaghan about her father. This mini-corpus of material provides insights into a sophisticated organisation, based on the twin pillars of secrecy and mutual trust on the part of the activists. What also clearly emerges is that both O'Carroll and Fagan believed themselves to be sincere and dedicated patriots. Not only were they active in the Scottish Brigade of the IRA, they were also members of the older, Fenian-inspired oath-bound Irish Republican Brotherhood, whose supreme council acted as the ruling authority of the then notional Irish Republic.[9]

Michael O'Carroll was born in Dublin's Rotunda hospital on December 6, 1901. Of the thrifty working class, his father Patrick, a carpenter, was from Inniskeen, County Monaghan. His mother, Margaret Healy, from County Meath, was a cousin of Joe Brady, a member of the secret society, the Invincibles, who was hung for the murders in Dublin's Phoenix Park in 1882 of the Chief Secretary to Ireland, Lord Frederick Cavendish, and the Permanent Secretary, Thomas Henry Burke. One of four boys and three sisters, Mick grew up in a strong republican household. The first photograph was taken of him in 1906 wearing a sailor-like hat with the words *Sinn Fein* – Ourselves Alone – embroidered on its rim.

In 1912 O'Carroll joined *Fianna Eireann*, the Boy Scouts of Ireland; but this was no affiliate off-shoot of Baden Powell's scouts. Founded in 1909, the *Fianna* was the first Irish republican organisation to come into the open. To a degree, it was a front for the IRB and it channelled the idealism of young lads like O'Carroll in the direction of the physical force tradition. The militant character of the *Fianna* was indicated by its declared objective of re-establishing the independence of Ireland. Its means were the training of the youth of Ireland, mentally and physically, through teaching Irish history and the Irish language, as well as through scouting and military exercises.[10]

O'Carroll attended its meetings in Dublin's Hardwicke Street under the captaincy of Sean Heuston. There he met Willie Pearse and Con Colbert, both to be executed at Kilmainham in May 1916. Attendance at the silent film, *Ireland, a Nation*, further moulded the impressionable youth's nationalist republican ideology. In his own words, Mick was 'well-primed for the nationalist side.'

He witnessed the 1913 labour dispute in Dublin. 'I saw the baton charges in 0'Connell Street. I can remember quite vividly Jim Larkin and all the members of the Citizens' Army, the lock-out and the Labour agitation. I remember Madame Maud Gonne MacBride and the women along the Liffey quay handing out parcels of food which came from the trade union workers' organisations in England. It was in this spirit and atmosphere that I grew up as a kid. The Dublin Metropolitan Police held sway. The workers were batoned off the streets. So were their wives and their children. Prams were upset. It was a rough time. History records that in 1913 Dublin was the most underfed city in Europe.'

O'Carroll became well-known to the leadership of the *Fianna*. He saved up enough money as a newspaper-boy to buy the haversack and the Fianna uniform of a green jersey with brass buttons and a beret. In uniform he went to the Rotunda theatre in November, 1913, to witness the formation of the Irish Volunteers, known in Irish as *Oglaigh na hEireann*.[11] He also witnessed the landing of arms by Erskine Childers at Howth harbour on July 26, 1914: 'I cycled with Martin Flanagan, my cousin, to Howth that Sunday. We spotted the Fianna's track-cart on Howth pier. We saw batons being dished out to the Volunteers. A cheer arose around the pier. It was the sighting of Erskine Childers coming in with the arms. I remember the boxes and the rifles being passed up from the yacht. I had the pleasure of handling one of those weapons. It was very heavy.'

O'Carroll recalled reading *The Evening Mail* in August, 1914, with its stark headline 'England declares war on Germany.' O'Carroll, though a pious Catholic, was not impressed by the calls of the leader of the Irish Home Rule party, John Redmond, or of the bishops – to join the British Army to defend 'Catholic Belgium'. He took the Fianna's pledge 'never to join England's armed forces', even though 'the atmosphere was behind the war, and Dublin could have been an English city.'

O'Carroll's next involvement was in July 1915 when the remains of the Fenian, Jeremiah O'Donovan Rossa, were laid out in state in Dublin. 'We were detailed to go up to the City Hall in our *Fianna* uniform as guides to the people who queued up. I remember looking at the coffin and watching the Volunteers who were guarding it.' After a huge funeral procession to Glasnevin Cemetery, Padraig Pearse delivered the oration that was to enthuse his generation. O'Carroll frequented St Enda's, the school founded by Pearse, and he took part in parades. He knew Sean MacDermott and Tom Clarke, whom he described as 'a John Mitchel in the flesh.'

Meanwhile, O'Carroll spent a lot of time at Liberty Hall, where he came under the influence of Helen Maloney, of the Transport and General Workers Union. Because of his closeness to the republican underground movement, O'Carroll was aware of what was likely to happen: 'I knew there was going to be trouble and I knew which side I was on.' His elder sister Maggie was working in Houlihan's Shop at 77 Amiens Street, where the leaders met in secret. Maggie tipped him off about a planned insurrection. 'I was only a nipper then but on Easter Monday morning in 1916 I was up at Liberty Hall and saw the Citizens Army move out. I remember the smashing of the windows in the GPO and the men inside putting the mail-bags in the windows, and the small crowd that surrounded Pearse reading the Proclamation on the stairs of the GPO. I was not in uniform and was told not to be in uniform. I was detailed to go to Abbey Street to put cases between Wynn's Hotel and Kelly's bicycle shop – we were building a barricade there. I was in and out from home until the Wednesday. I knew James Connolly so much so that I could call him 'Mr Connolly'. He was a wonderful man. He was very fatherly. He seemed to welcome young men like myself.'

British soldiers raided the O'Carroll home at 16 Charleville Avenue, Fairview, looking for Mick's father, who eluded them. The executions and internment changed the mood. By December, there was an amnesty. O'Carroll, working in a brush factory in Talbot Street, put up a Tricolour to welcome the returning prisoners. This gesture brought him into conflict with the management and he left the job in protest. In February, 1917, O'Carroll was detailed by the Fianna to assist released prisoners, including two Scots, Alec Carmichael and Barney Friel of Anderston. This encounter gave him the idea of moving to Glasgow. On February 15, he travelled with Friel on board *The Maple*, of the Burns and Laird Line. In Glasgow, Friel introduced O'Carroll into 'the proper circles.' Contacts were made with leading republican militants in the West of Scotland such as Joe Robinson, a painter who was 'the head centre of the IRB,' Seamus Reader, Paddy Moran, Sean and Eamon Mooney and 'many other lads.'

O'Carroll took up digs in Bridgeton with a family called Mullins from Northern Ireland, and secured a job in the Trongate. Every Saturday he attended Gaelic dances at the Old Hibernian in London Bridge Road, where he met Robinson, and was sworn into the IRB as its youngest member. Robinson administered the oath.

'I was assigned to move out to the different places particularly at the week-end in the mining districts. Joe Robinson accompanied me and introduced me. Each week I would return to Glasgow with a package weighing up to seven or ten pounds in gelignite. This was stored in a little place in the Saltmarket. You would be amazed at the amount of stuff. I made frequent trips to Dublin bringing parcels and containers with me. There was always a consignment for the Citizens Army and always one for the Volunteers.'

On his third visit to Dublin, on November 23, 1917, O'Carroll, accompanied by Sean Nelson, from Anderston, was sent with a quantity of explosives for Sean McGarry, the President of the Supreme Council of the IRB, and for the General Secretary of the Volunteers and for the Citizens Army. He had letters for each of them. The explosives and guns were in a box which was packed in the Saltmarket at Joe Robinson's place. The journey from Ardrossan to Belfast was a stormy night crossing.

'How that box did not go up, I don't know, because it was swinging all over the deck', O'Carroll said. 'On our arrival at Belfast we were apprehended by the RIC as we went down the gangway. We were taken to Musgrave Street barracks. We were permitted to carry the box. It was a good walk. They were nice types of fellows and they asked us all kinds of questions. I knew that there was one thing they were not to get was the letters I had in my pocket. I succeeded in tearing these up without being detected by visiting the toilets. What those letters contained I don't know. The main concern of the police was to open our box. They had a good idea what was inside but they were surprised by the stuff. A cutting in the newspaper said it was enough to blow up the town hall in Belfast's Donegall Square.'[12]

In response to police interrogation, O'Carroll invented the story that they were to meet a contact wearing an ivy leaf on arrival by train at Dublin's Amiens Street under the clock. Two policemen travelled to Dublin but on their return, empty-handed, the mood changed in the Belfast police cell. O'Carroll and Nelson were sent back via Stranraer to Glasgow Central Police Station. O'Carroll appeared before the Sheriff Court and was remanded in custody to Duke Street prison. The attention of the authorities was more on Joe Robinson, who received a 10 year prison sentence. On O'Carroll's release in February, 1918, he rejoined 'the group.'[13]

'Things were beginning to shape up. The Volunteers were forming companies all over Glasgow and the West of Scotland. Sinn Fein was taking on great proportions. I was now working in the Trongate in a brush shop. Barney McCabe, a businessman, acccommodated us in every way. The arms began to flow in and we established dumps, where these arms could be safely secured. We got cooperation from people who were not connected with the movement but who were militant ILP. At that time they were gathering arms too and we bought arms from them. They did have an idea of a physical movement in Scotland to bring about social revolution. Dumps were fairly well established throughout Glasgow, in Dumbarton, Wishaw and Uddingston, and other places. Places which recall to mind, where I gathered a lot of stuff and a lot of company volunteers, were Leith, Stirling, Dumfries, Hamilton, Blantyre, Bothwell, Carfin and Dundee. O'Carroll spoke highly of Henry Coyle and Joe Vize.'

'As the arms came in, we shipped them in a commercial way to Dublin. Those arms usually went to Liverpool. They were reassigned from Liverpool to Dublin. We were working in conjunction with London and Liverpool. Neill Kerr, who was an important figure in customs and excise, fairly organised things.'

The supply of arms became more prolific after the Armistice in the Great

War in November, 1918. 'There was a lot of stuff knocking about – rifles, Webleys; lads home on leave. The money was pouring in and we had the money to buy stuff. We were now sending the stuff across with passengers and divers ways – on cattle boats and other ships. We found out at different ceili from different girls where they were working. If they were in offices shipping material to Ireland especially to Dublin, we were able to get samples of their invoices and bill heads. We started shipping stuff to Dublin from Glasgow. The main artery was Tommy Tracey, an undertaker. Tommy had a branch in Parkhead, where we packed the stuff. That place was never tapped.'

'It is here that Liam Mellows stepped into the picture and also D.P. Walsh, from Fethard in County Tipperary, later the assistant quarter master general, the man who really established our commercial basis and who was also sent over by Collins. The reorganisation of the purchasing department took place. It was then that I went on the staff of the purchasing department. Our activities included Hamburg, Denmark, Brussels, all parts of England and Scotland. From that day on to the time of the Truce, there was not one round of ammunition discovered or captured, and we sent some considerable quantities of stuff home. I bought rifles from British soldiers – we had a price of £3 for a Webley.'

'We had two Albion lorries on the road. We had an old Austin touring car – that was the mode of transport down to Liverpool. We got in touch with the English regiment in Edinburgh. We were in touch with friendly detectives in Edinburgh whose jobs dealt with prostitutes and the underworld. We got in touch with a Mrs Gordon, who gave the police tip-offs. She gave us the whole set-up in Edinburgh. We knew who was who. She had a second-hand shop. Her husband was a runner for the book-makers. That woman had marvellous contacts. We were put in touch with the sergeant who secured arms for us and data where arms were stored. We were on the point of pulling over a great coup in Maryhill Barracks but the troops came in.'

'We got in touch with the Belgians who came into Leith. German automatic guns were very useful. I paid in readies to those people. Barney McCabe was our reservoir of stock. I often had to carry a ú1,000 which came from GHQ. We acquired lots of British officers' uniforms which we also sent over and proved useful at home. We shipped a lot of stuff from firms in Scotland such as Forsyth Glass Works which were oblivious to the fact that consignments were in their name. When boats were loaded in Glasgow, the dockers put our stuff on last and it was first off at the Dublin Wall.'

It was on visits to Blantyre that O'Carroll came into contact with Andy

Fagan, whom he described as 'a very shrewd and solid man, who would have gone to the scaffold' for the cause of Irish freedom. A great Irishman 'in the eyes of fellow IRA Brigade Council comrade, Jimmy McCarra.'[14] A 'remarkable man who suffered quite a lot of intimidation and victimisation,' according to trade unionist, James Jack.[15] 'A character' to fellow miner, John McArthur.[16] So remarkable was Fagan that he occupies a unique position in relation to the Royal Family : his moment of fame came shortly before he died in 1975, when the firm for which he had worked for fifty years recommended him for a British Empire Medal from Queen Elizabeth as the oldest working man in Scotland. Although then 89, Andy was still doing manual work for five days a week for Murdoch MacKenzie Ltd., a civil engineering and construction firm based in Motherwell. His award attracted extensive media coverage, as Andy posed on his motor-scooter for the cameras with one hand on the throttle and in the other a glass of whisky. The story that was missed was that this particular recipient of the Queen's Award was also the proud holder from the Irish Government of a Service Medal for his IRA activities.[17]

To give Fagan his official title, he was Quartermaster of the the Scottish Brigade of the IRA and a Director of Purchases for Scotland. Fagan, according to McCarra, an Irishman living in Cambuslang , was also 'the Centre for the IRB in Blantyre.'[18] McCarra, who formed a branch of the IRB with Fagan, credited Fagan with responsibility 'for the large flow of guns and munitions that went to Ireland to beat the Black and Tans during the War of Independence.' McCarra also revealed that in 1920 or 1921 Fagan travelled to Ireland to interview Michael Collins, at a time when there was a reward of £20,000 for the capture of Collins and he only interviewed people of importance.[19]

Born in County Meath, Andy Fagan was the eldest of sixteen children of the marriage of Matthew Fagan and Bridget Hoey. After eviction from their small farm at Kingscourt, the Fagans moved to the United States, but stayed only for a year before returning to Meath. Unsettled, especially after the death of his first wife, Andy moved to Scotland, where his first job was in Ardeer with I.C.I. which unwittingly tutored him in the use of explosives. He moved to Blantyre to work in the pits but, finding it increasingly difficult to obtain work, he became involved in politics and union work. Fagan fought injustice wherever he saw it, filling in forms, advising people of their rights, going to rent tribunals with them. He was an activist who incurred the anger and ill-will of the bosses.[20]

O'Carroll often stayed with Andy and Margaret Fagan, née Skelton, from Milltown, County Armagh, at their home at 7 John Street, with their three daughters. Fagan organised dances and raffles to raise funds to bring Irish speakers or politicians interested in the cause of Irish freedom to Blantyre. Among those who crossed his doorstep were Dan Breen (ardent and enthusiastic), D.P. Walsh (tall, highly-strung and constantly smoking) and Liam Mellows (forceful, with a distinct Cork accent.) In 1919 Andy was host to Countess Markievicz when she visited the Gaelic League Hall in Blantyre. The hall was supported by women teachers, including Miss Annie McBride, Mrs Milligan, Mrs Clifford, Mrs McManus and Miss Rose McCluskey. 'They ran raffles and raised money in every possible way to help the cause, but were never involved in actually purchasing or handling arms, although they must have known where the money was going,' Cathie Callaghan recalled.[21]

In 1920 Fagan was selected by the Lanarkshire Miners to attend the John Maclean college in Glasgow, where he studied English, philosophy, politics, the social sciences and trade unionism.[22] Among his classmates was John McArthur, from Fife. According to McArthur: 'Fagan had little or no schooling and arithmetic and algebra were completely foreign to him. But in the most difficult subjects, such as trying to get an understanding of Dietzgen's Science of Understanding and Philosophy, on which John Maclean lectured and which were part of the reading we had to do, Fagan curiously enough was the outstanding pupil in the college.'

Unlike most of Maclean's pupils. McArthur learned about Fagan's Sinn Fein connections. McArthur recalled the day that Fagan asked him for directions to a sweetie shop in the Kelvin Hall district of Glasgow. After college, the two walked towards the Kelvin Hall :

> Fagan had a parcel under his arm. We were not sure where the street was that Fagan was looking for so he said he would ask the policeman who was on point duty at a street junction. He just marched up to the policeman and asked where the street was, and was directed. He found the street and handed the parcel in at the sweetie shop.
>
> Next day he said to me, 'You wouldn't know what was in the parcel?'
>
> 'No.'
>
> 'Oh', he said, 'That was some revolvers and ammunition. I just drop it in there at the shop and the sailor picks it up and takes it in his kit bag.'[23]

Cathie believed that her father set up an almost fail-proof system for getting arms and ensuring they were safely transported to Ireland. He had numerous contacts in Irish clubs, business circles, dock areas, sailors, workers and even the within the military establishment where some were privately sympathetic to the Irish cause. He never used the same contacts regulary but instead used a rota to fool the police. He was very cautious, very careful.[24]

Cathie also left a memoir of the Bothwell incident of October 1920 :

My father, along with Jimmy Rodgers, James Coneghan, Willie Corrigan, Jimmy Grieve, Jimmy McCarra, and several others planned that they would collect ammunition from Hamilton Barracks, and gelignite from miners who worked at Bothwellhaugh mine. The people had been contacted for both ventures, and the price agreed. As always, it was decided who would go where, and what they would collect. They had to set out at different times, each to pursue his own way. It was autumn, and it had to be dark before each left. As always, my mother was on tenterhooks. She could never relax when there was a 'ploy' on. I was nervous myself.

Later I learned that the meeting was in front of the main gate in Elmwood. Luck was not with them – one of the men returning was stopped by a policeman, coming to the meeting place. The policeman was suspicious and phoned Blantyre. My father directed the men to run along the railway and if need be dump the ammunition and gelignite in the Clyde. They ran like blazes. My dad kept his gun for emergencies. He went through the hedge at Woodlands Crescent to see if any of the policemen were still in pursuit. Big Toby, a bluff, stupid man, was a few yards away. Dad fired impulsively and Big Toby dropped.

We, my mother and I, were waiting dad's return when we heard his feet running up the stairs. He came in, sweat blinding him, and shouted 'For Christ's sake, get rid of the gun.' Mother seized it and ran. She came back without it, and bundled me into bed. He had removed his cap and jacket, got his pipe lit and picked up his book. Half an hour later, the detectives arrived. They searched the house but did not disturb my grandmother. For days there was constant surveillance of Irish families suspected of Sinn Fein connections. Another policeman had been killed that night but we knew not to ask questions. Big Toby was in hospital for quite a while.[25]

In many respects, the crescendo of the republican activities of Fagan and O'Carroll was 'the Smashing of the Van' episode when they failed to secure the release of Frank Carty, the commander of the Sligo Brigade of the IRA. From Clooncunny, Ballymote, County Sligo, Carty had become renowned in 'the movement' for his daring escapes from Sligo and Derry jails. After remaining in Derry for about eight or ten days, he crossed in a coal boat to Workington.[26] From there he went up to Glasgow, accompanied by fellow-Sligoman, Jim Hunt. When they contacted the local IRA, they were put in touch with the house in Anderston where O'Carroll was then living:

I came home and was told two men from Ireland were looking for me. They got a cold reception. One came back because he was pleased at this. It happened to be Brigadier Frank Carty, who was a wanted man. He had escaped from Sligo and Derry jails. He was badly wounded in the arm. Frank stayed in the house for a few nights. I reported to D.P. about Frank's presence. A safe haven was arranged. A doctor attended to Frank, who was well again in a few weeks.

Frank meanwhile went to Glasgow Central Police station to get a driving licence for the taxi people, Wylie and Lockhead. He was also training young men.

At the end of April Carty was arrested by armed detectives at the house of Frank O'Hagan, 76 Abbotsford Place, Cumberland, Glasgow. While in Glasgow he had assumed the name of Frank Somers. As yet, the authorities did not know how big was their catch, but they knew he was dangerous and they prepared for any eventuality. Carty's arrest posed a major dilemma for the Scottish Brigade, which believed that he would 'certainly be for the rope' when extradited back to Ireland. The Brigade felt it had to work quickly. In their minds, too, was the likely fate of General Sean MacKeon, who was under sentence of death at this time in Dublin's Mountjoy Prison.

D.P. called me. We went into Abercromby Street right opposite St Mary's. Father MacRory was there – he knew all about our rescue plan.[27] Also there were Brigadier John Carney, a barber from Govan and Brigade Commandant of the Scottish Brigade, and Sean Flood from Dublin, Brigade Adjutant. The plan was to rescue Carty while under police escort while en route from Glasgow Central Police Station to Duke Street Prison. However, it transpired that Dublin was also working on this. George Armstrong from Derry was the courier between Dublin, Derry and Glasgow. George came in that night I think with a message from GHO in Dublin.[28]

But things were well organised by that time for the rescue of Frank Carty. Joe Brooker and myself were given the task of mobilising sixteen men for the ambush which would take place next morning. The night before I had no sleep. We visited the dump to get the necessary arms. Everything was staged and ready. There were two vans which would be leaving the police station. Joe Brooker and myself, we went to Springburn and Maryhill and round that area, and detailed them where to assemble the following morning. It was early morning by the time we got that done.

The next thing was to go to the dump and get sufficient arms to dish out to the lads. Some of them that I mobilised were in their beds that morning. We also spent time arranging with them the establishment of an alibi. Having done that that brought us to about 10 30 a.m. of May 4.

Meanwhile, D.P. Walsh was addressing the logistical problem of which of three vans would convey Carty between court and prison. Walsh arranged that Annie Murray, from Northern Ireland and a member of the *Cumann na mBan*, the woman's auxiliary section of the Volunteers, would cycle ahead of Carty's van. Murray was to be tipped off by an old lady, who was a cleaner in the central police station. This lady was given a description of Carty by Walsh. Her instruction was to throw out her bucket and mop as Carty's van was about to leave. This was the signal for Annie Murray, to start peddling up the hill and alert 'the lads'.

At about 12.15, Carty was hand-cuffed in a small cell to the front of the police van and the key was given to one of the officers placed in the rear compartment along with another prisoner. The outer rear door of the van was locked from the outside by a different key which was sent in advance of the van to Duke Street Prison. In the front seat was the driver, Constable Ross, flanked on the outside by Detective Macdonald, Sergeant Stirton and Inspector Johnston. At about 12 20 the van reached the vicinity of the prison after climbing the hill. The plan was to hold up the van as it slowed down at Drygate. Three groups of assailants were strategically positioned – to its front, its side and its rear, all ready to come out of lanes and shadows.

> As the van came up and changed gear – it was the old guage change – the position I had was right at the rear of the van, about thirty feet from where the van had stopped to change gear. It was then that Sean Adair and Eamonn Mooney came out to hold up the van. Stirton fired through the wind-screen. The minute he did there was a reply and Johnston fell mortally wounded out of the side. I saw him lying there. Stirton ran round to the front of the van across on the far side. I took cover behind one of the standards. I saw him coming. I took a random shot. I got him in the arm and the gun fell from his hand. He lifted it and ran back under a hail.

While the men in front attacked the escort with the driver, another party attempted to smash open the rear door. Johnny Coyne, who was a hefty man, was given a sledge-hammer. If there was any difficulty in extracting the keys from whoever had possession of them, his job was to smash the lock of the door. But after some minutes of strenuous effort, he failed to smash the lock of the door. In increasing panic, one of the attackers fired at the lock – but it still would not budge.

O'Carroll continued:

> Ross the driver of the van, fair play to him, he crushed himself down and threw his machine into gear and drove away up the street at a slow pace. We had to be careful in the cross-fire not to get the man we were looking for shot in the van. The van wheeled right to the gates of Dukes Street which were opened in a flash and the van went right in.

The attackers scattered in all directions and were soon out of sight. Stirton and Johnston were taken to the Royal Hospital, but the latter was dead. Carty later claimed he was beaten up by the police.

'What was I to do?' O'Carroll wondered:

> I had a Webley in which one shot had been fired and, incidentally, it was the same calibre as Johnston was killed with. I was wearing an overcoat and a cap.

I put the gun back in my pocket. The van was gone. A man was lying dead. There was no contact from the top of the rear. I was the only one at the rear. I just calmly walked down the street, stood at the green tram spot and got on the tram. I went to Bridgeton to the house of my friend Maisie Mullins. She happened to be washing out the close at the time. I asked her if anybody was around. She said no. So I broke the revolver and threw the cartridges and the revolver into the bucket and said to her 'You know how to get rid of this when it is convenient.' She never asked any questions but she would have heard about the incident later.'

I was not working at the time. I was signing on the broo. So I thought quickly. When I got to the Labour Exchange it was about 12.45. I signed the registrar. That came out in the evidence. I went to an Irish house, to Miss Cassidy's. I changed my overcoat, cap and a bit of my appearance. There was no such thing as people running about. I was played out. I had an early bed about nine o-clock. But about twelve o'clock there was a knock at the door. The boys were at the door and I was arrested. I was taken to Glasgow Central Station. D.P. Walsh, Father MacRory and John Carney had already been arrested. They had a fair nucleus of those who were involved in the incident.

On May 5, the *Evening Citizen* reported that Somers's real name was Frank Carty, whom it alleged was wanted on more than one charge of murder in Ireland, in addition to stealing a revolver from a dead policeman in Ireland, as well as his daring escapes from Sligo and Derry jails. The newspaper published the names of twenty accused who appeared at Glasgow Central Police Court but listed O'Carroll as 'M. McCarroll, aged 19.'[29] O'Carroll was charged with attacking the van and fatally wounding the police inspector and wounding the detective. Other familiar faces to him included Sean Adair, Thomas Tracey, Frank O'Hagan, as well as D.P. Walsh, Father McRory and Jimmy McCarra.[30]

Much of the publicity centred on Father MacRory, as there had been disturbances the previous evening when he was arrested in St Mary's Church, while hearing confessions during benediction. This arrest enraged a large crowd which gathered outside the church and blocked the road. Stones and other missiles were thrown at the police. Several times the police drew their batons to ward off attacks. At about 11 p.m. a contingent of soldiers, wearing steel helmets and carrying fixed bayonets, arrived as reinforcements. Such was the outburst of feeling in favour of Father MacRory that that IRA leadership denounced his arrest as sacrilege and vowed to take revenge on any policeman who was a Catholic.

Later, O'Carroll learned why the police concentrated on Abercromby Street. 'There was a call from Dundee from the parochial house – some time around one o'clock on May 4. It was supposed that the speaker spoke in Irish and that whoever transmitted that – or whatever tap or system they had at the time – the police followed up the call from Dundee to the presbytery in Abercromby Street. This led them to the arrests of Father McRory and D.P. Walsh. The priest in Dundee was Father John Fahy. He was Irish. The murder squad was after him. Father Fahy knew about the whole thing. He made that unfortunate phone call. He spoke in Irish – I would say that it was the result of the phone call that the police concentrated on Abercromby Street.'[31]

Andy Fagan was among those arrested in further police swoops and imprisoned. According to McCarra, Fagan 'saved some of us from execution in connection with the Prison Van trial in 1921. I well remember the day that he entered Duke Street prison; he smiled to me as he had a large Bible and a very large Prayer Book.'[32] It was not divine inspiration that Fagan was looking for : while in prison he worked with the legal team devising a stratagem to get the accused released. For eleven weeks over thirty accused were held in captivity. After the pleading diet, thirteen were detained for trial and the rest were released on July 22, including Fagan and MacRory. There were jubilant scenes of rejoicing by a vast crowd who had gathered to cheer their patriot priest outside the prison, not far from where the death of Inspector Johnston had scandalised Protestant Scotland.[33]

In the tense sectarian atmosphere in Glasgow – this was the biggest Irish scare since the Fenians tried to blow up Tradeston Gasworks in 1883 – it was known that a conviction would result in hangings. The parallel was drawn in the press between the Glasgow Van Trial and the case 54 years of a similar case in Manchester which resulted in the execution of Allen, Larkin and O'Brien, the Manchester Martyrs.

According to O'Carroll, the defence counsel, Neil Docherty from Derry, and his assistants, Turnbull and Clancy, ensured that the jury was packed to prevent the accused becoming the Glasgow Martyrs. The Governor of Duke Street Prison was disposed to them. So too were the 21st Lancers, who were guarding the jail.

Even if the jury had returned a guilty verdict, the prisoners were confident that they would be freed, because, in the words of O'Carroll, Michael Collins had 'The Squad' over from Dublin and were staying in the Calton. This group of elite hit-men, known as the 'Twelve Apostles', operated as an integral part of Collins' Intelligence Department, specialising in the execution of British agents or the rescue of IRA members from difficult predicaments. 'We knew that they were on the outside. We had the whole thing worked out,' O'Carroll said.

A few spine-shivering moments, however, were experienced by the prisoners. 'Ellis, the hangman, sized us up in Duke Street jail before we went for trial. We were told by one of the warders that this was the procedure. They took our height and various things like that. That was the atmosphere when we went to trial in Edinburgh.'

When the trial opened on August 8 in the High Court, one of the prisoners, Frank O'Hagan, was released, broken in health. 'Of the twelve who went to trial, four had not participated in the ambush,' O'Carroll declared. 'It was a formidable indictment. There were about 160 witnesses. Incidentally, they found arms in Abercromby Street and they were also used as productions as well as personal effects. I had a loose leaf notebook. Unfortunately, when I had whipped a page out, it had left an impression on the next leaf. The police were able to identify 'assemble at Rottenrow'. That identified me. I was implicated very much on that. That was one of the things that went against me.'

'The Crown case fell to pieces on identification. My Attorney, Sandeman, K.C. had me stand up in the court when Stirton – he was the principal Crown witness – was told by his Lordship to have a good look at me.'

'Describe the accused, O'Carroll.'

'Tall, sallow complexion, dark hair.'

'I had a big mop of hair at the time.'

'At the same time, Sandeman gathered his paraphenalia, made a gracious bow and left the stand. That was a very famous turn in the trial.'

O'Carroll was found not guilty on both charges of conspiracy and murder. The others were found not guilty or not proven. A Tricolour was thrown from the public gallery. D.P. Walsh , who had been identified as an escaper from Strangeways Jail, Manchester, with Austin Stack, was immediately re-arrested in the dock. Walsh's set-back did not dampen the jubilation of the pro-*Sinn Fein* Irish.

'The reception in Glasgow was absolutely fantastic. As that train left Edinburgh, right through the different stations – the crowds were at the stations – it was a through train – didn't they give us the gee–up passing through different stations. When we got to Glasgow Queen Street station, we were lifted completely off our feet. There were receptions all over Glasgow for the next two weeks. I remember I lost my voice and it was a wonder I ever got it back. The Truce was on between Lloyd George and Collins. That is what got us released.'

Ironically, the *Smashing of the Van* was the Last Hurrah of the IRB tradition in Glasgow. The Truce silenced the Irish question in Scotland. Although Fagan was arrested in November 1921 for smuggling explosives to Ireland, he slipped into the humdrum daily life of engineering work. O'Carroll returned to Ireland to join Carty with the de Valera anti-Treaty forces in the civil war.

The ironic legacy for the Scottish Brigade was that Sean Adair who had risked his life for Frank Carty was killed by Carty's column in County Sligo. For Mick O'Carroll, Sean Adair's death symbolised the tragedy of the Irish Civil War, and he looked back on his Glasgow days as glorious days. O'Carroll wrote the epitaph of the Glasgow Irish when he said: 'The people of Glasgow and the West of Scotland – the first, second and third generations of the Irish – I will always remember them – their loyalty, their sincerity and the ideals which were in their minds. They were wonderful.'[34]

REFERENCES

1. The ballad of 'The Smashing of the Van' is recorded in 'The Songs of Past and People 11' by Dreoilin Community Arts in association with Mid-West Radio and Knock Folk Museum, County Mayo, Ireland.

2. J. Handley, *The Irish in Modern Scotland* (Cork, 1947), 297.

3. T. Gallagher, *The Uneasy Peace* (Manchester, 1987), 90–1.

4. I.D. Patterson, 'The activities of the Irish Republican Physical Force Organisations in Scotland, 1919–21', *Scottish Historical Review*, Vol.LXX111: No. 193 , (April 1993), 39–59.

5. For the general outlook of the Dublin HQ on Scotland in early 1921, see Piaras Beaslai, *Michael Collins and the Making of a New Ireland*, (Dublin, 1926), Vol.11, 161–3, and C.D. Greaves, *Liam Mellows and the Irish Revolution*, (London, 1971).

6. Handley and Patterson misdate the Carty episode as 1920.

7. The Michael O'Carroll quotations are edited from three hours of tape-recorded reminiscences and interviews, plus notes. I am also indebted to Stephen Coyle and Liam McIlvanney, for some written source materials, and to Alan MacFadyen and Sean Boyne for assistance.

8. J. House, *The Heart of Glasgow* (Glasgow, fourth edition, 1978), 175–6. He called the incident 'The Battle of the Bell of the Brae.'

9. Henry Coyle, Joe Vize and Neill Kerr, were members of the IRB.

10. The National Association of the Old IRA, *Dublin Brigade Review*, n.d.g. See unsigned article on Fianna Eireann, 65–70.

11. F.X. Martin (ed.), *The Irish Volunteers 1913–1915*, (Dublin, 1963).

12. They were carrying 230 two-ounce sticks of gelegnite and a considerable amount of blasting power. See Patterson, 56.

13. In interviews O'Carroll denied possessing material incriminatory of Joe Robinson, but he confirmed that Robinson was behind the operation.

14. Letter from McCarra, to Cathie Callaghan, December 4, 1975, postmarked, Ballinade, County Monaghan.

15. Cathie Callaghan Cuttings.

16. Cathie Callaghan Cuttings.

17. Profiles of Andrew Fagan in *MM News*, Vol 1. No 3, (July 1970); R. Shears, 'Honours for Lord Vic and Old Andrew', *Daily Mail*, January 2, 1974. G. Anderson, 'Taxing Battle for a BEM (89)', *Glasgow Herald*, January 2, 1974 and J. Cooney, 'IRA Man Andy, a Royal Medal and the Road to an Era of Peace, *Irish Press*, April 29, 1995.

18. McCarra to Callaghan, December 4, 1975.

19. McCarra to Callaghan, December 4, 1975.

20. Cathie Callaghan, personal interview.

21. Letter of Cathie Callaghan to John Cooney, September 9, 1986.

22. Andy Fagan is pictured with John Maclean in I. MacDougall (ed.), *Labour in Scotland: A Pictorial History from the Eighteenth Century* (Edinburgh, 1985), 209. The question arises as to whether Fagan had an input into Maclean's pamphlet, *The Irish Tragedy : Scotland's Disgrace*, published in 1920.

23. The extract is from McArthur's *Recollections*.

24. Cathie Callaghan personal interview.

25. 'The Bothwell incident' – Note by Cathie Callaghan, July 1986.

26. Frank Carty's 'Statement of Military Activities', written in 1935, in Military Archives, Cathal Brugha Barracks, Dublin.

27. Bernard J. Canning, *Irish-born Secular Priests in Scotland, 1829–1979* (Inverness, 1979), 273–6. See also *Ulster Herald*, September 20, 1980, 'Recalling a remarkable incident in the life of an Omagh-born priest.'

28. For Dublin's anger, see Charles J. McGuinness, *Nomad* (London, 1934). O'Carroll did not sense real antagonism from Dublin. He felt that had the plan to rescue Carty at sea gone ahead, the anti-IRA clamour that accompanied the police van trial could have been avoided.

29. *Evening Citizen*, 'Sinn Fein Outrage Sequel,' May 5, 1921.

30. McCarra's importance emerges in a letter from Andy Fagan, dated, March 14, 1965 – 'he was one of the most active and diligent workers in the cause of Irish independence in this country. He was specially active in the IRA, was specially appointed to a position of trust and responsibility on the Brigade Council. Placed in charge with others of Purchases and Transport, he was an unqualified success.'

31. Canning, 96. Fahy founded the 'Land for the People' movement in Ireland.

32. McCarra letter, December 4, 1975.

33. According to O'Carroll, the priests in St Mary's Abercromby Street were sympathetic to Ireland. 'They saw the impact of the whole thing in the resurgence of faith among the Irish which gave them no choice anyway.' This link between 'Faith and Fatherland' deserves further study.

34. Michael O'Carroll died in March 1989. See, J. Cooney, 'An Escapade Recalled', *Irish Times*, April 8, 1989.

8

THE NORTHERN IRELAND PROBLEM
AND SCOTTISH-IRISH RELATIONS

Graham Walker

Whatever shape the future relationship between Scotland and Ireland takes, it has to address the Northern Ireland problem. Northern Ireland has to be central to that relationship or it will be built on evasions and delusions. Scotland's links to Ulster are too close, too deep and too complex simply to skip over, or to discard and disown out of feelings of shame or guilt[1], or of bafflement and despair about a solution to the Province's troubles ever being found. Over the span of the Northern Ireland troubles since 1969 the Scottish voice in debates about the problem has hardly been heard. We may have been busy asserting our Scottishness politically and culturally, but as far as Northern Ireland was concerned it was fine by us that the responsibility for working out a solution should magically emerge out of an 'Anglo-Irish' process. We breathed a sigh of relief as the more that term – 'Anglo-Irish' – was used, the more we slipped out of sight. Who cared about history? Intimate we may once have been, but now we were strangers.

Of course, this was only really true of 'official' Scotland. Unofficially there was plenty of moral – and sometimes even practical – support given to both sides by their respective constituencies in Scotland. Around us there was plenty of writing on the wall – slogans imported from the Shankill and the Falls – to provide awkward reminders. And some at least were well aware in any case of the depth of 'Orange and Green' antagonisms in certain parts of Scotland – at all costs we had to distance the Northern Ireland troubles or they would set alight the combustible material stock-piled at home. Some hitherto sanguine observers of the strength of Scotland's 'civic' political culture were won over to this perspective in the wake of the Monklands by-election of June 1994.[2]

However, if we are serious about re-forming relationships on these islands and exploring new possibilities, such fears have to be overcome and

155

such disingeneousness curtailed. I want to see a flourishing Scottish-Irish relationship but I believe it can only truly happen if it is part of a wider series of positive explorations to develop in the context of these islands as a whole. In addition, I believe it can only start to happen when we as Scots start to engage with all aspects of our Irish experience, and, most urgently, with the Scottish dimension to the Northern Ireland situation.

Scotland is a vital dimension to the Northern Ireland question because it is important that that question is not pushed simply into a one-island context. For Irish Republicans it has always been a simple matter: the object was, and remains, to break the connection with England. For Republicans, and indeed for most constitutional Irish Nationalists, 'Britishness' means 'Englishness' and the Union is equated with the English connection specifically. They are therefore at a loss fully to understand what motivates Ulster Loyalists; as even the Nationalist newspaper the *Irish News* has recently acknowledged[3], the failure to appreciate the strength of social and cultural ties between Protestant Ulster and Scotland has been a central weakness in the Nationalist outlook. I would add that there has been a concomitant reluctance to acknowledge the importance of Scotland to the experience of many Irish Catholics. The political sterility of the 'anti-imperialism versus loyalism' dichotomy has carved needless and arbitrary boundaries through the cultural mosaic of Northern Ireland, and has inhibited appreciation of the cultural cross-fertilisation which has shaped both places' history. The more we introduce Scotland to the debate, the more we might chip away at spurious ethnic absolutes and exclusivist historical myths on both sides. We as Scots should welcome the chance to contribute constructively in this way; in so doing we might learn a lot about ourselves and strengthen our own political and civic cultures. The more the debate in Northern Ireland is prevented from turning in on itself the healthier it will be, and Scotland is in pole position to widen that debate.

With the advent of a Scottish Parliament, that sense of opportunity will be more pronounced. A Scottish Parliament will provide a focus and a means for Scottish opinion on Northern Ireland to be given better expression. It will provide Scots with a platform to exert more influence and to disrupt productively the cosy Anglo-Irish (London-Dublin) framework. Contemporary issues of constitutional change bring Scotland and Northern Ireland closer together, and there may well be benefits for both in co-operation in the context of a constitutionally re-structured UK. Controversies and debates around the theme of devolution have borne down on both places since the 1970s.[4]

I have already indicated that Republicans and Nationalists in Ireland do not pay enough attention to what lies behind the Unionists' claims to be

British and their displays of loyalty. Scots could bring it home to them that Britain and Britishness have developed as very complex phenomena, encompassing diverse national and ethnic voices. Republicans have never grasped this: they are comfortable only with the idea of England as colonial oppressor. Scotland, with a history which combines friction and tension with England on the one hand, and an Imperial 'Golden Age' and a largely stable union with England on the other[5], is ideally placed to stress the limits of English colonialism. Moreover, they may help even impeccably constitutional Nationalists and fair-minded statesmen such as John Hume to appreciate that the object should be to address the desires and aspirations of Unionists rather than just 'assuaging' their 'fears' about the prospect of a united Ireland.[6]

Scottish influence on Ulster Unionists has the potential to be even more far-reaching. Protestant Ulster is often portrayed as out of step with British norms, although it is seldom noted that there is no such thing as a British norm. Ulster Unionists are undoubtedly pushed to the margins and it has to be said that they have not helped themselves to be understood. They have rhetorically claimed to be British with little acknowledgement of the many meanings and definitions of that term. Conversely, they have been labelled as 'un-British' or 'not quite British' by many people in Britain who have adopted an arbitrary definition of Britishness and ignored the reality that this concept means different things in different contexts. In short, the Unionist position within the UK has been undermined by the failure on the part both of themselves and their British critics to appreciate fully the diversity which characterises issues of British identity.

What is important to grasp here is that the more Unionists are marginalised the greater their insecurity and the less likely it is that they will compromise. Awareness of their marginalisation has made them all the more unbending in their relationship with their Catholic Nationalist neighbours. The Ulster Protestants must be allowed and enabled to engage positively with what they rhetorically claim to be part of, and I believe they will have to do this before they can come to terms with Irish nationalism and forge a lasting peace. If Ulster Protestants are treated as if they belong, they will be more disposed to build a better relationship with Nationalists and perhaps explore more positively their Irishness. The sense of pessimism about their community's cultural survival which runs so deep in contemporary Protestant Ulster is one of the most dangerous aspects of the current political situation, and Ulster Protestants have to feel more confident about the survival of their identity if peace is to be achieved.

Scotland might be in a position to help here. Scots should break with the tendency to 'distance', or 'disown', the Ulster Protestants, and instead encourage them to explore political possibilities and to feel less isolated. Most Scots today are disposed to be critical of the Unionists and to extrapolate, arguably too easily, from a Scottish constitutional debate in which the Union has been roundly attacked, to the Northern Ireland context. Nevertheless, Ulster Unionists may still be more willing to listen to Scottish voices. The extent of the Ulster Protestant regard for all things Scottish could become a positive resource; today there are parts of Protestant Ulster which appear to be outposts of a heightened sense of Scottishness, complete with pride in the Scots language.[7] If this resource could be massaged beyond sentimentality and cliché, then it is possible that it could form a basis for dialogue. Within this context Scots might help Ulster Unionists to learn the virtues of reason and dialogue and the importance of civil society and broader concepts of justice and fairness, qualities which an important recent intervention from a Unionist thinker has identified as sorely lacking.[8]

A distinctive Scottish voice in Northern Ireland deliberations may also bring home to the Unionists the reality of the new Britain and the need for them to adapt to it and, indeed, contribute to its re-shaping. As the critic and commentator Edna Longley has put it: 'Belonging to the UK means engaging with what might be its crisis, what might be its mutation'.[9] Longley has also observed how the sense of loss and disorientation resulting from the unravelling of the old Britishness might be viewed as a connecting theme between different peoples in the UK, particularly the Ulster Protestants and a significant portion of Scots. When a mutual sense of frustration regarding English ethnocentrism is added there would thus appear to be substantial common ground between the peoples; and for those so motivated there may be scope for Scottish influences to impress upon the Ulster Unionists the potential benefits of a decentralised, and perhaps federalised, UK and the necessity of behaving in less traditional Unionist fashion in the interests of the Union's survival in the wider sense.

Scotland's voice, if it encourages Unionists to engage with debates about change in Britain, will provide a much-needed sense of balance in the Irish peace process. As it stands, the Unionists view that process as hopelessly biased against them, and underpinned by a dynamic towards an all-Ireland context and eventual solution.[10] Ulster Unionists need to move beyond political minimalism, and change could rub off on them if their Scottish neighbours made the effort to engage them in dialogue and to show them that interaction between all the peoples of the two islands is the way forward.

Scots, in this respect, should be wary of the trenchantly expressed views of Southern Irish author and commentator Tim Pat Coogan who has focused on the possibility (likelihood in his opinion) that Catholics will outnumber Protestants in another generation and that a Nationalist triumph is inevitable.[11] Coogan's line of argument perpetuates old patterns of thinking on the subject, notions about the conflict only coming to an end when one side triumphs over the other: in this case when Unionist hegemony achieved through sectarian headcounting is reversed, and Nationalists inherit their place in the sun by virtue of a Catholic majority. This reflects old, outdated and unhelpful concepts such as ultimate victory/ defeat; majoritarianism in the nation-state as the basis of governance; a preoccupation with 'destiny' and 'inevitability'; 'unfinished business'; and absolutes. We need to get beyond the 'all or nothing' characteristics of traditional nationalism, and this applies to Scotland as well as Ireland. The story goes that when Bernadette McAliskey was told that the day of the nation-state was over, she replied: 'Hang on, I haven't had mine yet'. I suspect that more than a few Scottish nationalists would sympathise with her, and it was revealing that Alex Salmond should recently quote approvingly the ringing declaration of Parnell that 'No man has the right to set a boundary to the march of a nation'.[12] This desire for nationalistic redress – almost, it seems, as a matter of honour – is part of the problem rather than the solution. This is the nationalism of certainties, which talks of 'destinies' and becomes intolerant in its purist impetus.[13] Ironically, Unionists are at one with Nationalists (both Irish and Scottish) in signing up to this 'all or nothing' school of thought.

If more Scots pay attention to the Republic of Ireland, they may be intrigued by the way the latter country has begun to throw off the dead weight of its Nationalist past and to exorcise its 'ghosts'. Among the intellectual figures who have contributed to this process is the Dublin political thinker and philosopher Richard Kearney whose 'post-nationalist' ideas[14] and model of a 'Council of the Islands' should command our attention. In Kearney's scheme of things only such a Council, of Britain and Ireland (based on the Nordic Council example), could take us beyond old debilitating struggles over sovereignty and territory, and provide a structure in which the multiple identities of the peoples of these islands could be expressed at the same time as the things held in common could be affirmed. We need political arrangements which reflect the mongrelised cultural realities of these islands and we need, therefore, to push through to a post-Nationalist and post-Unionist world.

The stress placed on east-west links in the current Irish peace process, as well as north-south links, has resulted in due scrutiny of ideas such as Kearney's. The growing number of east-west connections and ventures, not least the Irish–Scottish Academic Initiative, in conjunction with the imminence of constitutional change in Britain in the form of devolution, has encouraged the Irish government to give thought to such a 'Council of the Islands', and the Ulster Unionist leader David Trimble has pronounced in favour of the idea.[15] This would appear to open up an avenue of possibilities and of hope. *The Belfast Telegraph* recently editorialised on the issue as follows:

> There is a new realisation that Strand Three matters – originally confined to London-Dublin relations – may usefully be expanded to include the complex relationships between all the regions of these islands, including Northern Ireland, the Republic, Scotland, Wales and England. All have interests in common – particularly so, as more countries join the European Union – and there must be possibilities for harmonisation and co-operation which should not be confined to Ireland.[16]

The Scottish-Irish relationship is one of several on these islands. It may in a sense be the key one in determining the future meaning of the term 'British'. Some commentators seem to assume the decline of Britain and Britishness to be permanent. That may be, and a future Scottish-Irish relationship will surely reflect it if it becomes fact. However, I am somewhat sceptical of visions of a new Scottish-Irish relationship which see it as emerging naturally now that both have emerged from the 'shadow' of England and/or 'Britishness'.[17] First, it is highly debatable that both were overshadowed in the way this suggests. Arguably what is more striking is the way both Scotland and Ireland have exercised influence on England and the wider British context; and secondly, it rather assumes that Britishness as a concept or as a living form of identity has run out of steam.

I am inclined to conceive of a new Scottish-Irish relationship as one among many on these islands, and to argue that the stress on the 'archipelago' picture is an appropriate one in these days of multiple and multi-layered identities, and a hopeful one regarding the conflict in Northern Ireland. The constitutional re-structuring process taking place in Britain seems geared towards keeping the different parts together as well as providing for diversity and this can be a catalyst for new relationships between all parts of the UK and the Republic of Ireland. As Vernon Bogdanor has argued recently, the development of a UK federation may turn out to be the saviour of the Union[18], and I would add that it may also hold the key to peace in Northern Ireland and better relationships within Ireland and between Ireland and Britain.

It is also more than possible that constitutional changes and cultural pluralism might result in 'Britishness' as a form of identity being renewed. I would contend that Britishness has not yet shrunk to English nationalism, and that it is a worthwhile project to rescue it from doing so. I think we have to address the question of whether Britishness matters enough to enough people to be positively reconstructed, and if it does then what the implications of this for the Scottish-Irish relationship will be. Britishness has proven to be quite tenacious in the past and my hunch is that it will survive as one of the multiple identities to be given expression. Even if it fades away I would say that we cannot escape dealing with the legacy of something so complex and so contested for so long.

Returning to the Northern Ireland problem, any refusal to admit Northern Ireland to the wider UK or British context only falsifies the nature of that British concept, only suppresses the issues that the Northern Ireland question raises about nationality and sovereignty on these islands, and suppresses important historical forces shaping British identity and UK structures of government. The Northern Ireland problem is very much a British problem (and within that a Scottish problem), as well as an Irish problem. We need to explore the Britishness (in particular perhaps the Scottishness) of the Irish Catholic as well as the Ulster Protestant experience, and to counter the tendency in all nationalisms towards reductiveness, over-simplification and essentialism.

In conclusion, I would emphasise again the extent to which Scotland has affinities with both communities in Northern Ireland, and with Ireland as a whole, North and South. Scotland is thus in an ideal position to play a more dynamic and constructive role. It can draw on these close ties and, crucially, on the experience derived from tensions within its own society, to offer more penetrating insights and alter the terms of the debate. A new Scottish Parliament provides the means, and removes the excuses for doing nothing.

REFERENCES

1. See comments in diary column of *The Scotsman*, 10 July 1997; also A Noble, 'Blarney, Dogma, Hatred and Fear', *The Herald*, 7 December 1996.

2. For an account of this episode see G Walker, *Intimate Strangers: Political and Cultural Interaction between Scotland and Ulster in Modern Times* (Edinburgh, 1995), 179–184.

3. *Irish News*, 11 June 1997.

4. Walker, *Intimate Strangers*, chapter 6; also P Lynch, 'The Northern Ireland Peace process and Scottish Constitutional Reform: Managing the Unions of 1800 and 1707', *Regional and Federal Studies*, vol 6, no 1 (Spring, 1996), 45–62.

5. See F O'Toole, 'Imagining Scotland', *Granta*, 56 (Winter, 1996), 59–76.

6. See interview with Hume in *Irish News*, 23 September 1997.

7. See debate on 'Ulster–Scots Identity' in Northern Ireland Forum for Political Dialogue, *Record of Debates*, no 23, 10 January 1997.

8. N Porter, *Rethinking Unionism* (Belfast, 1996).

9. E Longley, 'What do Protestants want?', *The Irish Review*, no 20 (Winter/Spring, 1997), 114.

10. See A Aughey, 'The Character of Ulster Unionism', in P Shirlow and M McGovern (eds.), *Who are 'the People'? Unionism, Protestantism and Loyalism in Northern Ireland*, (London, 1997), 30–31.

11. See, for example, Coogan's articles in *Scotland-on-Sunday*, 21 September 1997, and *Ireland-on-Sunday*, 14 December 1997.

12. *The Herald*, 27 September 1997. Parnell's words were perhaps more ambiguous than Salmond appears to believe.

13. See report of speech by veteran Irish Republican Martin Meehan in *Irish News*, 8 August 1997; also O'Toole, 'Imagining Scotland' for a discussion of Scottish Nationalist envy of Irish heroics.

14. R Kearney, *Post-Nationalist Ireland* (London, 1997).

15. See *Irish Times*, 6 December 1997 and 13 December 1997.

16. *Belfast Telegraph*, 25 November 1997.

17. See A Noble, *op cit*; also L McIlvanney, 'Dismantling of Prejudice', *The Herald*, 12 July 1997.

18. V Bogdanor, 'Sceptred Isle – or Isles?', *Times Literary Supplement*, 26 September 1997.